CONTEMPORARY AMERICAN FICTION

CHARLEYHORSE

Author of a collection of stories, *The Quiet Enemy*, and a novel, *The Live Goat*, winner of the Harper Saxton Prize, Cecil Dawkins was born in Alabama and grew up there. She received her B.A. from the University of Alabama and her M.A. from Stanford. She also received the Stanford Writing Fellowship, a Guggenheim Fellowship, and an NEA grant. Her play, *The Displaced Person*, based on stories by Flannery O'Connor, was produced off-Broadway. Her stories have appeared in *Paris Review*, *Southwest Review*, *Sewanee Review*, and other magazines. Cecil Dawkins lives in New Mexico.

CECIL DAWKINS

CHARLEYHORSE

PENGUIN BOOKS

PENGUIN BOOKS
Viking Penguin Inc., 40 West 23rd Street,
New York, New York 10010, U.S.A.
Penguin Books Ltd, Harmondsworth,
Middlesex, England
Penguin Books Australia Ltd, Ringwood,
Victoria, Australia
Penguin Books Canada Limited, 2801 John Street,
Markham, Ontario, Canada L3R 1B4
Penguin Books (N.Z.) Ltd, 182–190 Wairau Road,
Auckland 10, New Zealand

First published in the United States of America by
Viking Penguin Inc. 1985
Published in Penguin Books 1986

LIBRARY OF CONGRESS CATALOGING IN PUBLICATION DATA
Dawkins, Cecil, 1927–
Charleyhorse.
(Contemporary American fiction)
I. Title. II. Series.
[PS3554.A943C5 1986]   813'.54   86-5023
ISBN 0 14 00.8010 4

Printed in the United States of America by
Offset Paperback Mfrs., Inc., Dallas, Pennsylvania
Set in Electra

CHARLEYHORSE

1

Charley is in the habit when short of cash of remarking over her oatmeal, "I run a ranch half the size of a township and I do it for room and board." She hates oatmeal, but Belle has read where it cleans out your arteries.

Her mother, at the other end of the dining room table, sits balancing her accounts. Sometimes she eats breakfast and sometimes she doesn't, depending on how she feels about her weight. Her weight is always the same, but the way she feels about it changes from one day to the next. "You don't pay any rent," she says without looking up. "You can do a few chores."

"I've run up some bills that if I don't pay them they're coming after me."

"What bills are you referring to?"

But she knows what bills. Charley has been complaining to Lady, "It's like pulling teeth to get anything out of her." But Lady is committed to keeping the peace. "You know she still grieving, and grieving can make you mean." But Charley thinks it doesn't take grieving to make Belle mean. In her opinion Belle is peeved because if she had to lose one of her children why did it have to be Clay?

Charley dumps sugar from the bowl into the oatmeal and moves it around, feeling the bright blue eyes down the length of the table avoiding her face but running over the rest of her. "Look at that hair. Do you cut it with the ax?"

But Belle is as dissatisfied with her own as she is with Charley's. On top of the buffet, like honored, high guests at every meal, sit a half-dozen Styrofoam heads wearing wigs: a red one, a brown one, a blond one, a black one, a bouffant, hennaed one, and a gray one with bluing in it that Belle has decided she purchased prematurely. Sitting there with Lady behind her in the kitchen, she often looks in the round cosmetics mirror on its pedestal before her and weeps. "Where did I get this hair?" And Lady says, "Nothing wrong with your hair 'cept you fried it with permanents." And Belle says, "Momma said a woman's hair should be her crowning glory." And Lady says, "Your momma said a lot of things." And Belle says, "I never knew was it crown-*ing* glory or crown *and* glory." And Lady says, "It don't make a lot of difference."

Charley has heard it all before. She blows on her coffee and over the edge of the cup stares down the lineup of heads. The heads, though featureless, stare back. Each morning after the table is cleared, Belle tries on one wig after another, choosing for the day, while Lady, behind her, tends to the dishes and Charley sits hunched at the other end of the table watching, pinching her lower lip, trying to figure out how to get out of Belle whatever she needs most desperately at the moment. But to Charley's perspective the round mirror stands in place of Belle's face and renders it blank as the faces on the heads, and the fluorescent ring circling it gives it a stark, colorless halo.

Lady is their housekeeper but Belle introduces her as a friend of the family. They tell anyone who is interested that they are both East Texans trapped in the plains of Kansas. Belle says she feels like a foreigner who happens to speak the language, but Lady says she's not even sure she speaks the language. When they're alone they bicker a lot, but they perform a number of routines like this for strangers.

In addition to East Texas, they also have in common their lost sons, Clay Burden and Lady's son Tearl. There is no doubt at all that Clay is dead. He's lain for some time in an unmarked grave in the Tula cemetery waiting for Belle to decide on a monument to put over his head. About Tearl, missing since Vietnam, they cannot be sure. But though no longer in residence, both sons are presences in the two-story white frame house sprawled with its outbuildings on an acre enclosed by a three-deep windbreak of trees—one row evergreen—that blocks out the gale sweeping Kansas most seasons of the year. For Lady often quotes Tearl on whatever subject comes under discussion, and Belle frequently remarks to Charley, "If only your brother had lived."

And Charley says, "He'd never a run this place. Went to Manhattan to learn animal husbandry but all he studied was boozing and screwing."

And Belle replies, "I wish you wouldn't use that language. A place this size takes a man to run it. You're not a man."

"Every man you had around here either stole you blind or laid out drunk or tried to break down your bedroom door. You won't hire a man. You'd have to pay a man. You get me free."

"Free! Stud fees for those mares, hundred-dollar boots, new pickup every year . . ."

The pickups are alternately red, white, and blue. The last one was blue. With this red one she starts all over again. Belle argued for a little Japanese import but Charley bucked for a three-quarter-ton and won. On certain things she knows she can always win. She doesn't know why. The pickups are one of them.

". . . new sports car out there under a plastic tarp!"

For the thousandth time Charley tries to get through to Belle and explain something she hasn't yet succeeded in explaining to herself. "I never wanted a sports car! It was Clay wanted the sports car! I want something, give it to him! He wanted something, give it to me!"

Clay had been the favorite because he was the son. But Charley had felt sorry for him anyway. She had understood Clay. He was born wanting everything he wasn't supposed to want—a fast car, a can of beer, and Reenie beside him, flying through the night, a big city, a cool pad, and loud music going all the time. And Charley wanted the horses, spring calving, tending the cattle, flying the plane, driving the combine, running the tractor. She'd understood her brother because they were alike in this: they were both born wanting what they weren't supposed to want.

———

Belle is coming home today from the hospital in Kansas City where she's had plastic hip sockets installed after driving her T-Bird off an embankment over a fifteen-foot culvert while under the influence. Charley is flying her home this afternoon in the little single-engine Cessna tethered against the wind at the end of the landing strip out behind the house.

She was up early this morning, barreling along the two-lane blacktop at six a.m. in the fire-engine-red pickup, a saddled horse in the truck bed, driving with one hand and playing a tattoo on the door with the other in time to the country western blaring from her stereo. She was not really listening. She was impatient to get to where she was going, though that didn't account for the speed at which she hurled the bright red pickup toward her destination. She always travels at the same speed, coming or going, day or night, impatient or not.

The truck turned off on a section road and then on a dirt track that traveled cross-country till the prairie began to swell and the road dipped into a coulee. At its head stood an old log house with chimneys at either end and a roof pitched out over the front porch. At the bottom the draw opened toward the horizon beyond a sprawling, weather-grayed open shed and a pond with

4

cottonwoods where a dozen white mares grazed with their foals, Arabians in Quarter Horse country.

She lifted her chin to the old vaquero squatting in the shade of his hat. He rose and approached the rear of the pickup and unfastened the tailgate. The mare stepped down and he unsaddled her and dropped the gear into the truck bed. Wet from working, for Charley's been cutting heifers out of the herd, she trotted off toward the pond.

Charley embraced the steering wheel with both arms and contemplated the filly tied to a fence post inside the corral, her coat turning—it looked like a bright blue roan—and so shiny she might have been raised on eggnog. *"Que bonita, Juan."* It was easier to say things like that in Spanish. The wind was already coming up so she took off her hat and sat framed against the gun rack with her rifle lying across the top bars and, across the bottom, her pool cue in its long, thin leather tube.

She approached the filly, talking to it softly while it danced. Its ears swiveled toward her. She untied the reins and stepped into the stirrup.

She knows no better feeling than this, her legs forked over the barrel of a filly she's bred herself, paying an arm and a leg for the stud fee. A barely perceptible trembling runs up the horse into her thighs. The filly could let go any minute and sunfish all over the place. But she settles tentatively into a walk along the fence with Charley light on her back and easy on her mouth. She's been scared of the bit. She's tried to tongue it out and succeeded only in frothing up her mouth. Something tells her it could come down hard on her tongue and against her lips, this foreign, funny-tasting thing only now beginning to warm up. But it rests easy. As long as she doesn't fight it, it doesn't come down on her. At the corral corners, the reins slant gently along her neck. It happens each time she has to turn a corner. She's beginning to catch on. But then, out in the center of the corral, away from any

5

corners, it happens again. What does *that* mean? Tentatively she turns. Charley's hand falls softly on her neck. "You got it, babe." The filly is pleased. She leaps around a little with Charley laughing on top of her. It's not mysterious anymore. Charley's heel nudges her. She spurts forward. The reins lie on her neck at the corner. That's easy. She turns.

Squatting on his heels against the gatepost, Juan watched Charley circling. He taught her to ride when she was five. He tried to teach her brother as well, but Clay was a different breed of dog, shy of horses when he was little and, as he grew up, liking cars a whole lot more. The boy talked a lot and Juan could never follow. And the father—always meddling, never satisfied, leaving the boy frustrated and ashamed. But nobody cared if Charley rode or not so Juan could take his time. She'd turned out just the way he wanted. He went once a year to the races in Ruidoso, where he had worked when he first swam the river at El Paso and entered the States and established himself. He thought she could ride those horses if she wanted to. She was little and light and tough enough. Of course she was a girl.

When she'd put the filly through its paces, she propped her hands together on the horn and raised herself out of the saddle to lengthen her muscles and looked at Juan. He nodded. She swung her foot over the filly's head and slid off backward and dropped in one motion to kiss the ground. Juan led her over to the fence where the black colt Saud—Juan called him Negrito—was running hard along the fence line, tossing his head and stopping on a dime when anything caught his attention. She hoped he'd be good enough for studding. It was too early yet to tell. Something about the colt excited Juan. When he turned an expectant face toward her, to please him she nodded.

"That one can run," Juan said.

"They're about out of pasture," Charley said. It only meant moving the electric fence and driving the mares and their foals a little way down the draw.

At seven they sat in the kitchen and Lady, in from her trailer parked out back of the house against the windbreak, fed them bacon and eggs and hash browns and buttermilk biscuits with her own preserves. They were off to inoculate the yearlings. Charley tapped one on the shoulder to distract it, threw the needle in the neck, screwed on the syringe, shoved the plunger, removed the apparatus, and tossed the empty into the trayful of serum bottles that Juan, behind her, held.

Before noon she ran the tractor pulling the small baler going *chucketty-chucketty-chucketty* behind her up the windrows. She had borrowed the baler from Will Askew because she wanted square hundred-pounders for the horses. He would borrow her big one later, for the big, round bales, taller than a man, that she used for cattle feed. She twisted around on the metal seat and watched the bales kick out behind her into the fresh-cropped field. Mowed and raked, it looked like a lawn. Up ahead, the dark green windbreak rose with the house roof above it, and alongside, the strip with its wind sock. The little plane parked at the end of the runway reminded her she had to go get Belle. So she parked the tractor, climbed down, and trotted back to join Juan, who was driving the old Ford flatbed slowly across the field. She scrambled atop the prickly load. A teenage boy hired for the day walked behind the truck, grabbing a bale when the truck passed it and bucking it to another boy on the tailgate, who bucked it to Charley, her knees sprung and her legs spread for balance, three tiers up.

When the last row was finished, the old truck crawled with its terraces of hay toward the high pole shed just outside the windbreak. It was August. She was getting a second crop from the irrigated section. She walked into the field alongside the house to meet the giant sprinkler rotating in big, slow circles. The moving monster approached and passed, leaving her soaked and spent and satisfied.

Lady, on the back step, wiped her hands on her apron and called, "You better get going!"

She knew it. She swooped down and picked up a rock and chucked it at a crow hitching a ride on the departing sprinkler. She had to gas up the plane at the pump before taking off. She hoped Belle would be ready and waiting when she got there, but she thought: Fat chance.

Lady had risen from her siesta out in the white trailer house surrounded by its picket fence with its yard of flowers—zinnias, four o'clocks, marigolds, hollyhocks in all colors because the soil favors them and, over the trailer door, morning glories on their vine-covered trellis. She'd had her bath and put on a checkered print with an apron over it to protect it and gone into the house to start dinner. She was busy washing the beans. They were pinto beans, still green, that she would cook like string beans, still in their pod, with a little white meat, which if you're from East Texas is what you call salt pork. They were Belle's favorite vegetable. Her favorite meat, already in the oven, was a leg of lamb.

She had the radio on. A forlorn singer was vowing how he loved her but he's gotta be moving on. They were always vowing how they love you but gotta be moving on. She thought of Charley and Belle up in the clear cornflower sky somewhere, knowing it was a peaceful ride because Belle was scared of flying and wouldn't rock the boat. Only time Charley's ever at the controls, she reflected. Only boat Belle hesitates to rock.

She sliced eggplant for a casserole and put it in a pan to soak. Charley ought to get out more, see some people, make some friends. A girl like that, she could do anything, if only she knew it. Around the place she knew it. Around Belle she didn't.

She scrubbed the sweet potatoes and rubbed their jackets with butter and poked a fork in them so they wouldn't explode in her oven. They never had but she'd heard somewhere they might. All this preparation was premature but she liked to be doing something and it was too early to get in the garden and pick the salad and start watering.

She had cherry pies cooling on the sideboard. The trees in the little scrap of orchard were producing more than she knew what to do with. And cherries were the early fruit. Next she'd have to think about Jonathans and MacIntosh and Golden Delicious, and just when the garden would be folding and she'd have days of canning. Well, she liked having so much planned ahead. It made her feel pacified.

She got the beans on. She would slow-cook them now and heat them up later because you can't rush beans and expect to have anything worth putting in your mouth, and she was thinking of going after some weeds in the flower beds when she heard the plane. She leaned over the sink and looked out the window. Charley burped her engine. She slammed out the screen door into the yard to stand looking up, her hand shading her eyes, squinting into the light. The wind pulled at her skirt, a fretting, entreating wind. It brushed against her legs like a cat. It purred around her while Charley skimmed low over the house and dipped a wing, then fell out of sight north, over the windbreak, where she would circle and set down.

She hurried back inside and grabbed the dish towel hanging on the handle of the refrigerator door and went through the dining room, swiping once more at the table and the top of the buffet around the Styrofoam heads, stooping to look in the mirror running along its top, smiling to see herself reflected in such stately company. She pushed at some hair at the side of her neck. The eyes looking back at her were sad. Maybe they'd always have to be sad about Tearl. And in the eyes she also saw his, because the son favored the mother, only Tearl's were mad, mad as hops, mad at everything. "Howcome you always mad?" she used to ask. Now, too late, she knew how come. It had taken her a long time to see

9

things as Tearl was born seeing them. She wasn't mad, but now she understood his anger. It felt like, once Tearl was missing, he took up lodging inside her. Now, at times, she saw with his eyes, heard with his ears, and stepped back and felt his acid irony. Not long, for she had, as she explained to him, a happy nature while he had an angry one. "The world ain't never *not* been rotten," she told him. "But as it is the only world we got, if you gone be happy, you gotta be happy inside it somewhere. No telling when things'll change. We could be dead and gone." That last still popped out of her, and when it did it made her sad.

"Yoo hoo! Lady! I'm home!"

That was Belle. Lady hurried back through the kitchen in time to see Charley wheeling her down the path through the windbreak. "I thought this time you'd take the roof off!"

Belle laughed her noisy laugh. Charley handed her two aluminum crutches that came to her elbows, and slowly she stood up. Lady tensed, watching. While Charley piled suitcases into the wheelchair, Belle steadied herself, then stood triumphant, propped on her crutches, in a shocking pink pantsuit and a new gold wig and a hat with an enormous brim. Lady eyed the hat. Belle always looked more dressed up than dressed. She was a small woman who looked taller than she was by virtue of some unspecific largeness in her composition.

Slowly she began to move forward, talking as she came. "How you like my aluminum legs!" She paused and put up her face to sniff the air, her bright eyes swimming. "Aw, Lady, what's that I smell? I've laid awake nights dreaming of a leg o' lamb."

"What they feed you at the hospital?"

"I never recognized it. I suspect the surgery adjoins the kitchen and they never waste a thing." She cawed her laugh that sounded like a crow, and Lady gasped and giggled. Belle could take your breath with the things she'd say.

Charley set the suitcases down at the back door. Belle dropped back in the chair, weary, and while Lady stepped outside to get the suitcases, Charley followed the mechanized wheelchair around on the walk to the front where they'd had Ben Bunsen build a ramp over half the front steps so they could get her in and out.

Lady brought in the suitcases and hurried through the house, listening through the open dining room windows to Belle as she rolled alongside on the walk. "But oh, it was a lovely place. Mural paper on the walls, everything carpeted. Figured drapes. They don't paint hospitals white anymore."

Yeah, Lady thought, white would show the dirt.

Charley pushed the wheelchair up the ramp and across the porch that wrapped around two sides of the house. Lady held the front door open and Belle, pausing first for effect, drove in with a flourish.

Charley handed her the crutches again, and in the cool, shadowed hall beside the gun case, between the sliding doors opening on one side into the dining room and on the other into what used to be the parlor, Belle stood up.

"How you like my new pantsuit? I couldn't resist it. Though now that I'm back in this place it's unlikely I'll have occasion to wear it again." She took a few tentative steps. "Smell that!" She meant the leg of lamb.

"We moved your bedroom furniture downstairs," Lady said, "like you wanted. Hope we put things in the right place."

"Oh, look!" Belle said, turning toward the old parlor. "My new bed's come!"

"It's right there waiting for you."

"It's identical to the bed I had in the hospital. I fell in love with that bed. It massages your back, lifts your knees, raises and lowers your head . . . there's nothing that bed can't do." Charley snorted. Belle whirled on her. "It's electric!" She moved toward her new bedroom. "But oh, it's too open. I never thought of that." She pulled at her short chin. "Lady, pull out one of those old sliding doors."

11

They hadn't been touched since Charley and Clay were children driving everybody crazy on rainy days playing with them, but the door rolled smoothly out to leave half the original opening.

"No," Belle said. "Pull them both out a little way and that'll leave the door in the middle."

Lady made the adjustment and looked to see if Belle approved. Belle put her hands together in front of her like a silent clap. She liked things symmetrical.

She slowly made her way into the dining room. She ducked and looked at herself in the buffet mirror. "I'm not crazy about this hat," she muttered. She took it off and dropped it askew on one of the heads and stood propped there on her crutches, looking around. "Now that I'm to be restricted to the ground floor, I might do a little remodeling."

Lady threw up her hands. "Here we go again!"

"You'd never dream," Belle said, moving alongside the buffet toward the head of the table, "how we're unconsciously influenced by our environment. . . . I read the most interesting article in the hospital."

"Where you want this?" Charley asked, leaning on the wheelchair.

"We just got put back together!" Lady said.

"I think I'll remove this wall between the kitchen and the dining room."

"Kitchen's where the mess is! I wouldn't want all that opened up."

Charley sat down in the wheelchair. "One of these days you'll take down a bearing wall and the roof'll come in on you."

"Houses don't have dining rooms anymore. Dining rooms are old-fashioned. I'll tear out the wall and turn all this into an old-timey country kitchen. They're coming back in."

"Last year it was add-a-den," Lady said, "but we still sitting in the dining room."

"This article I read maintained that country kitchens bring the family together."

"You can get too close together," Charley said. "I read where up in Maine they dammed up a harbor mouth so they could dump in their lobster catch to wait for prices to go up. . . ."

"Before the den it was extra bathrooms!"

"When the prices went up, wadn' any lobsters left. All crowded in that way, they turned cannibal and ate each other up."

Belle dropped heavily into her chair at the head of the table and opened her purse and took out her compact. "Since when are you so interested in lobsters?" She pointed with her lipstick at the corner over the old rolltop desk. "I think I'll hang a TV up there where I can see it. They hang them that way in the hospital."

"That's where they hang them in bars," Charley said, wheeling herself past Belle into the kitchen.

"Then it ought to make you feel right at home. Up there they're out of the way. You can see what you're looking at. They think of everything at the hospital. Little individual speakers on your pillow . . ."

"Somebody coming," Lady said. An automobile had turned off the blacktop.

"I was in the new wing. Just like the Holiday Inn. Except for the food, the hospital was a vacation for me."

"Vacation for us, too, wadn' it, Lady?" Charley got a carton of milk out of the refrigerator. She stood up out of the wheelchair and took a swig.

"Looklike we got us a visitor!"

Propelled by a jet of dust, the automobile rushed up the quarter-mile aisle of sunflowers toward the house.

"My insurance called for a private room, but you know me, I wanted company. The first woman they put me with was a rotten patient. They all said what a wonderful patient I was. Perfect strangers, and couldn't do enough for me. It occurred to me while I was in the hospital that families would be better off if they were perfect strangers to one another."

"I always thought it'd be better if they wadn'," Charley said.

"I'm glad I had you forward the paper to me. It allowed me to keep up with what's going on in Tula."

"What's going on in Tula they don't put in the paper," Charley said. She took the milk carton with her to the front window and stood looking out. "It's Theron Turner's taxi."

Belle looked in the mirror of the compact and arranged her lips for the lipstick. "Where'd you put the living room furniture?" She stretched her lips and slid them against each other to get the lipstick spread.

"We moved it up to your old room upstairs," Lady said.

"Yeah," Charley said. "I've got me a sitting room up there across from my bedroom. I've got my thirteen-inch set in there and I hung up my dart board and my elk head."

Belle snapped the compact shut. They heard it in the silence, for the taxi outside had just shut off its motor. "Now that the Lord has seen fit to render me immobile ten miles out in the country from a town with grain elevators for skyscrapers, I'm going to need a little company."

"Looklike you got some," Lady said, going to the door.

"They got the wrong place," Charley said.

Belle put her lipstick away. "I read in the newspaper where they've hired a new teacher for the elementary school."

Lady watched the passenger slide up and sit on the edge of the seat and lean over toward the driver. Then the back door opened and a leg slid out. It had on a tire-soled Mexican sandal and faded stovepipe jeans. Then slowly the whole passenger emerged and straightened up. The top she wore was flamingo-colored and as she turned toward Lady her long earrings caught the sun and glittered.

"Stuck way out here with just you all and the cows," Belle

14

said, "I'll be in need of some lively intelligent company, someone I can talk to. I wrote a letter to this new second-grade teacher."

"Thinking of taking a refresher course?" Charley asked.

When the taxi rumbled over the cattle guard, it took her so by surprise that she gasped and lifted her bottom an inch or two off the seat. Ordinarily, realizing what she had done, she would have collapsed laughing. But she was aware that the driver kept an interested eye on her in the rearview mirror, so she restrained herself and stared out the window. She had passed a number of these places all wrapped up in trees, the roofs just visible, and she had found them otherworldly and mysterious. "Windbreaks," the bus driver had said, but she suspected they were not so much to keep out the wind as to stop the eye, give it some boundary against the limitless space.

"Will you wait?" she said. "I don't know how long I'll be." The stillness, after the motor, after the wind, was eerie. She grasped the top of the front seat and pulled herself forward.

The driver, a short, elderly man in a baseball cap, turned a pale eye upon her. "Miz Burden know you're coming?"

Did he think she was some poor relation, that she might be going to ask these people for her taxi fare? She had heard they were suspicious of strangers out here. She rummaged in her purse and dropped a sheaf of bills, more than the meter called for, onto the front seat beside him and turned to get out. The beak of the baseball cap tipped down, but when he looked back up at her he was no less suspicious. "You planning to go back into town?"

"Yes. No. I'm not sure."

She opened the door and got out and stood looking up at the house. It was a big white house with dark trim around the doors

15

and windows. Over the porch roof the windows of the upper story caught the light of the falling sun and glared out over her head.

Inside the windbreak both sunlight and wind were muted. She passed a red pickup and opened the gate. She peered curiously at the long shed backed up against the trees on one side. The rear end of a light blue car bulged out from under the roof. The stall beside it housed a huge green farming vehicle with an enclosed cab, and next to that what might be another, smaller automobile—she couldn't tell because it was all wrapped up in some kind of cover—and then some large pieces of farm machinery of the kind you hook onto the back end of a tractor. She glanced at the taxi driver and gave him a bright, sudden smile as if he were the one needing encouragement. But he only picked up a newspaper from the seat beside him and spread it on the steering wheel and peered down at it through his bifocals.

A red dog came down the walk toward her, a young dog with its head held up comically on its long neck. She had been wary of dogs since Mexico. She hoped she would get over it. But you could tell this one was friendly. The tail, she thought, certainly in this case wagged the canine. She put out her hand and he smelled it and dropped a long pink tongue out one side of his mouth and smiled.

She heard voices. They sounded angry. A woman was standing at the screen door looking at her, a pretty woman, not coffee and cream, more coffee and milk, with her hair in tight marcels like the queens of the silent movies. She was smiling a little nervously as the voices behind her swelled.

She moved on, reassured by the flower border around the house and lining the walk, profuse and unpremeditated, as if someone had thrown fistfuls of seed and everything had come up—delphiniums that held their heads up, not the new hybrids too heavy for their stalks, and zinnias, nasturtiums. And larkspur! She couldn't believe it. She bent down close and picked one small blossom from a flowering purple spire and raised it to her face and there it was, the rabbit in its pulpit. Morning glories with their deep blue fluted horns and creamy throats climbed the porch railing, and running low along the walk, moss roses, portulaca. The grass didn't grow so well. It straggled, leaving patches of sandy yard bare. Someone looked after the flowers, but nobody bothered about the grass.

She began walking again, but the voices cracked inside. She avoided looking at the woman in the door. A ramp covered one side of the steps, a ramp for an invalid—new, she could see, the paint was quite fresh. In the other side yard, where the windbreak thinned, something fluttered in the wind on a pole. She feared it might be a flag. She caught sight of the edge of a trailer out back, white and surrounded by flowers. She hoped for a moment it was the trailer that was for rent. But the letter had said a room.

———————

Lady's smile was beginning to feel like plaster. Belle and Charley behind her didn't seem to be running down.

"It's not vacant, I tell you!"

"Please, I'm just back from the hospital."

"I'd like a little privacy for a change!"

"Any more privacy, you'll be unfit for human companionship. You live with those horses as it is."

"I don't want a schoolteacher living up there with me."

Lady was afraid the stranger had heard that, for she paused on the walk. KC, Clay's dog, had wagged himself up to her and now was following her. They made a slow procession between the flower borders. KC was supposed to be a watchdog but he acted more like a welcoming committee.

"Strange, idn' it,' Belle said. "Tula never used to import schoolteachers. Second grade was just taught by somebody's wife."

"I'll move out to the tack room!"

"You'll be in for meals, I suppose."

Lady kept her smile on. The stranger climbing the front steps looked uneasy. She had a small, delicate chin with a dimple in it the size of a thumbprint, and her eyes behind wire-rimmed spectacles were cinnamon-colored. Her hair, reddish brown and parted in the middle and held at her temples by little silver clasps in the shape of feathers, mantled her shoulders, so curly it wouldn't wave. She looked both old-fashioned and very up-to-date. Lady thought she was very pretty. She peered at Lady over the tops of the glasses and shoved them up with her finger, at the same time sniffing them back in place.

"I'm Juna Evers?" she said. "I'm looking for a Mrs. Belle Burden?"

Lady's sympathy went out to her. She didn't know what to do but open the door.

Juna hesitated, trying to look more casual than she felt. No doubt about it. The voices were definitely angry. She looked in their direction and the woman who had met her at the door ushered her to the big double door of what appeared to be the dining room. The voices fell silent. The person at the table seemed dressed for an amateur theatrical, and over at the window an undersize cowboy stood with his back to the room.

"My," the woman said. "You're a little young thing, aren't you. I'm Belle Burden. Welcome to the Wild West." She laughed.

Enthusiasm welled up in Juna. "I'm so glad I took the bus. Though the trip was sooooo long." Her shoulders slumped forward and her tongue fell out to illustrate. She straightened and got her mouth closed, but too late. Belle Burden's eyes brightened as if she had glimpsed some exotic creature in the foliage. Juna blushed and tried to retrieve the moment. "I've been all over the world. I'm just back from Latin America. But I've never seen anything remotely resembling Kansas. It's majestic!"

The black woman said, "That's what they call the picture show in town."

It was clearly meant to be encouraging, and Juna was grateful. She laughed. "I've been here less than an hour and already I sound like a Rotarian."

Belle Burden, with her round face and large eyes and the plump mole snuggling up under the edge of her nose for protection against the elements, was looking her up and down and drawing conclusions. "Nothing wrong with that," she said. "You can thank your lucky stars you were born wherever you were born and not in one of those little off-brand countries that all they've got to export is revolution. You travel light."

"I left my things in lockers at the bus station till I could—" It annoyed her that she blushed so easily.

"My daughter Charlene here will drive you in to get them," Belle said. "You can let the taxi go."

Juna glanced confused toward the window. "You're going to love it here," Belle said. "Lady's a wonderful cook."

Juna looked at Lady. "I'd hoped to do my own cooking. I'm a vegetarian."

Belle Burden's laugh sounded like an extended bellow. "This' a cattle ranch," she said. Juna was drawn to the laugh. She liked its vitality.

Lady said, "I always put in a garden big enough to get a family of twelve through the winter."

When Juna eyed Lady again, Belle said piously, "Lady is not a servant. She's a friend of the family." Juna could see that Belle was a mind reader and used this skill to her advantage.

"Then howcome nobody else ever does the dishes?" Lady asked, and Juna smiled. She had a slow, head-ducked smile that made her seem to be smiling up at you. It looked either very seductive or very shy. Lady guessed it was probably the latter. Matching the thumbprint in her chin, two more appeared in her cheeks. It was a face of high color, like a particularly appealing peach.

"You're going to love the room," Belle said, and added, inspired, "It's a bed-sitting room."

A snort came from over by the window.

"It's a good bed," Belle said, and then added solemnly, "My children were conceived in that bed."

From over by the window an outraged, choking sound.

"You'll only share the bath with Charlene here," Belle said, throwing Juna into confusion. "But you won't see much of her. She's off and gone most of the time. She's more at home—ha ha—on the range."

Juna glanced toward the window and saw a twitch that looked electric spiral up the figure standing there.

"Could I maybe see the room?"

"It was my bedroom," Belle said as if defending it, "from the day Fletcher Burden carried me over the threshold a bride. I'd never have given it up, but I've just had plastic hip joints installed. The result of a rare condition . . ."

A thin scrap of a laugh escaped the figure at the window but Juna restrained herself from turning.

". . . and I can no longer climb the stairs. Lady, take her up and show her the room."

She was glad to follow Lady toward the stairs.

"I'm real pleased," Belle said when she thought the coast was clear. "She's an original, but so feminine. You can learn a lot from her if you pay attention."

"Rare condition!"

"Now I'm warning you. You'll just have to adjust to a new situation. It's broadening to adjust to new situations. She'll be stimulating company for me and a good example for you. You can see she's got style. Every eligible bachelor in the county will be after her."

"Yeah, all three. Tom Jenkins going on eighty and Pig Miller. And then there's Joyce Perkins."

Belle guffawed, then sobered. "Don't forget Warren Hubble."

Charley exploded. "Howcome nobody else has any say around here?"

"Nobody else pays the bills."

Juna, lingering on the stairs, had gained the upper hall. Charley's footsteps headed for the door. "I'm going to Smoky's!" The screen door slammed and she rattled down the front steps. "I'm gunna get drunk!"

Belle called after her, "Crack up that pickup, you're on shank's mare! I mean it, Charley!"

With dismay Juna heard the taxi outside crank up. The driver must have finished his paper and got tired of waiting. She ran into the bedroom where Lady had gone and watched the rocket of dust shoot the taxi back toward the blacktop and town. Now what? Below her Charley stormed down the walk. For a wild moment she thought of flinging up the window and crying out, "Wait for me!" But then an old man in a battered straw hat straightened up from where he'd been working on a tractor and called out something she could have sworn was Spanish, and Charley got out of the red pickup and left the truck door hanging open and walked over to see what he wanted, and Juna got her first good look. Short, dark hair sprayed out from the crown of the head, where several twigs stood up. A fringe fanned down over the forehead. Wide cheekbones made the face look short, and black eyebrows dipped over her nose into a steep V that attached them across her face like a set of wings. The lips were as long as the eyebrows. She stood listening, then bent to see what he was showing her on the tractor. Then she took off her denim vest and folded it over the seat and slid under the tractor to look at something. After a minute she reached out a hand and the old Mexican laid a tool across her palm. Juna was impressed.

21

She felt Lady watching. She turned and looked around at the room. It was furnished with a brass double bed, an easy chair with a hassock, a floor lamp peering over its shoulder, an old-fashioned library table with a straight chair, and a square oak rocker. These things pleased her. But there was also a television set—she abhorred television—a dart board on the closet door, some weight-lifting devices on the floor, and a stuffed elk head with staring glass eyes and flat-plate antlers on the wall over the bed.

"You don't have to put up with that," Lady said. "It can go back where it came from. Go ahead. Try the bed."

Obediently she lay down, then felt foolish. The elk head from that angle startled her up again.

Lady laughed, kicked off her shoes, stepped up onto the bed, took down the unwieldy head, and, balancing its weight, stepped drunkenly around on the springs, laughing. Juna laughed too. Lady started barefoot across the hall and Juna hurried to help. As she passed the bath she let go the elk and paused to look in. The tub and sink were bright red with brass fixtures, and the carpet was pink and fuzzy. A book lay open on its face beside the toilet. She stepped closer and read the title: *Outstanding Studs of the Year*. Her hand fluttered to her throat.

She found Lady rehanging the head over Charley's white iron bedstead with its thin mattress, the sheets and blankets pulled tight and tucked square. The bed was the only neat thing in the room otherwise strewn with socks and boots and horse magazines. A wide-brimmed straw hat hung on one bedpost, a vest on another, and on another some sort of leather harness. Along one wall an old-fashioned clothes press stood with its door hanging open, disclosing chaos. Beside it was an untidy boot rack.

She bent over the dresser to look at framed photos of horses, some with blue ribbons attached. Out here she meant to acquaint herself with horses. Stuck in the side of the mirror was a fading photograph of a girl about ten in a cowboy outfit, matching six-

22

shooters strapped to her legs, their handle butts forward. The girl was squinting unhappily at the sun. She had a short face and high cheekbones and a long upper lip, the center node prominent, vulnerable-looking, like a bee sting. Beside it was a newspaper clipping of somebody coming off a bucking bronc, caught in midair, the face toward the camera, surprised. The caption read "Bronc Bucks Burden." The picture was mounted on cardboard and edged in black.

Lady walked over and looked and laughed. "That's Charley," she said. "One year she got herself in the bronc riding at the rodeo." Lady walked toward the door. "Make yourself at home. Look around. Take your time." She left Juna and went back down the stairs.

Belle looked up expectantly as she descended. "Well?" she said. "How she like the room?"

"She a little puzzled. She don't know what to make of this bunch."

"She might as well get used to us," Belle said. "I intend to make her one of the family."

"Idn' she lucky!" Lady said, heading for the kitchen.

Belle took off the gold wig. Her own hair was pinkish and thin. Her homecoming was so suddenly over she felt let down. She picked up the phone and dialed.

When Lady heard the long dial for long distance and then "Marlon?" she stopped listening. "Futures," filtered through, and "margins" and "municipals." And once Belle asked, "Is that over the counter or through the exchange?" Then she hung up and dialed again. "Ben? That you? This Belle Burden," and Lady, in the kitchen, was all ears. "Well, I haven't *been* around. I've been in Kansas City having my plastic hips installed." A pause. Then Belle's guffaw. "How do *I* know what color!" Lady chuckled. She added a quarter-cup of water to the beans. "Ben, look, are you available?" A wait, then another laugh. "Y'ol lecher. You're going to have to get out here. I've got a wall that

23

might have to come out." There was a pause, then a shriek of laughter. "You shouldn't of been a carpenter. You should of gone on television."

Upstairs Juna sat on the bed and looked out the window at the horizon line beyond the blacktop a quarter-mile away where she had so recently turned off in the taxi under the high entry made of logs with one cross beam on which was mounted, dead center, the dry, white skull of a cow with perfectly matching horns.

She had, of course, pictured the place. The fantasy had pitched her into confusion when she confronted the reality. She felt suddenly overcome with that hollow sense of loneliness born of being plunked down inside an unfamiliar place where nobody knows you and you haven't got a friend and where you know you are going to be for some time. Still, she liked the rambling old house with its good smells of cooking. She liked Lady. Then she looked down and saw the rug. How could she have missed it? Where could it have come from, so out of keeping with the rest? It appeared to be very old. The warp showed through. It was so beautiful she wanted to bend and lay the palm of her hand just lightly upon it. In the light of the late sun it was like looking at a garden under pale wine, and it reminded her of the flower borders outside in the afternoon sun. She decided to give the place a try.

When she came downstairs, she was startled to see a stranger at the head of the dining room table, but when the stranger looked up it was only Belle Burden in a different wig. "Well," Belle said. "What do you think?"

Juna stopped at the foot of the stairs and clutched the head of the newel post for support and said, "I'll take it."

Belle tried to bounce once in her chair. "I knew you would! Lady!" Lady stuck her head in from the kitchen, a dish towel in her hand. "See if Charley has left yet. Tell her I want her in here."

Lady ambled through the dining room past Juna to the front door. "Charley!"

"Tell her I want her to run Juna into town to get her things."

Over Lady's shoulder Juna saw Charley slide out from under the tractor, throw down the tool, climb onto the seat and start up the motor. It chugged a minute, hiccupped, then ran smoothly. She climbed down and Juan took her place and she stood hunched a little forward with her hands on her hips watching him drive off toward the implement shed. Then she strode over to her truck and got in and started the motor. Juna was sure she would drive off and leave her standing there embarrassed, but though the motor gunned again, the truck sat waiting. She grabbed her purse from where she'd left it on top of the gun case and flew past Lady out the door and across the porch and down the steps.

———

All the way into Tula, country western blared from the radio and Charley stared straight ahead at the road. Juna, uncomfortable, looked out her window at the countryside. She was wondering if she'd made a terrible mistake. But that's bound to happen when you've taken a giant step that is irrevocable, she told herself. Yet she longed for trees. She could all but see the wind. The windows were open and it whipped through the cab and tugged at the roots of her hair. Along with the wind there was the noisy music. She felt so lonely she could have cried. She thought of Muriel Gebberfield, her best friend from high school, now married with three small children, and a hollow gaped inside her she missed Muriel so much. Actually, whenever they'd seen each other in the past ten years, their talk had consisted of *oh Juna* and *oh Muriel* and *it's so good* over and over again. They'd come to have so little in common. But now it seemed to her that if she

25

could only spend an hour with Muriel Gebberfield she would be restored.

Moving only her eyes, not her head, she stole a glance at Charley. Just then Charley's hand fell on the gearshift knob and hung there by the fingers. It was small-boned and squarish with long, narrow fingers, the nails bitten to the quick, and still smeared with grease from the tractor. The faded blue work shirt cuffs were rolled back a couple of turns and the arms and wrists were smoothly brown. She eyed Charley's feet in their slant-heel boots with pointed toes and her own in their sandals felt suddenly naked. She cut her eyes till she could see Charley's middle sunk concave into the seat. She wanted a look at her face up close but she didn't dare. She thought of trying to engage her in conversation but the idea filled her with a sense of futility. Charley's company intensified her loneliness.

The pickup passed the rodeo grounds with billboards heralding the fall event. One had a gigantic figure of a cowboy thrown high on the humped back of a bronc. She thought of the photo stuck in Charley's mirror. The cowboy's head and raised hand leapt up off the billboard, a cutout against the cloudless sky. Charley speeded up. She never turned her eyes from the road. They passed a Ford dealership with bunting whipped by the wind, an implement sales yard full of John Deere tractors, and a truck stop with a lot of semis parked outside.

The pickup slowed when it came to a sign that read TULA, with an arrow pointing to the right. Opposite the sign, across the blacktop near the railroad siding, grain elevators like Siamese quintuplets soared to dominate the landscape. The pickup turned off past a roadside tourist rest—a couple of picnic tables under little pitched roofs on poles, two fiberglass privies, some garbage cans chained to a concrete slab, and a few wind-bent trees—and into Main Street, which, lined with diagonally parked pickups, split the town as it rushed toward the courthouse square and circled it. The pickup swerved in parallel to the curb in the Greyhound bus stop. Charley didn't turn off the motor. Juna hesitated. "I'll just be a minute," she said, because she had to say something, and slammed the door without looking at Charley.

Inside the café that doubled as the bus stop, buttocks of every shape, all of them in jeans, hung off the counter stools. A cowboy stood at the expanse of plate glass watching for the bus, his tooled saddle on the floor beside him. She opened a locker and loaded up with a couple of suitcases. She tried shoving the heavy door open without setting anything down, said "Damn" under her breath, and managed a smile when the cowboy opened the door and held it for her.

Charley sat in the truck while she dumped her things into the truck bed and returned to the depot for another load. She opened a second locker and loaded herself down with her portable typewriter and portable sewing machine, her backpack, a canvas duffel bag, and a winter coat. She dumped everything over the tailgate and then fell over it herself and hung for a minute like a discarded rag doll. When she straightened, she saw Charley's head cocked toward the rearview mirror. She heard the ignition switch off. The radio went out with it, then came back on. She could feel Charley's impatience. She headed inside again, opened another locker, and grabbed out a worn and bulging briefcase, a rolled exercise mat, and a carton of books.

The cowboy shouldered his saddle and headed out the door ahead of her. A bus had pulled in behind the pickup. It blew its horn impatiently as she unloaded her burdens into the truck bed, sounding, she thought, like it was blowing its nose. She hurried around to her side and got in just as Charley gave the bus driver a finger. She gasped and laughed.

And back they went past the tourist rest and the grain elevators and the railroad siding, past the truck stop, the implement sales yard and the Ford dealership. It was all beginning to look familiar. She stole a look at Charley and caught Charley at that mo-

27

ment stealing a look at her. They both looked quickly back at the road.

They repassed the rodeo grounds. "I've never seen a rodeo," she said. But Charley didn't answer. Bite your tongue, she told herself.

Charley thumped the buttons on the radio. An announcer came on chanting crop prices. Wheat was up, corn was down, hog bellies soared, and beef futures held. It was another language. They turned off the blacktop and raced up the drive. When they crossed the cattle guard, she felt again the impulse to lift her bottom off the seat and giggle, but she controlled herself. The truck skidded on the gravel to a stop and she got out and started taking things from the truck bed. Charley sat for a minute with the motor running. Then she got out and began setting things from the truck bed onto the ground. Juna smiled tentatively, but Charley never looked at her. When her things were all out of the truck, Charley got back in, slammed the door, and sped off on a tunnel of dust toward the highway, leaving her standing there alone.

———————

A couple of miles in the other direction down the blacktop, facing catty-corner to an intersection, stood a long, low, sleyed-log building with a sign across its weather-gray wood-shingled roof that said SMOKY'S in big individual wooden letters painted yellow. The roof slanted out over a boardwalk and along the boardwalk ran a rail like a hitching post. The fire-engine-red pickup nosed in between a hybrid vehicle part-car, part-truck, but actually neither, and a dark, three-quarter-ton king cab pickup, both of which she recognized. She reached up and got her pool cue in its black leather case from the gun rack.

As she started in, a young man with tan, crinkly hair and tan, ruddy skin, in jeans and a blue bib shirt, started out.

28

He stepped to the door. She had to stop.

"Charley."

"Warren."

"Hi you been?"

She lifted her shoulders. "Pretty good. Hi 'bout you?"

He lifted his. "Pretty good I guess."

She looked at the top of his chest where the smooth blue front of the bib stretched taut and snapped. For a minute he didn't move. Then he moved and she smiled up at him, a bright, quick smile, polite, and went on in.

He turned and stood in the door looking after her, and as she sat nervously on the bar stool and waited for her beer, she felt him there. But after a minute she heard the motor of the king cab start up.

She put her elbows wide apart on the bar and propped her chin on her laced fingers between them and sat hunched. Whenever she ran into Warren Hubble, he made her feel like something was her fault.

Smoky was drying glasses behind the bar. He was a balding, bearish man with a lot of hair on his arms through which, on one, a red-and-blue tattoo showed indistinctly like an old wound faultily healed. It was a long, dark room with rafters where on hot days sparrows sometimes fluttered, and the walls were lined with wooden booths. It was empty except for Smoky, doubled by the big mirror behind him, and Harvey Sears down at the end of the bar. He was a young man with hair long on his neck, a very smooth face, eyes too close together, and a mustache with ends that drooped on either side of his red-lipped mouth. Charley avoided looking at Harvey's mouth. It struck her as a part better not exposed. He was the owner of the Ranchero parked outside. He sat at the end of the bar watching her wait for a bottle of beer then walk with it toward the pool table. She set the beer down and got her cue out of its case and fitted its parts together. She racked up the balls and broke them. They rumbled over the table. She stood chalking her cue and studying the emerging constellations. When she sank a shot that had to be banked off the side of the table and then launched by means of a second ball, she looked up, expressionless, at Smoky. Smoky, also expressionless, had paused to watch. He took up his chore again.

She drank her beer and studied the table while Harvey Sears played a silent ditty with his fingers on the bar and studied her. One by one she put all the balls away. He walked over and tapped her on the shoulder. She laid down her cue. They walked outside. She took the rifle from her gun rack in the pickup, aimed at the stop sign across the dirt crossroad, and fired. A new bullet hole appeared among its brothers in the center of the O. She offered the rifle to Harvey, but he sighed and shook his head. She replaced the gun in the gun rack and they walked back inside the bar where Harvey held up two fingers to Smoky and dredged money out of his pocket while she returned to her pool.

When he'd got the beers from Smoky, he took them over to where she was racking up the balls again and set hers down on the rim of the table. She picked it up and drank.

"I was hoping we could have a little talk," he said.

She carefully removed the triangle and hung it on the rack on the wall. She leaned over the table and sighted along the cue.

"It could do you a lot of good."

The balls broke and rumbled over the table.

"I don't see what you've got against it. It'd just be an experiment." Damn it, wasn't she a girl? When you want something from girls you just take them dancing and sweet-talk them a little. But not this one. If she'd been her brother, they could have gone out drinking, and maybe hunting in the fall and tended to business that way. But you couldn't go hunting with a girl, not even if she outshoots you every time. Especially not if she outshoots you every time. He ran his hand through his hair, as frustrated as ever, sighed, and took a cue off the rack. "How 'bout a game?"

Charley wanted to be alone, but she had to be practical. "Same as before?"

He nodded. He had no more chance of winning here than he'd had outside. He always ended up buying the beers. Otherwise she wouldn't have put up with him. But Belle kept her short of cash and Smoky sometimes got nervous about her tab. He was soon at the bar for two more beers even though Charley couldn't keep her mind on the game. She was burning about the invasion of her space by Belle's new boarder, who was at that moment wandering in the lengthening shadows around the backyard, peering into the implement sheds, exclaiming over a late litter of kittens she found nuzzling up to their mother in a corner full of empty feed sacks. The mother, black and white with slanted green eyes, seemed friendly. She picked up a kitten, all black except for a pursy white muzzle. It went limp against her breast and began to purr. The purr was so small she felt rather than heard it. She stroked the kitten and held it up to check its gender. The mother cat was watching, her head laid back and weaving on her neck like a snake's, as if she might be nearsighted, so she laid the kitten back with its little pug muzzle forward in the nursing lineup.

She wandered through the vegetable garden, down one row and up another. The sun sat on the horizon. The air already had that moldy chill that comes after sundown, and she made a vague connection between that and the damp of the recently watered garden. The big squash vines were full of zucchini and crookneck and winter squash about the size of softballs—pumpkins and those gray-green globes. She recognized radish tops and the furry tops of carrots, and beans strung on string, and lettuce and spinach. And along one side, the permanent beds—big, leafy, red-stalked rhubarb and asparagus gone to seed. She loved gardens. Outside Lady's picket fence she stopped and looked at the flowers. A lamp was on in the trailer. It looked cozy inside. She'd never seen a trailer house up close.

"I'm not home," Lady called from the kitchen door across the yard.

Juna was embarrassed, as if she'd been caught snooping.

"Supper's about ready. Come keep us company."

The kitchen smelled like Thanksgiving. "They'll be plenty vegetables," Lady said, "and a salad. And I fixed you a batch of rice. You won't go hungry."

The old man was sitting on a stool beside the stove smoking, his pipe completely enveloped in his fist, his elbow on his crossed knee and his big knob-toed work boot swinging.

"This here's Juan," Lady said. At the sound of his name he looked up and nodded. His curly black skullcap with its widow's peak matched circumflex eyebrows over deep-set eyes and cheeks like arroyos.

"*Buenos días*," she ventured.

"Ah," he smiled, lifting his face by way of hello. "*Bueno. Como esta?*" His voice was a pleasant, soft tenor.

"Juan helps out around the place. Probably a wetback, but plenty dry by now," Lady said.

"Oh, good! I can practice my Spanish!"

"You speak it?"

"A little."

"I can say *bueno* and *en mas* and *una poquito*. Charley can talk it some. Her and Juan run the place together."

"Imagine!"

"Howcome you teaching school way out here?" Lady was bending to peer into the oven. She slid out the roast and spooned the drippings over it.

"I'd have stayed in Mexico except for the state of women there." She shrugged. "So I went home for a visit."

"Where's home?"

"Long Island." Lady looked blank. "New York."

32

"Who-ee," Lady said.

"But I've outgrown the East. It gives me claustrophobia. I guess I wanted an adventure."

Lady set the roast on the kitchen table. "You seen too many Westerns."

She smiled. "Not that kind of adventure." She looked hungrily at the big platter full of sliced carrots and cucumbers and tomatoes on a bed of ruffled garden lettuce. She studied the illuminated Coors clock on the wall over the sink, its face a waterfall that by some trick of internal lighting actually bubbled.

"We ready to eat," Lady said, "but where's Charley!"

"She doesn't seem very friendly."

"Charley?" Lady made a trip to the dining room, loaded down. The table was already set. Juna counted five places. "She got her nose out of joint just now. Don't let that fool you." She returned empty-handed, picked up the roast, and headed back. The wigged heads on the sideboard watched.

Juna stole a sprig of parsley and ate it. There was the mother cat, at the door. Lady let her in and she came and stood in front of Juna, looking up, her head weaving a little to see better. "She'll notice anything new to the place," Lady said. "Bring in a bag of groceries, she'll note everything comes out of it and then climb in the empty sack. Howcome you left your babies, Mary Jane?" Mary Jane went over to the bowl of milk under the sink and folded her tail neatly around herself and drank.

"You're not from Kansas, are you?" Juna asked.

Lady picked up the bowls of vegetables—the green beans, the rice, and the eggplant casserole—and headed back again to the dining room. "Naw. I'm not from Kansas."

"What brought *you* here?"

Lady straightened and checked the table, wiping her hands on her apron. "A breakdown."

"Oh," Juna said, her voice hushed. She debated a moment over the propriety, but then she asked, "Mental? Or physical."

Lady laughed. "Mechanical. Me and Nap—that's short for Napoleon, his father was a little man—we was headed for California in this old Ford, Tearl on the way. So here we were. Stuck. Had to make enough to fix the car. Before we could do that, here come Tearl. One thing after another . . . you know how it is. The worry got to Nap. He took sick. Then hospital bills, doctor bills. They ate us up. They say money don't matter but they wrong. We the slaves of money—the poor getting it, the rich keeping it."

"If you've stayed this long, you must be fond of this family."

Lady chuckled. "I don't ask too much of people." She checked the table again and raised her voice toward the front of the house. "Supper's on the table!" She closed a window where the wind had taken the curtain and billowed it over the back of a chair. "How'll you get to school and back?"

"I can ride the school bus."

"Lucky you!" Mary Jane was at the door. Lady let her out. The aluminum canes thumped toward the dining room.

"I won't mind," Juna said. "I missed a lot growing up. I want all those experiences."

"Some things better missed."

Juna spied the pies where Lady had set them out of the way on a shelf. "Look at that crust! What do you use for shortening?"

"They ain't but one thing to use in a pie crust and that's lard."

Juna raised her eyebrows doubtfully. "I'm really fond of food. Imagine the emotions of the first woman to stumble onto a soufflé."

"If she'd a stumbled on one of mine," Lady said, "she'd a broke a toe."

"Oh, they're easy. I'll show you."

"Don't show me. Just go ahead and make 'em."

Juna surveyed the big, old-fashioned kitchen with new interest. The glass-front cabinets soared. It would take a ladder to get to the highest shelves. There were acres of counter top and a table in the center for extra work space. She saw herself and Lady sitting there shelling peas or paring fruit and swapping recipes. The big old-fashioned sink with its enamel drain board was attached to the wall, and under it, on the floor, was the bowl of cream and a larger bowl of water. Tall windows on the east and the garden, and others on the south, would fill the room with light all day, though now all you could see through them was the dim outline of the sky over the top of the windbreak. She was suddenly overcome with a sense of well-being. She doubted it would last.

Belle appeared from the hallway and stood on her crutches in the door, looking cranky till she spied Juna and remembered. She still had on her pink pantsuit, though it was crumpled now from her rest.

Juan got up and knocked out his pipe in the palm of his hand and threw the dottle out the screen door. He put the pipe down on the windowsill and walked into the dining room, not looking at anybody, and took his accustomed place. Belle lumbered toward the head of the table. Lady said, "Sit there," and pointed, and Juna sat on Belle's left, with Lady across from her, next to Juan.

"So. Long Island," Belle said, whipping her napkin open. "What's it like, Long Island?"

Juna was at a loss.

"What's your father do?" Those inquisitive bright eyes were on her.

"He's retired," she said.

"Retired from what?"

"He was a stockbroker, but he retired from that to devote full time to drinking."

Belle hooted. "I come from a largely military family myself," she said. "My husband Fletcher Burden used to say if he'd had it all to do over, he'd of joined the military. He said it's the only place left where a man's still free to shoot from the hip." She offered the platter of roast to Juna but Juna declined. Belle re-

35

membered, "Oh," and passed her the rice. "Fletcher was the last of the great beef barons. You could look at him and tell he was a dignitary. When Fletcher Burden went to town, they stepped into the street to let him pass. And he did it with just the look of his eye."

"He's . . . I take it he's passed away?"

"He didn't pass away. He died with his boots on! A hunting accident. Pass the beans."

Lady passed them and pushed her chair back from the table to check on the corn bread.

"What you're going to miss most out here is cultural events," Belle said. "Concerts and things."

"Well, I like movies and I'm not much into western music."

"Believe me, I'm not either, but it's all you get out here when you turn on the radio."

Juan reached across Lady's place and helped himself to more gravy. He ate steadily and purposefully, with clean, careful manners, without looking up.

"I mean western in the sense of . . . I'm not into classical music," Juna said.

"Oh, well," Belle said, and Juna could see that Belle wasn't either but didn't think it was the kind of thing to admit to. "What *do* you like?"

"Well, I'm into . . . I've gotten interested in things like . . . the Bora drum."

Lady returned with a pan of hot corn bread and put it in the center of the table. Juan's polite hand reached out and claimed a wedge.

"It's this Amazon group. They play mostly drums," Juna said. "And they chant."

Lady said, "I think I saw that group on the tube. White satin pants? Lots of rhinestones?"

Juna chewed thoughtfully and swallowed. "Not that kind of group. It's more like a . . . tribe."

Lady was butt ing corn bread. "Like in the woods?"

Juna took a sip of water and nodded.

"Not much clothes on?"

Juna shoved her fork under the rice and nodded again.

Lady said, "Oh."

They all heard Charley's pickup coming. They went on eating, passing things. Belle complimented Lady again on the lamb. She said that in spite of having married a beef baron, her favorite piece of meat was leg o' lamb. And Lady said it was hers, too, next to pork, and Juna said she loved pork but she'd always been scared to eat it because when she was little her mother had told her people who eat pork sometimes get tricky noses. "To this day," she said, "after I eat pork I find myself touching my nose or looking in a mirror." Belle bellowed. She said it was the best joke she'd heard all week. They communicated out here a lot in jokes, Juna saw. She thought she might pick it up.

They all heard Charley's truck door slam. Belle's mouth took on a stern, disapproving look. Lady went to get a glass of milk and set it at the empty place opposite Belle at the other end of the table. Conversation languished. Then they all started to say something at once. They were waiting for Charley to come through the door, which presently she did, banging it closed behind her. She took her seat without a word and began helping her plate to the food.

"I'd like to know where you've been," Belle said.

"Smoky's. I told you."

"I don't like the idea of you in that bar alone."

"I wadn' alone."

"Who was there?"

"Lots of people. Harvey Sears."

"Harvey!" Belle said. "Now he's an interesting man, not unlike Fletcher Burden at that age. He's a man of vision, gumption, get up and go. A big, good-looking thing, too. At your age"—she looked from Juna to Charley and back—"Harvey Sears would have been my ideal. Except, of course, for the one thing."

"What one thing is that?" Charley asked.

"I suspect he might be Hebrew."

Charley snorted. Juna's fork paused halfway to her mouth.

"I don't have a prejudiced bone in my body, but I have to live in this community."

Lady, buttering her corn bread with the carving knife, could have told anybody that Belle lived very little in the community and did not much care whether she pleased or outraged it, and if she'd had a preference it might well have been the latter. But Lady didn't say anything. She didn't meddle with Belle unless she had to.

"Harvey's an independent driller," Belle explained to Juna.

Charley said without looking up, "He's an aging hippie-turned-Hindu's got this diviner divines she's sitting on the biggest bubble of natural gas in Kansas."

Juna was startled. It might be construed that Charley was addressing this remark to *her*.

Belle belched behind her napkin and laughed. "All these raw vegetables, I could be persuaded he's right."

Charley said, "He's offered her a fortune and just keeps upping his ante."

"That don't sound nice," Lady said.

"I admire you," Juna said, "for not selling out to oil interests."

"Gas," Charley said without looking up. "And Reenie, she come in."

"Don't mention that name in this house!" Belle said, setting down her glass of water with such force on the tablecloth that a little bit slopped over. "She is responsible for Buddy's death and you know it!"

Charley went on cutting her meat.

Belle got hold of herself and turned to Juna. "Buddy—Clay Burden—was my son. He accidentally shot himself."

Charley said, "Five people and a bird dog witnessed him putting the gun in his mouth and pulling the trigger."

Belle said, "He didn't know the gun was loaded."

Lady said, "I hope I live to see the day when there's a gun on this place that's not loaded."

Belle said angrily, "I'll get my grandson away from her if it's the last thing I do. She's no fit mother."

"Howcome?" Charley said. "She keeps him burped and fed and dry. She keeps him away from you."

"She's nothing but a hippie. She uses drugs."

"Aw, hell . . ."

"She sleeps with men!"

"What you want her to sleep with?"

"The current one is Mexican!"

Juna glanced at Juan and was aware that Charley and Lady did the same, but Juan just went on pushing up his beans with his corn bread.

"Not a prejudiced bone in her body," Lady said.

"No," Charley said, "it's in her head."

Belle said, "Humph. Barefoot, in rags, they came in off the road one at a time and first thing you know, what've we got? A commune!"

"That all seems like a long time ago," Lady said.

"Called herself a refugee from Wellesley College! She seduced my son."

Charley said, "Aw, for crissake. She never would of had him if she could of got rid of him."

"That's it! That's why he did it!"

Charley, leaning on one elbow on the table, holding her fork out over her plate with a bite of lamb upon it, looked up and said, "Hear what you just said? You just admitted he did it on purpose."

Belle gave a little cry, like a sob. "All you want is to hurt—*hurt*—HURT people!"

Juan wiped his mouth thoroughly, folded his napkin, and slid out of his chair, finished. Lady got up and headed for the kitchen with a couple of empty bowls. "Who needs some coffee?"

Nobody answered.

"It's very good . . . the corn bread," Juna said. Nobody else said anything. "Would you like to hear one of my tapes?" She'd said the first thing that came into her head.

Belle looked at her blankly. Tapes were something that if you had them you called the vet.

"My machine's upstairs." Juna slid out of her chair, needing badly to escape. When she returned, Lady was making the rounds with her coffeepot and Juan had lit up his pipe again out in the kitchen. Juna set the tape recorder at the empty place beside her on the table and pushed the play button. A low, husky chant filled the room, backed by intermittent hand drums. Lady imagined them in a ring on the forest floor, the trees so high overhead she couldn't see their tops and so thick up there they cut out the light. She paused a moment, then went on pouring. Belle stared at her new boarder. But Juna closed her eyes the better to hear the rhythm.

At a point where the chant renewed its vigor, Juna opened her eyes and found herself looking straight into Charley's. It was the first time Charley had looked directly at her. She did so with a face from which all expression had been laundered. She had something in her mouth, but in the interval she had stopped chewing. Juna smiled uncertainly, whereupon Charley turned back to her plate and went on eating. But after she turned away, Juna was left with an after-image of eyes the palest gray she'd ever seen, with a violet rim around the iris, and paler still for those dark, loop-de-loop eyebrows. They reminded her of hot ice.

2

Outside the windbreak Charley lived all the way through to her center. Inside the windbreak she surfaced and lived on her skin. She could feel the change when it came over her, like something incredible or bionic, like her forehead bulged and she grew long in the tooth. Outside the windbreak she was herself. Inside, somebody else, somebody mean and contrary and devoid of good will, shoved her aside and took over.

"Get out the T-Bird," Belle said. She'd been up early. She was already dressed in her new gold wig and her new large-brimmed hat. Lady was pouring her a second cup of coffee. "I got to get in to the bank."

Aware of the boarder coming down the stairs, Charley said without looking up, "I can't take you to the bank. Some cows got out last night. Some fence is down."

"Considering all I do for you, you can take me to town," Belle said. "Let Juan fix the fence. That's what I pay him for. He is perfectly capable of mending the fence without you."

That was true, but Charley didn't want to go to town. "He'll have to pull wire with the block and tackle," she said. "He'll need help on it. It's five posts down."

"I don't care how many posts are down, get out the T-Bird. You're going to have to drive me now. I can't drive myself."

"Can I ride in with you?" the boarder asked in a small, distant voice.

Charley's eyes slid over and stopped on her. She had on a skirt that swung down around her calves. It was brown with little purple granny flowers. And then those sandals.

"Of course you can," Belle said. "I'll be glad of a little pleasant company."

"I can't leave till they bring the bull," Charley said. "They're delivering him this morning."

"What *time* this morning?"

"They didn't *say* what time."

"Oh, honestly," Belle said, but as she said it, Charley heard the rattle of the stock trailer coming up the drive. "That's them now," Belle said.

"I'll be ready in a minute," Juna said. "Just let me get my things." She ran up the stairs.

"I'm going up to get my boots on," Charley said. "Tell them where to put him."

"That's right. Leave me to deal with everything. Where do you want him?"

"In the stubble. Tell him to go down to the south gate and wait for me."

They grew corn on the half-mile strip between the house and the Askews' place. It had been harvested and she'd run in a few steers to clean up the stubble. She wanted to put him in there to cool down before she introduced him to the cows.

This frequent bull-swapping was a nuisance. Ever since Fletcher's death, despite good sense and all advice to the contrary, Belle had sold or swapped bulls every year or two. It started one day when Charley was moving the herd to the winter pasture. Belle had walked out to the rise behind the house to oversee the operation and Charley had ridden up to find out what she wanted. The bull, frisky in the frosty morning, mounted a cow before Belle's eyes. It was a small cow and the bull was as large

42

and square as a meat block on little low legs. Belle's eyes narrowed. She drew her shawl around her and said, "How long has he been on the place?"

"Who?"

"That bull."

"We had him for some time," Charley said.

Belle's eyes narrowed to slits as the bull fell sideways off the cow with his long, pointed penis unholstered and red. The cow scuttled off with her head down, and the bull trotted after her.

"Sell him," Belle said.

"*Sell* him!"

"Get rid of him."

"Why? He's a good bull."

Belle turned a veiled eye upon her and said, "Get rid of him at once. That cow could be his daughter," and walked stiff-backed away toward the house, her arms wrapped in her afghan. Charley sat dumbfounded in the saddle watching her go, then shouted after her. "They're *cows*, dammit!" But Belle had made up her mind.

Charley had one boot on when she heard Belle out on the porch directing the driver back down the drive. They were all out there. The boarder said, "He looks prehistoric." Charley curled her lip. "He's huge," Lady said. Belle said, "He ought to be. He cost a fortune."

She heard the driver having trouble backing and turning. It didn't sound like he knew what he was doing. She limped out in the hall with one boot on and the other in her hand. Belle called up, "We can get on into town. He's got a boy with him to help him."

She sat on the top step and pulled on her other boot and then went downstairs and out on the porch and watched with the others as the driver maneuvered. He finally got the rig headed in the right direction. "Right down yonder," she shouted, pointing. "Just back up to the gate and I'll be there."

43

"He's mean-looking, that bull," Lady said.

"Just a bull," Charley said. "Damn fool driver."

The gate into the stubble field was about halfway down the drive toward the road. She went to the shed and backed out the T-Bird and drove it up to the house. Lady wheeled Belle down the ramp and got her up on her crutches, and she made her way to the car. She stepped up close, eyeing the hood, the door, the roof. "They did a better repair job on the car than they did on me."

Lady got her inside. The crutches went in back with the boarder. Charley drove toward the rig, watching the driver back up to the gate and let the kid out. The boy ran around and opened the gate into the field and swung it all the way back to the fence and fastened it and then ran up to the tailgate on the stock trailer.

Charley had an awful premonition. "Christ!" She stepped on the gas but it was like going in slow motion while Belle screamed, "Stop it! Slow down! What are you doing!"

"Drive on in the field!" Charley shouted with her head out the window, but the wind rushed over her words. She sat on the horn, but the driver just waved. He had parked with the end of the trailer barely inside the gate, and the boy was letting the bull out.

Charley's foot went to the floor. "Stop this car!" Belle shouted. The bull trotted into the stubble and she thought for a minute it would be all right. The boy turned and closed the tailgate on the stock trailer and shouted something to the driver. She skidded the T-Bird up to the truck and yelled, "Wait!" but the driver pulled out anyway onto the road, leaving the boy behind in the field and the gate wide-open. The bull had stopped and turned. It stood there and looked around and bobbed its head a time or two at the boy.

Charley swerved the T-Bird sideways and plugged part of the

gate opening. The bull swung its heavy head toward the car and scratched at the ground with his hooves like a hen.

"Get that gate closed," Charley shouted, but the boy had wired it to the fence so the wind couldn't blow it to. All thumbs now and one eye on the bull, he fumbled at the wire. "Dammit, get it closed!" She opened the car door.

"You get back in this car this minute!" Belle said.

She stood on the ground with the open car door between her and the bull. It trotted a few steps toward her and stopped.

"Get back in this car, do you hear me?"

The bull lowered its head and swung it lazily around, then shook it like he had water in his ears, then feinted once at the boy and charged.

Charley snatched her jacket off the back of the seat and ran out with it in front of the bull, yelling over her shoulder "Get under the fence!" But the boy stood frozen against the barbed wire and the bull was turning toward her.

Juna sat pressed against the back of the front seat, holding her breath. "Oh, do something, do something!" she said.

"Roll under that goddam fence, Arthur," the truck driver yelled.

The bull pawed the ground and eyed Charley with its head low. The boy—a brittle-looking boy with pimples—threw himself down and rolled in the weeds to the safe side of the barbed wire.

"Come out of there, Charley!" Belle cried.

But Juna didn't see how Charley could.

The truck driver, a man with a dark beard shadow and a heavy belly hanging out into his T-shirt like a melon in a basket, cleared his throat and hitched his trousers and took a step toward the fence and stopped.

The bull charged. Charley flashed her jacket at it but it came on straight. She balled up the jacket and ran with it under her

45

arm like a football, the bull right behind her. They did a tight figure eight around the field, Charley sprinting as hard as she could, her knees churning high and her head back. The jacket came undone and flapped behind her in the face of the bull, and the bull kept jabbing at it with his horns. Charley headed straight toward them there in the car. Belle screamed. Charley looked like she would run right into the automobile. At the last minute she leapt. Juna saw it from the back seat through the windshield. A hand came down on the hood. They heard the thump. And Charley vaulted, somersaulting over the car, and landed on her feet on the other side while the enraged bull struck the fender with his horns. The car rocked. Belle had her hands up to her face. She was screaming. Juna reached over and rolled up the window on the driver's side. The bull backed off, his horn broken, bleeding a little at the skull. He turned and, wagging his head a lot like KC, lumbered off into the corn stubble. He nosed the ground and picked up a piece of husk and, looking back at them, began to chew calmly, like a cow.

Charley closed the gate and turned on the driver. "What the hell you think you're doing?"

The driver knocked his pack of cigarettes against his hand and pulled one out and tried to light it. "Didn't nobody get hurt," he muttered. He motioned the boy into the cab and climbed in the truck without looking at them and drove off.

Juna thought Charley looked shaky when she opened the car door and slid in, but Belle said angrily, "I don't know what gets into you! Why couldn't you let the men handle it? That's what they're paid for."

Charley turned a face mottled red and white and looked at Belle. "Just dry up, will you."

They pulled out onto the road and Juna slid up to the edge of the seat and said, "I thought it was marvelous. I'd have been petrified!"

Charley's head jerked up and the pale eyes met Juna's in the

46

rearview mirror, the dark furry V frowning steeply over them. Then they looked back at the road.

"What was that you did—over the hood? Does that have a name?"

Belle snorted. "When she coulda been taking home ec, she was taking gym."

"Gym*nastics*!" Charley said.

She set the speed at eighty and revised it upward to pass. "Slow down!" Belle said. "Watch out!" But Charley did not slow down. The robin's-egg-blue T-Bird was Belle's favorite possession and she enjoyed handling it roughly. It was the last car they'd made, Belle said, that had any class, and she wasn't going to swap it until she could afford a Lincoln Continental.

They dropped the boarder off in front of the new school. It was brick with expanses of glass and bright panels in primary colors. It didn't go with another thing in town. It was not the school she and Clay and Tearl had attended. That school, a two-story red brick with a gingerbread cornice, had been gutted and turned into a gas plant.

She swerved the T-Bird into a parking space outside the bank and stopped. Belle was thrown forward but Charley got out before she had time to turn on her and lecture. She rounded the car and opened the door and reached in and took Belle by the arm. Belle yanked her arm away and then had to sit waiting for her to offer it again. Charley didn't. "*Will* you help me out of here!" she had to say, so Charley leaned down and Belle grabbed her arm and pulled herself up on her feet. She took the aluminum canes and made her way determinedly up the walk. Charley fell a step or two behind, her jacket pushed back and her hands in her pockets. People greeted Belle respectfully and noted what she was wearing. Their eyes ran her up and down. And she returned their greetings graciously, with a bow, like a queen among peons. Charley pulled open the heavy glass door of the bank and Belle, canes and all, swept in. The vice-president rose from behind his desk and came forward, smiling. Belle ignored him, heading past the receptionist frustrated in her function and straight for the door marked PRESIDENT. Charley followed, looking neither left nor right, a reluctant dinghy in tow.

Curtis May, Jr., a large, affable young man with psoriasis in his eyebrows, leapt to his feet. He'd been filing his nails and he threw the file into his desk drawer and slammed it and pulled up a chair for Belle. Belle ignored the chair and took the seat he had vacated behind the desk to sit imperious while he was forced to take the more humble place meant for her. He looked very uncomfortable. Charley leaned on one shoulder against the wall by the door with her hat tipped over her face and watched.

"Uh, Mrs. Burden," Curtis said, "as I wrote you, we've had lots of new help join the staff lately. It was all just a slip-up. Nothing to trouble yourself about. You know I always handle your investments personally. Of course, we can deal with the matter as you suggested on the phone, if that's the way you want to work it."

Belle said, "Do you want me to keep on banking with you?"

"We certainly want to keep on serving you, Mrs. Burden."

Belle went through an elaborate personality change that achieved as its finale a certain flirtatiousness. Charley could never tell how she did it. "You know, Curtis," she said, "I'm getting to where I don't miss your daddy here anymore. I'm getting used to *you*."

Charley shifted to her other shoulder. Curtis was only an instant at a loss. Then he grasped the role she had cast him into and, though a negligible actor, stammered out the lines he thought his father might likely have delivered at that moment. "I declare, Belle, you're looking so well. Why, you and Charley could almost be sisters."

Charley only saw the flush when it reached the thinly sown crown of his head. The flattery would have fallen easily from his father's lips. The old bastard would even have congratulated himself on his originality. But Curtis had failed miserably. The stranger who moved Charley over and took up residence in her skin enjoyed such entertainment. And Belle found the failure more interesting than the father's success would have been. It gave her a sense of power that came more and more frequently but still surprised her. She laughed with pleasure.

At the office of Belle's CPA, Charley sat on her spine outside the cubicle, her arms crossed and her legs, stretched out in front of her, crossed at the ankles. Darrel Thigpen, an elderly man of the strictest integrity, was saying, "But Mrs. Burden, you know I can't complete the quarterly returns unless you supply me with—"

But Belle interrupted, pouting. "Can't we be just a little creative, Mr. Thigpen?"

A rumbling sound, half sigh, half snort, shoved out past Charley's lips, and Darrel Thigpen stared at Belle with a look of incomprehension.

"You are my conscience, Darrel Thigpen," Belle said with a pretty sigh, "and I wrestle with you accordingly."

At the gas company, which carried on a business in monuments on the side, a round-headed young man with black hair and a fresh complexion showed Belle the catalog while Charley propped her seat against the door frame, waiting. They had been here many times before, but Belle claimed to want just one more look. She had promised to make up her mind.

"Idn' this one beautiful," she said in a voice she reserved for polite, small children.

The dealer was clearly pleased. "You'll never regret choosing that one," he said. "I never seen more classic lines."

"Yes," Belle said, and a little low hum issued out of her mysteriously, like the purr of a cat. "That's the one I love and keep coming back to, but this"—she flipped back to a page she'd kept a finger in—"is the one I'm going to get." She looked earnestly into the young man's dashed face. "I believe in putting my money on the living." She rested a hasty hand on Charley's shoulder. Charley made a sound through her teeth like air escaping a maimed tire and rolled her eyes to the ceiling.

At the five-and-dime Charley leaned against the popcorn machine while Belle wandered the aisles, picking up teddy bears and rattles and little shirts in case Reenie should ever bring the child to see her. She had boxes of such presents at home. She was continually upgrading them because the child aged and outgrew the clothes and the toys. The boxes were a sad reminder of her plight, but still, sometimes she sat by the hour going over them. Sometimes she got something to him by way of Reenie's friend Creep, but she never knew if the clothes suited him or if he played with the toys.

At the dry-goods store Charley stood with her hands in her pockets looking out the plate-glass window while Belle tried on hats. She watched enviously a black-and-white mongrel lift his leg on the fire hydrant and trot away. There was a pile of hats around Belle on the table and on the stacked hatboxes on the floor. They'd been at it for some time.

"How 'bout this one?" Belle asked Charley.

"Just take 'em all, why don't you," Charley said.

And Belle said, "That's a thought!"

The pinched little old maid clerk hovered over Belle's shoulder, ducking to look at her in the mirror. "You're looking awfully well, Mrs. Burden," she complained. "Health is wealth. That's what I always say." She was thinking how wonderful, to be able to buy a new hat anytime you felt like it. She herself could barely afford one a year, even with her discount. She had her old mother at home on oxygen that cost a fortune, ninety-four years old and too hooked on television to die.

It was almost noon when Juna, watching for them, saw the T-Bird swerve to the curb outside. She stood with her arms crossed a little back from the window, out of sight, and watched Belle slowly make her way up the walk while Charley leaned back against the fender, picking her teeth with what looked like a matchstick. Her lower lip caught under her upper teeth, Juna studied them thoughtfully.

She met Belle at the door and held it open while she maneuvered her way inside. "My, times have changed since my children's day," Belle said. She already knew Mr. Maple, the principal. He hurried from his office to do her honors, a stocky, short-waisted man continually hitching up his trousers with his elbows stuck out behind him, preparatory, it seemed, to some further undertaking. He had a wife and three daughters at home, he had six female teachers on his staff at school, but in spite of all this experience he felt nervous around women and vaguely guilty about something. He tried to greet Belle heartily. He congratulated Juna again on the luck of her living arrangement.

"You needn't worry, Milton," Belle sang in a voice that floated back down the hall after her like a scarf. "We'll take good care of her." He watched with relief as their backs retreated.

"I've been down to the pet section of the dime store," Juna said, showing Belle her homeroom. "I went ahead and got the tropical fish and set up the tank. I want them settled in before school starts—to avoid any traumas."

Belle leaned over the tank, then straightened and looked around her at the ceiling. Juna watched anxiously. "Is anything wrong?"

"It's the quiet," Belle said. "It's unnatural."

Juna laughed, gathering up her things. "It won't be quiet much longer."

As they made their slow way back toward the car, Belle asked, "How'd you ever get into schoolteaching? You could of been an airline stewardess."

Juna was watching someone come toward them down the sidewalk, someone with a basket on her arm and a kerchief on her head whom Juna first took to be a child playing dress-up.

"Hi, Creep," Charley said.

51

Juna was startled, but it sounded like a nickname. Her attention was arrested by Belle's face. It went through elaborate changes to arrive at pleased surprise. "Why, Eveningstar!"

"I'm Keeta now." She spelled it. "It's an Indian name."

She was a little thing, an urchin, a waif. Her large wet china-blue eyes took up most of her face, a face fringed on three sides with white hair and glowing like that of a child who's been out in the cold, red-cheeked and glazed with chap.

"Well, how *are* you!" Belle said. "And how—how is the baby?"

"Baba is meditating with us now." The clear, childlike voice pouted. "Hogarth made him his own little pillow. He sits on it in a basket, and meditates."

Belle looked as if she were swelling up, but whatever it was, she assimilated it and smiled. "Well, when are you coming out to see me?" She spoke very brightly.

The young woman's whole small body swayed languidly like a flower on a stalk. She had on a dress that might have been made out of window curtains. She held the basket in front of her with both hands. Her large eyes looked at Belle till they seemed to go out of focus and look right through her and beyond. "Oh," she sang vaguely, "one of these days."

"One day *soon*, I hope," Belle said.

But she was edging around them with her basket till she came out on the other side, waving good-bye with only her fingers waggling. They watched her go. "She claims to be close to Irene," Belle said, her narrowed eyes following the small figure down the walk.

Charley said, "They're all close. They call themselves The Family." She laughed.

"Humph," Belle said, getting in the car, "they'll call themselves anything."

At the Plainsman Hotel they sat at a table for four, Belle cheerily greeting people at the surrounding tables. The place was more crowded than Juna would have expected. The tables were covered with white cloth and there were white cloth napkins at the places. Nothing was made of paper. The waitresses were middle-aged women who seemed to know their customers personally. When their orders came, Belle looked down at hers and exclaimed, "Why, Mildred, I didn't order this."

"It's the crab au gratin, Mrs. Burden," the waitress said.

"Why, I didn't expect it to look like that," Belle said. "I've never eaten anything that color in my life! We'll have to start all over."

The waitress smiled and handed the menu back to Belle and took away the crab au gratin. Belle thought she'd have the prime rib, and Charley said, "You never start out with it but it's what you always end up eating." Belle ignored Charley and handed back the menu. Juna sympathized with the waitress, but the waitress patted Belle on the shoulder and said, "It'll just be a minute, Mrs. Burden," and Belle said, "Take your time, take your time."

A tall, upright, elderly man at a table for two against the wall nodded to Belle, and Belle said, "Mr. Thigpen! Mrs. Thigpen! How *are* you?" And Mrs. Thigpen, just out of the beauty parlor, smiled and put her hand to her newly done-up silver hair in its invisible nylon net.

A rancher—plump and short, his chin merging into his stomach—rolled past in Western suit, boots, and hat, smoking a big cigar. He winked at Juna, patted Belle on the shoulder, and said in a voice like a bullfrog's, "How'sa girl?"

"Raymond!" Belle cried. "Aren't you looking wonderful!"

"Hey there, Charley," he said. "When you gone get married and put on a dress?"

As Raymond rolled away a young man with a drooping, soft mustache loomed up out of a nearby booth where he'd been lunching with a very large youngish man with something wrong with his eyebrows. "Belle, my lovely! Charley!" But despite his exclamations, he was eyeing Juna.

53

Juna gave her attention to her club sandwich. Belle's eyes danced back and forth between them, missing nothing. "This' my boarder, Juna Evers. Juna, Harvey Sears."

The large young man with the red eyebrows rose a little out of his seat clutching his napkin and bobbed at them, murmuring, "Belle, Charley," and also eyeing Juna.

Harvey said. "*Four* women way out there alone?"

Charley said, "We just born lucky, Harvey."

Harvey's smile never faltered, but Juna thought she saw a subtle displacement, like a slide, in his eye. She was fascinated by these new forms of life.

On the way home they passed the rodeo grounds again. "Right there's where Charlene like to made herself immortal," Belle said over the voice of the stereo and the wind to Juna in the back seat. And Charley jammed down on the gas till her foot met the floor and she couldn't jam any further. The T-Bird held back an instant and then shot forward. At first it seemed to be going very fast, but then it was like a plane the moment the wheels leave the ground. It surged slowly into a new dimension, and Charley left the rodeo behind.

It was not as if it had happened yesterday. It happened the fall after she graduated from high school, when Clay went off to college and she stayed home. She was looking for trouble. It was a happening she both wanted to forget and wanted to remember. She wanted to forget because if she remembered she had to go through a kind of inner writhing that at times had made her vomit. The instant it flickered at the edge of light, her impulse was to close it out—by ramming on the gas, by turning up the stereo, or by thinking doggedly of something else. She could say one thing for it, it had given her control over her mind. It was not just shame, like the memory of the time she wet her britches in first grade. It was also her sense, not of injustice, but of a meanness done her. She might have singled out this one or that for particular blame, but it had been the collusion that hurt, not just the other riders, but the whole crowd, the stands laughing at her as if she'd got her comeuppance. When the flicker of it touched the edge of her consciousness where it blurred like a heat wave, she wanted to cry, to curse, to hit something again and again. It was the only time in her life when she felt nobody wished her well, nobody. So, contrarily, she also wanted to remember, and in this interest she had stuck the picture in her mirror. It had happened because she wanted what she wasn't supposed to want and that set all of them against her. So she had to remember. As long as she remembered, she would never let her dukes down that way again, for that's what leaves you wide-open.

The Tula rodeo looked like any of the other rodeo grounds strung out from Kansas to California, but it wasn't. Though it looked public enough there beside the highway, it was the private property of Abner Askew, the pens and corrals, the ring, the chutes, the stadium, and the land. Abner Askew, going on ninety and her onetime friend, never tired of explaining that he had no use for rodeo as public entertainment. He had built his rodeo as a continuation of what it had started out to be, a sensible competition in their line of work for the cowboys of this part of the state to show off their skills and work off their mischief—not in the middle of July, their busiest season, but in the quieter time that had once followed roundup. If his son Will had turned it into a carnival, it was none of his doing. And that had gone about as far as he meant to let it. He didn't intend to be written down as the founder and patron of any scheme to bring drifters and gamblers and the sporting element into Kansas. Pros could come if they liked, and watch. Maybe they'd learn something. Anybody caught betting on his rodeo would be ushered off the property by Brady Culpepper, the county sheriff, who was also his nephew. The same with anybody caught drinking hard liquor. Beer had been sold on the rodeo grounds for the past several years. Abner didn't like it, but he explained that he got fifty percent of the profits from the concession, and though he didn't need the money, he believed in things paying their own way. The beer allowed the rodeo to pay its own way and kept him from having any further outlay on the doings.

While they were still friends, he'd been fond of telling Charley that he came of the *stock that stayed*. Through panics and Indians and brush fires and twisters and Canadian locusts, *they stayed*. And the state of Kansas was the result. While Charley came from Johnny-come-latelies only out there after the War. The War he meant was the Civil War. On days when he was in good temper he agreed it wasn't as late as others he could mention.

The Askew place was the next one east, toward Tula, and a mile down the road. It straddled the highway with the house on the same side as the Burdens', wrapped around with as many trees, and the rodeo set back opposite, across the blacktop.

Charley had hung out over there all through high school. The Askews raised Quarter Horses and Charley broke the horses for them alongside their son Knute, till her misfortune at the rodeo. There had always been a competitive spirit between her and Knute over the horses, over who was better than who. Though it was left unspoken, it manifested itself in their dares, each urging the other on till more than once one of them barely escaped a broken neck. Then one day a summer shower came in with a little thunder to break up the heat on a still afternoon, the kind of afternoon when they kept a lookout for twisters. They had taken refuge in the barn to wait it out, and Knute had made a surprising suggestion. Like the competitive spirit, the suggestion had not been spoken. He had simply reached out and grabbed her in a certain way. Tearl thought nothing of grabbing her, and then they would wrestle. Or Clay might grab her, or her him, for if either of them was mad or frustrated they took it out on the other. But when Knute Askew grabbed her, it had something smirky or nasty about it and she shoved him and he happened to fall over backward on top of some fresh, steaming horse apples, and she made the mistake of laughing. After that, he was her enemy and she knew it. She had been glad when he joined the Navy. He must like it, he was still in. His mother spoke righteously of his making a career of the service, but Charley just saw him grabbing at girls in kimonos, girls in sarongs. Knute had had a hand in her one rodeo experience. He'd thought she made a fool of herself and it served her right. His father thought they all ought to laugh it off. His grandfather was so outraged in his sense of propriety that it couldn't be mentioned in his presence. He thought a girl who'd do a thing like that ought to be whipped. What Charley thought, she wasn't telling. And now their connection was down to a formal, polite one of swapping balers and the like, and conducted mostly by telephone. Belle handled it all because it gave her something to do, and Juan trundled the slow farm machinery back and forth along the section road running north and south about a mile behind the house, and Charley stayed out of it.

While Charley and Belle did their errands, Juna, shopping for goldfish and paper clips and little gold stars and poster paper, had taken stock of Tula. Walking its few streets, going into its stores, she had looked eagerly at the people, who looked back less hopefully at her. She realized with annoyance that she was not quite seeing them as people like herself. Sometimes she hated being a New Yorker. It was true they were provincial and judged other parts of the country against the sets of Broadway musicals and found them blurred and undefined and somehow not quite right. She didn't want to be like that. Still, as she walked down Main Street she kept expecting the cast to burst into song.

She saw clearly enough that she had to modify herself for Tula. She bought a skirt at the dry goods store and a couple of plain white blouses at the dress shop. When she tried these on upstairs in the big bright bedroom, she added a wide belt and a scarf at her throat and then determinedly took them off and put them away. She would have to accustom Tula gradually to herself as she really was. That would take time. Meanwhile she twisted her hair into a bun and fixed it at the nape of her neck.

As she came down the stairs she heard Belle saying to Lady, "All young people conform to their peers." Juna slowed on the stairs while Belle went on: Hadn't she herself once worn bobby socks and sloppy Joe sweaters and saddle shoes and beads to the waist tied in a knot between her breasts? If only Charlene would conform to something! These hippie types at least looked like girls.

She waited to be sure Belle had finished before she crossed the hall.

Belle's mouth fell open when she saw her, but after a little intake of breath, she laughed. "I see you've Tularized yourself. Lady, come look! It's something I've refused to do," she said. "And of course I've had to suffer for it. But then I've been spared the necessity of holding down a job." Her eyes narrowed over Juna's blouse, her skirt, and landed on her sandals.

"How do I look?" Juna asked when Lady stuck her head in.

"You look fine," Lady said. "I like the way you look."

"My hair's too short on the sides to stay put." She tucked it back wherever she could.

"You look like a sweet young schoolmarm," Lady said.

Belle said, "At least put on your earrings."

Juna had felt that with her hair up the earrings were too dramatic. "Do you think I dare?"

"Out here," Belle said, "you've got to dare."

So she ran back upstairs to get them and descended slowly, her hands up and her head tilted, putting them on. Belle's eyes pounced on her tire-soled sandals. "Now those can go," she said.

Juna was doing the other ear. "But what'll I put on my feet?"

She settled for some brown low-heel pumps with tongues sticking out toward her ankles. She got them at Tula's one shoe shop and Belle made a face when she saw them but Lady was satisfied.

In her little low pumps she modeled her new wardrobe downstairs in Belle's parlor bedroom, Mary Jane, the mother cat—her kittens almost weaned—sitting in judgment on the foot of the bed, watching. Belle approved this, banished that, matched up outfits, and, dissatisfied, made notes of things they had to shop for. She eyed a new dress from the Bon Marché in town that Juna had bought for the fall teachers' meetings. "Momma would have said you could dress that up or dress it down." Lady brought in a tray of coffee for herself, tea for Juna, and a diet Pepsi for Belle, ensconsed in her bed with clothes strewn all over it, looking bright and content. "I haven't had so much fun since the last time I saw Thelma," she said. "Why, it's like having a daughter." She looked misty-eyed at Juna. "Fashions come and go and come again," she said. "We used to wear skirts just like that." She picked up a hem and dropped it. "Only when we washed them we wrapped them wet around a broomstick and let them dry with the wrinkles in. We called them broomstick skirts. They were all the rage." She described in detail the outfit she was wearing the first time she'd set eyes on Fletcher Burden, and she made Lady look for her wedding dress and take it out of its tissue paper. It wasn't a bit yellowed. She had saved it, she said, for her daughter to wear at *her* wedding. She paused. She laughed.

They hadn't noticed Charley in the door holding a carton of milk in her hand. She had come in through the kitchen and stopped by the refrigerator. She turned up the carton and drank. Juna waited with a feeling akin to dread for the gray eyes to fall on her. But Charley turned the carton all the way up and drained the last of the milk and reached around the edge of the sliding door and tossed it into Belle's wastebasket. Then she turned and went up the stairs two at a time, to change into something clean and get out of there.

School started. Morning and afternoon, yellow school buses plied the long, straight roads, their red lights flashing at stops where they picked up or put down children swinging satchels and pummeling each other and calling against the wind. Behind the buses resigned ranchers hunched over steering wheels in dusty pickups and contained their souls in patience. The wind pulled Juna's hair, leaving her scalp sore and ravaged. Her hair came undone around her face and blew in wisps in front of her glasses. It blowsed along her cheeks till she looked old-maidish. At preschool conferences, as boring in Tula as anywhere, she met her colleagues, whom she soon divided into those attracted to teaching by the summer vacations and those whose children had grown up and left them with time to fill. She'd been curious to find out why she'd been hired from so far afield and was disappointed to learn from Mr. Maple—clearing his throat, hitching his trousers—that there weren't any other applicants. The children were ciphers yet to be read. Plump and pretty or owl-eyed and spectacled, they looked at her with neither love nor hostility. In the wisdom of their years they withheld judgment, biding their time.

It was true that she'd junketed around Europe, and then Central and parts of South America, pretty much alone but making friends along the way. One summer in England she'd hitched a ride on the back of a motorcycle and ridden there till fall. She'd had drinks on a yacht in Nice and not debarked till Palermo. She'd been protected in her travels by fearlessness born of innocence and trust. And once, when that didn't work, she tried her karate. It wasn't very good but it was worth something in shock value. The friends she'd left at home admired her vagabond life, not guessing that beneath it lay a deep, abiding discontent, a discontent she never showed, not out of pride alone but because she felt it was unkind to dampen the general enthusiasm for life. It was so necessary, a bank to deposit in when you're flush and draw on when you're drained.

Maybe she should have married, like Muriel Gebberfield. She liked neither celibacy nor promiscuity. But men either helped you in and out of cars like you were an invalid or went striding three steps ahead of you to insist on some imagined autonomy. Say what you will, at no time was it equal. If you found the best man in the world and he helped you with the dishes, there it was, written all over his face, he was wonderful and you were lucky, just lucky. And people congratulating you on such a catch!

Her days themselves were not unhappy, but their happiness lay in the hopefulness with which she conducted her quest while having no idea what she was looking for. She thought it might be a life that contented in its everyday morning-to-night pursuits. She hoped it wasn't some bovine kind of life. If it was, she would have to despise it. She knew she had often confused being useful—she'd been in the Peace Corps in Honduras and taught English in the Yucatan—with using all of herself, which was one way she'd tried defining happiness, but that had at least given her a certain variety. And the restlessness of travel gives you a sense of having a goal, a destination. At the end of the day you have to arrive somewhere.

The town that had seemed so inexplicable, there in the middle of nowhere, became familiar. She explored Main Street with all its shops and stores for locals only, unlike small towns on the Cape and in New England that tried to disguise themselves as real, pretend they weren't all just little boutiques for the tourists. No tourists ever came to Tula. They sped through Kansas, with neither mountains, deserts, oceans, nor truly navigable rivers, on their way to places they could photograph.

She had hesitated over the ad in the teachers' journal, thinking a place so far removed from all shores would be impossible: she required an ocean. But something in the prairie began to satisfy

61

that need. Was it the light, so constantly changing, in the morning fading the landscape to soft pastels and in the evening deepening it into striated shadows purple, blue, and gold? Or the huge expanse of sky? Or the clouds, easily the most spectacular features in the landscape, towering, piling, caroming. Kansas, she decided, cooled her out.

When she first crossed the state line, and then reached Tula, she had thought of it all as way out somewhere far removed from everything. But now that she was here, she discovered it was a hub, the geographic center of the country and the geodetic center of the continent, that everything radiated out from.

She frequented the courthouse square at lunchtime. Though plain and unlovely, now, in the fall, as at most times of the year, the grounds with their benches and the retaining wall over the sidewalk was a meeting place for farmers in town to go to the co-op and women tired out from shopping and local professionals on their noon break. The courthouse had been built from plans peddled by salesmen who traveled through that part of the state in an earlier day with several courthouse plans to choose from in their sample cases. Tula's town council had picked a three-story red brick building with a sawtooth gable. She thought it was rather nice.

She saw the Burdens, Charley and Belle, as exotics, while Lady was familiar and homey. She and Lady were already friends. And lately Juan managed to busy himself inside the windbreak toward late afternoon when she got off the school bus, and they talked together in Spanish.

She wasn't expert at it like he was, and her a schoolteacher, too, so he grew expansive and informed her on things having to do with crops and the weather, and he told her a great deal about himself. His abundant hair, still mostly black, came down to a widow's peak over his forehead. Clearly he had been handsome. He still walked with a kind of lazy strut, a middle-size man you could see had always been muscular and light and compact.

62

He showed her his *casa*. It had once been a carpentry shop and before that, when they still mended wagon wheels and fitted their own horse shoes, a forge. It was attached to one end of the implement shed. A lot of tools—a grindstone run by a foot pedal, which Juan used chiefly to keep Lady's kitchen knives sharpened, a mechanical drill, drawers of nuts and bolts—still occupied a heavy wooden counter along one wall that was also his kitchen, for though he usually ate his meals in the house, sometimes he liked to fix a bite for himself. After it was a carpentry shop it was a storage shed, and he found in it everything he needed. He had a plug-in coffeepot and a two-burner hot plate and an old round-shouldered Frigidaire that was once, years ago, in the house. He told her he used to live in town, but he started taking naps in slack times in the storage room and in stages took up residence. Nobody mentioned it, so he stayed, and Lady began setting another place at the table. He had two prize possessions, one that he'd brought with him, the other that he'd found in the storage room. They were a guitar and a radio. He played one or the other every night, favoring the guitar outside in warm weather on his stoop, and the radio in cold weather indoors. He wasn't very good on the guitar. He never sang but simply strummed, remembering other voices. He preferred the radio to the television Charley had given him one Christmas, so small he could lie in his bunk with it on his stomach and watch in the dark. Charley hadn't given him this tiny television out of stinginess. Juan was partial to very small things. He'd once owned Chihuahuas. He'd mooned as a child over the village midget. But he only used the television for sporting events, prefering the radio for everything else. Was it not more grand, made of wood with its rounded top like a shrine, like a church? He saw things more clearly, more to his liking, with the radio. With the radio every scene took place somewhere in Chihuahua.

In addition to sporting matches, the television was good for one other event. This was a wild chase in automobiles through city streets, through intersections where traffic parted to let them pass, up hills where you could see their entire undercarriages lifting over you before they nosed down, along twisting mountain roads beside precipices, missing head-on collisions by a hair. Several times each evening with the radio going he turned on the television without the sound and spun the channels to see if he could locate this spectacle.

They had tea in Lady's trailer house, and Lady told Juna Juan would soon be packing his grip and leaving. She learned that once a year he packed his yellowed tan cardboard suitcase with a change of socks, an extra shirt, and a clean pair of pants, and Charley took him to the bus station. And Juan said sometimes he then took the bus, but sometimes he waited till Charley had gone and then he walked back out to the truck stop on the highway and set the suitcase down and waited for a trucker to ask where he was going. He was going to the races in Ruidoso. He fooled Charley this way because Lady always gave him betting money and he wanted to have all of hers and his own still with him when he arrived in Ruidoso. Only once had he come back empty-handed. That had been in the beginning when he took the advice of others. After that he depended solely on himself and he always returned with great sums for them to hide under their mattresses.

In Ruidoso he met boys from home who had walked across and now earned their keep as exercise boys just as he had when he was younger. With Jose, Manuel, Emilio, he enjoyed a week of talk about home, the horses, the weather. It had to do him for a year. "Kahn-cis!" they'd say. "*Por qué* Kahn-cis, mon?" He'd tell them he had a *casa* all to himself where nobody slept but him and a pretty woman to cook for him just like his *mujer,* and yet he didn't have the upkeep of that woman. He said that his *patrona* was young and ignorant and let him do as he liked, that without him this big rancho would not progress. He told of the small herd of horses they had started in these last dozen years, of the luck they'd had, or the blessing of the Virgin, in fillies every spring but one. These horses had short heads and short backs. He measured in the air with his hands and enjoyed their astonishment. They have souls, he said, these *caballos*. He would like to train one for racing. Two summers ago they'd had the misfortune of a colt, but this little colt was black with a star on his forehead and he was fast. These horses they turned gradually gray, then white as they got older, but he didn't think this colt would turn white. *She* thought he might be a stallion for the mares, but he, Juan, thought this colt might race.

Each year in Ruidoso Juan also fell in love—once with the governor's lady handing up a trophy, once with a Thoroughbred filly, once with an almond-eyed nymphet from Juarez whom he followed everywhere till she told her brother. He never spoke to his love or tried to touch, but the feeling was better than marijuana or mescal. Each year he looked and looked till whatever he would love caught him in his midsection and sent him flying up a string like a message on a kite. He treasured this feeling and savored it all year. He told Lady and Juna all about Ruidoso except about falling in love.

Juna passed Charley's door on the way to her own, but it was always closed. They shared the bath, but the only signs of Charley in there were the stud book and a tall bottle of horse liniment in the medicine chest.

They never bumped into each other coming or going, for no matter how early she got her start, Charley was up and long gone, and no matter how late she bathed and got to bed, though in her robe and furry slippers she sat up late reading for pleasure or preparing lessons, she heard Charley's pickup crunch up the gravel drive, back home from Smoky's, a great deal later.

As for Charley, once Belle had gone off to be mended, before the advent of Juna, she'd felt easier in her room upstairs. She had never used it for anything but sleeping and changing her clothes. The idea of expanding, opening her door, having the upstairs all to herself, had led her to explore areas she had always taken for granted. Now she would have a real indoor space, not like the fields and pastures, yet familiar and private and all to herself. With all the doors standing open, she had frequent glimpses of the surrounding ranch. She'd never left her door open when Belle was across the hall. Though she hadn't really claimed the space, to have it snatched away, given to a stranger, was worse than a disappointment. Her own reach had begun extending. Contracting again, she felt her childhood room, her narrow bed, not as a return to normal, but as a bitter regression. Worse. With a stranger across the hall the space she had lived in all her life seemed shrunken, as if it contained not enough air to fill her lungs and she only with difficulty got her breath.

Growing up had changed Charley. As a child she was always riding or running full tilt or else sitting perfectly still on the side porch, her head resting halfway up the tall, green wicker back of one of the porch rockers, her feet, once they could reach, propped against the banisters. Sitting still, she was always daydreaming. Her dreams grew out of old movies they showed on Saturday afternoons at the Majestic or old books from the Tula library where Mrs. Maple, the principal's wife, knew Charley's taste and gave her Crusoe on his island and Tarzan in his jungle. She was not an up-to-date reader. She had no interest in outer space. And since television was an indoor sport, she had no taste for it. She was, of course, always the hero of her daydreams, and when randomly it flickered at the outer edge of her consciousness that girls are heroines, she ignored that feeble flare till it went out. Heroines were simpering idiots, mere decoration, there to be uselessly rescued. Finding herself a heroine would have made her consider hari-kari.

As a child she sat by the hour, her eye on the plains beyond a break in the windshield of trees, because the plains were just so much undistracting nothing, and the thing at the edge of her consciousness rarely intruded. But as she grew older, it threatened to come out of its corner and thumb its nose at her. Then she turned to running and riding full tilt and to working around the place and breaking horses over at the Askews. After her father died—she had not much liked her father—she watched Belle fight with foremen and one by one run them off the place, till she, Charley, then barely twenty, effectively ran the place while her brother Clay ran around the countryside in fast cars with fast girls, drinking too much. It had been no great matter for her to take on the ranch. She had Juan. Juan, she suspected, had really run the place, anyway, not her father.

She and Clay had been close as children and understood each other's plight, neither fitting the roles laid out for them at birth like costumes on a bed, ready to be put on when they grew into them and meanwhile serving as reminders. As they grew up a distance widened between them because, she suspected, though Clay didn't want the job meant for him, he resented seeing her move into it so readily.

If Juna's arrival meant that Charley spent even less time around the house—and she'd never spent much—she had one consolation. She'd lately come to dread that, now the family was so diminished, Belle might one day reach out a dimpled hand to claim her. Juna's presence made that event less likely.

3

"This family is afflicted," Belle said. "Prominent families often are." She was sitting at the head of the table with her account books piled around her. But she wasn't doing the accounts, she was plucking her eyebrows and raising her hairline a little, the cosmetics mirror tilted before her with its light on. She'd been down in the mouth all day and Lady had been humoring her with patience wearing thin.

"I never had to get prominent to get afflicted," Lady said. She was at the kitchen table shelling peas into a pan. Belle had been gloomy since a lengthy, long-distance fight with Marlon over some*thing*, not some*body*, named Ginny May.

"Not a day goes by that I don't grieve for Fletcher Burden. And Buddy. I guess I was meant to be a woman alone."

"You got Charley. You ought to thank the Lord you got Charley."

"A sweeter boy never breathed than Clay Burden. *Why* did he have to do it?"

Heartsick suddenly for Tearl, Lady said, "No telling why things got to happen like they happen."

Belle said, "Humph. I come from people proud to give their sons to the defense of their country." Belle's mind reading annoyed Lady. It stripped her of her privacy.

"People I come from," Lady said, "they sons join the army because they can't get jobs."

"Well, you have to know how to *do* something before you get a job."

"Tearl said they don't give jobs to black boys so they'll have to join the army where they'll all get kilt."

"Tearl was so pessimistic." Belle was beginning to work with her tweezers on her chin. When she was young she thought it unsightly to see a woman pulling at whiskers on her chin with her fingernails and now she did it herself. Things like that made her feel uneasy. Nowdays she felt worse about her age than about her weight. You can keep your figure and hers was still good, but there's little you can do about your age. It was a recent revelation. "You still haven't given him up," she said.

Lady sighed and straightened her back, squaring her shoulders to get the cramp out, glancing past Belle out the front window and down the ranch road. "Sometimes, with the sun in my eyes, I'll think I see a boy in a soldier suit walking down the road." She turned her attention back to the peas. "I guess that's crazy."

Unseen by Lady, Belle matter-of-factly nodded. "I know that's what keeps you here. If you were to give him up, to stop looking for him to walk down that road, in spite of all I've done for you you'd be out of here like a shot." But Belle was losing interest in the conversation. She was watching Harvey Sears' Ranchero approach the house and stop beside the cattle guard where Juan was raking leaves. Juna got out, turned and smiled at Harvey, and slammed the door. Harvey waited a moment, as if hopeful of being invited in, but as Juna stopped to talk to Juan he shifted gears, backed, turned, and drove off down the drive toward the highway.

"Here come Junie," Lady said. "You'll cheer up with a little gossip from town."

"It's at this time of day," Belle said, "with someone to talk to, that I crave a little refreshment."

Lady took the pan of peas to the sink. "You can have you a Coke."

"Co'colas are full of sugar."

"Not half so full of sugar as what you got in mind."

"I am tired of being bullied in my own home!" Belle said. She grabbed up her eyebrow pencil and stroked two swift diagonals up her forehead like insect feelers that gave her, in the mirror, an angry look. She turned this face to Lady.

Lady couldn't help laughing. "Better," she said, "to be bullied at home than at that other place." They had twice taken Belle to the drying-out center in Topeka, once after Fletcher Burden's death and once after Buddy's. It was not her favorite resort.

The phone rang. They both looked at it there by Belle's elbow on the table but made no move to answer. After the fifth ring it stopped.

"That could have been Marlon," Belle said, "and I'm missing his call. I pay for that phone and I'm afraid to answer it." She picked it up, got a dial tone, and hung up.

"What's she doing out there?" Belle grumbled. "Why idn' she coming in?" She looked out the window to where Juna was practicing her Spanish. "All those books. You think they even read in the second grade?"

The phone began again. "Thought he had the wrong number," Lady said, "so now he's trying again."

Belle snatched it up and listened, then said angrily into the receiver, "If you call here one more time I'll sic the law on you!" and slammed it down.

"Whu'd he say?" asked Lady.

"I wouldn't repeat it." But there was a hint of satisfaction in her eyes as she looked in the mirror and tried on another wig.

"Must of said something," Lady muttered.

"He left nothing unsaid. Men are filthy-mouthed." She tore

70

the wig off and threw it on the table. "This one has to go see Thelma. She'll have to dye it and restyle it."

"If you want it to go to Thelma's, let Charley take it to Thelma's."

"I haven't seen Thelma once since I got back!"

"You stay 'way from Thelma," Lady said. "You and Thelma got too much in common. We ain' going through that again." It was on the way home from Thelma's that Belle had had her crack-up.

She grabbed up her buffer and went after her fingernails. The phone started up again as Juna crossed the porch and came in. She stopped in the door and looked from one of them to another while the phone rang insistently, as if it were angry. She set her books down on the end of the table, her eyebrows raised.

"We thought we was shut of him," Lady said.

"Does he sound like anybody you know?" Juna asked.

"He sounds like everybody I know," Belle said. "Everybody in this godforsaken place talks alike. Through the nose."

"You ain' been outchere but thirty years," Lady said. "Look-like you'd be getting used to it."

"If I live to be a hundred, I'll never get used to it. All women *say* they'll follow their man to the ends of the earth but *I* was the one required to *do* it."

"What can he be after?" Juna asked.

"What they're all after," Belle said. "Men are driven. Take the load off your feet. Have a diet cola. Lady, get us some diet colas."

Juna sat down and took off a shoe and massaged her foot. "No thank you. I never eat chemicals."

Lady said, "I put the kettle on a while ago. Won't take but a minute to heat it up again. You can have your cup of tea."

Belle mouthed *tea* silently with such distaste that Lady had to laugh.

Juna eyed Belle's antenna. "Are you made up for something special?"

71

Belle examined herself in the mirror. "I should of gone on the stage. If I'd wanted a career, that's the one I'd of chosen."

"So what did he say?" Juna asked.

"She hoarding his exact words to herself," Lady said.

Belle said, "I wouldn't be caught dead repeating that kind of language."

Lady said, "The dead not so particular."

"Idn' it time you thought about supper?"

"I thought about supper long ago."

"What's the gossip in town?" Belle asked.

"Supper's been in the oven going on an hour now."

"No wonder I've been suffocating."

"I wonder what's prompting him to call *here*?" Juna said.

"His britches prompting him," Lady said. "He too big for his britches."

Belle said, "They'll do anything out here to amuse themselves. The wind drives them crazy. Empty space drives them crazy. We don't have the crime rate you have in New York, but when we do have a crime, it's a lulu. That's Kansas!"

They heard the pickup cross the cattle guard. Lady looked out the window. "Here's Charley, back from town. Looklike you two could get synchronized. She coulda give you a ride home."

"She *had* a ride home," Belle said, but Juna ignored her.

"I hope she didn't forget the sugar," Lady said.

"You can bet she forgot it. Sugar's what you sent her for, idn' it?" Belle started working on the antenna with cold cream. Then she drew the mirror close again and began to replace her eyebrows with a pencil.

"Are you going somewhere?" Juna asked.

"She making up for her new admirer," Lady said.

"If he sets foot on this place, I'll call Brady Culpepper."

"Might be Brady calling you," Lady said. "The sheriff's a ladies' man."

Juna said, "I'm afraid that's what'll become of Billy John Etheridge."

"You worry too much about Billy John Etheridge," Belle snapped. "He idn' but a second-grader."

"A re-peat," Juna said. "He induces the girls to play doctor in the cloakroom by giving them sticks of chewing gum. He's got a regular clinic going back there. I have to watch him all the time." She rose. "Well, I've got lessons to plan."

Belle said, "You work too hard! Not everything worth doing is worth doing well." More and more now Juna went upstairs soon after she got home. To prepare lessons, she said. She was a conscientious teacher and wanted to start the year off right. Belle missed the days of the teachers' meetings when Juna had come home and sat at the table with her and she got to go into her life story with all the central characters she found so interesting—her momma and poppa and Big Momma back in Texas. Juna had been an appreciative audience.

But Juna picked up her books and headed for the stairs.

"Aw, come on," Lady said, "wait for the tea." Lady had liked the visiting too, and it kept Belle off her back.

But Belle snapped, "Where's Charley?"

Lady said, "She talking to Juan."

"If Juan is constantly engaged in conversation, he'll never get his work done. Get out on the porch and tell her I want her in here this instant."

"Lemme wash my hands."

"You don't need to wash your hands!"

"I know when I need to wash my hands."

"Oh," Belle whimpered, "*why* must I be aggravated to death?"

Lady, wiping her hands on her apron, ambled toward the porch. "I'm going fast as I can go." The screen door slammed behind her. "Charley! Your momma want you!"

Charley looked up frowning. Hugging a bag of groceries with

the day's mail sticking out the top, she headed toward the house. "What she want now?"

"She didn't tell me what she want. Come see for yourself what she want!"

Charley climbed the steps and crossed the porch, passing Lady, who turned and followed her in. "Ten minutes earlier, you coulda picked up Junie and brought her home from school."

"I'm not studying schoolteachers." She looked up and saw Juna on the stairs, clasping her books to her breast and looking down at her. She marched into the dining room and dropped the groceries heavily on the table.

"Those belong in the kitchen," Belle said.

Charley skidded the mail across the table toward Belle. "What ch'ont with me?"

"Bills, bills, bills . . ." Belle said. She held up a letter as if to identify it through the envelope. "What's this?"

As she tore it open Charley pushed her hat onto the back of her head and hitched her thumbs into her belt. "I ain't got all day." Behind her, Juna, still holding her books, descended the steps one at a time.

Her attention on the letter, Belle said, "I want you to take your father's rifle and shotgun out of the gun case. I want you to check them and oil them and fire them so I'll know they're in good working order."

"Who you gone shoot now?"

Lady said, "He been on the phone again."

"Who?"

"Her secret admirer."

"It's a letter from a friend of Clay's! They were at the commune together."

"Whu'd he say?"

"He says he's a sculptor and he's sculpting me a bust of Clay. Says Clay is the symbol of The American Dream turned national tragedy. Now what can *that* mean?"

74

Charley said, "I mean Honest Abe. Whu'd he say this time?"

"She say she can't repeat it," Lady said.

But Belle said, "I said who is this, and he said Chuck, can you make a rhyme with Chuck? And I said Muck. It's what you get on your shoes when you cross the barnyard." And she whooped with self-appreciation.

Lady sighed. "I'moan go cut flowers for the table. We won't have them much longer."

"Maybe it's Joyce Perkins," Charley said.

Juna asked, "Who's Joyce Perkins?"

"He's one of our eligible bachelors," Charley said without looking at her.

Belle said, "He said four women out here alone, don't we need a man sometime?"

"Hell, maybe it's Harvey."

Belle looked at Juna with a smirk. "We can be sure it isn't Harvey. He was right out there by the cattle guard when the phone rang."

"Hell, he wouldn't do the calling himself. I mean one of his goons. He's tried everything else, now he's trying scare tactics."

"I might just let him sink a test well on the place," Belle said. "What harm would it do?" And seeing Charley's face, she added piously, "It'd make jobs for a lot of men with families."

"Families!" Charley said. "Those roustabouts are like rodeo riders that travel with nothing but an extra pair of socks."

"Charlene's our expert on the rodeo," Belle said. "Just think how rich I'd be. I could remodel this place, purchase a Lincoln. . . ."

"You could rebuild the place from the ground up and buy out the dealership and it wouldn't make a dent in what you got now."

"I know you think I'm rich!"

"I don't give a damn about your money! All I want's the old place and a few acres to run the horses. You can leave the rest to Clay's bastard!"

"Don't you dare use that word in this house! I'm warning you, Charlene! I'll leave everything to Clay Burden Junior!"

"He ain't Clay Burden Junior!"

"I don't care what they call him!"

"I'm a Burden too!"

Belle shrieked with laughter. "*Now* you've got it!"

"You promised me the homestead. You heard her, Lady."

But Lady had disappeared.

Belle smiled into her mirror, doing something to the top of her wig, both arms circling over her head. "That'll be the day," she said, and added, inspired, "The day you win the bronc riding I'll divide the ranch."

Charley turned her back on them and headed angrily toward the door. "Lemme out of here."

"Where are you going?"

"I got a mare in foal that might be in trouble."

"What do you know about mares in trouble! Call Will Askew if a mare's in trouble!"

"Will Askew calls *me*!" She paused on the porch to calm herself and light a cigarette.

Juna followed excitedly to the door. "Can I go with you? Oh, please. I've never seen anything born."

Belle said, "Just a stinking mess. Why waste your time on it?"

"Oh *please* take me!"

"It'll turn your stomach!"

Charley pulled on her cigarette, looking out toward the windbreak, seeing a chance to thwart Belle.

"I'll just be a minute," Juna flung over her shoulder as she ran up the stairs.

Charley took a drag and flicked her match into the yard.

Belle called angrily out to her, "You waste your time on those horses and neglect the herd!"

"Time I spend on the horses is *my* time." She felt calm now, in charge.

"Whose money do you spend on them! They don't pay for the hay they eat!"

"I raise the hay they eat. You never have to buy any hay."

"A place this size takes a man to run it. You're not a man. If only your brother had lived. Just look at that hair!"

"I'm not studying hair."

"You're not a woman!"

Charley flung herself down the steps into the yard where Lady was putting together a bunch of flowers from the border along the porch. "You always let her get your goat," Lady said, plucking a fading zinnia from her bouquet.

"She can go to hell."

"We all can if we try hard enough."

"What's she mad at now?"

"She just jealous."

Juna hung out the upstairs window and called down, "Wait for me!"

Hands in the back pockets of her jeans, Charley watched the toe of her boot shove a pebble around. "Howcome she hates me, Lady?"

"She don't hate you. You ought to hear her brag on you when you not around. 'That girl can do anything!'"

"She never says nothing like that to my face."

"I ast her," Lady said, "howcome you don't give that girl something? Brag on her behind her back but to her face nothing but pickety-pick. And she said, I don't want to spoil her."

She searched Lady's face but finally she scoffed. "You're lying, Lady."

"I'm just repeating what was said to me."

"You two're just alike—make it up as you go along. Tearl used to say women can't take too much reality."

"Quit talking like that. I won't have it. You're a woman too!"

"Tearl had your number."

"Don't mock me with Tearl. He mock me enough as it is."

77

Charley looked away. She was ashamed of herself, and that made her cranky. "Howcome you waste your time on honkeys?"

"You got to waste your time on somebody, Charley, or your heart'll shrivel up."

The trees in the windbreak were beginning to turn. Before long they'd live in a golden circle. She laughed suddenly, remembering. "He used to holler at me clear across the courthouse square, 'Hey, black-like-me!' *He was lonesome!*"

"Mad and lonesome. Like somebody else I might could mention."

"I miss ol' Tearl. He was rank."

"I always knew children ought to listen to they parents," Lady said. "How else they gone learn what's right? But since he's gone I have come to know it's also true the other way around. The world is changing so—how we gone keep up with it 'less we listen to our children? Now you listen to me, I'd say to him, laying down the law. He'd get so mad. *And* he'd yell! Sometime I can hear his voice, still yelling. And I tell him, I remember the day, the very hour, where you were standing and the look on your face when you first tole me that. *Then* I didn't know. *Now* I do. It quiets him down. I can see him . . . sitting on a log in some woods, sitting there slinging his knife and sticking it up in the ground, over and over and over . . . like that game yawl used to play. . . ."

"Territory."

"Now I listen. And he sits quieter on that log."

"Tearl wouldn't ride nothing tame as a log. Hot nights, we used to lay out by the cattle tank and drink till daylight. If it was winter we'd build us a fire in the old house. He'd tell me what-all he'd been riding. Only black boy in Tula, these Kansas girls got off on it. He was some cowboy!"

"Now I know how hard it musta been. Parents and children ought to understand each other."

78

"Shoot," Charley said. "Just biology. Where we go wrong is trying to make it"—she sneered—"a re-*lay*-shunship."

"I hope I see the day you and your mother come together in love."

Charley hooted. "She's the last person I want to come together with." She reared back and looked up at Juna's window. "She coming with me or what? I got work to do."

Inside, Belle rolled herself back into her bedroom. There were still signs it had recently been the parlor—tall drapes at the windows, carpet on the floor. She got herself into her electric bed and lay there pouting and abandoned.

Juna hurried down the stairs and stopped at her door, dressed in riding pants and knee boots and a little black coat with a scarf at the throat and carrying a hard black-billed cap. Belle had never seen anything so absurd. Juna went to her dresser mirror to put the hat on.

Belle said, "This will certainly be a treat for the horses."

Juna spit on her finger and swirled a little limp strand of hair behind an ear. "I'm going to talk Charley into giving me riding lessons. I wanted to be prepared."

"No place around here you can't get to on foot or in a pickup," Belle said. "You couldn't pay me to bounce around the place on a horse."

Juna's eye fell on the framed photos of Belle's children on either side of the dresser—a studio portrait of Clay, a handsome boy with those same pale eyes, and the slick enlargement of the newspaper photo of Charley coming off the bronc. She was startled. She paused with the hat still in her hand.

"That's my son," Belle said. "And that's my favorite picture of Charlene. I bought it off the newspaper reporter that snapped it." She laughed. Lips parted with horror, Juna looked at Belle in the mirror. She ran out of the house and down the steps, passing

Lady coming in with her flowers. Charley gunned the motor, but Juna paused and asked Lady nervously, "Do I look all right?"

"Where'd you find that get-up?"

"It's what we wore for riding lessons in college."

Lady eyed the costume. "Just come up on the horses nice and easy," she said. And Juna rushed down the steps while Charley revved the motor. She cimbed in the truck and slammed the door.

"Don't yawl be late for dinner," Lady called, "or you'll have to eat it cold!"

The truck sped off, crossing the cattle guard with a swift rumble, and Juna's hand out the window waved a scarf.

Lady stood on the steps and watched them go. The talk had got it going again. He's dead, she told herself. He's *been* dead. It had got to where that was a comforting thought. But what if he wasn't, where was he? Maybe he had that sickness that was forgetfulness and doomed you always to wander, looking for a home you couldn't remember how to find. Sometimes she put it out of her mind for days, then weeks, but it still came creeping back. What had they done with him? Had they made him suffer, and was he suffering still? But you can't suffer that long. But she knew you could. Then she wished him dead, but that was hateful. And finally she looked down the long, empty drive toward the blacktop to see if she saw a soldier limping home. It was the only thing brought her out of it and gave her a little peace.

The first few years, sometimes he called out to her in the night, "Momma!" in a voice completely bare of his old lifelong irony. "Momma! Momma!" And in the dream it was his voice, screaming, but when she woke it was her own, waking up the neighborhood, and Belle in the morning saying, "Honestly, what're we going to do with you! I don't see how you can survive first sleeplessness, now these nightmares." She sat down on the top step with the flowers in her lap and cried a little before she went in. She glanced into the dining room but found it empty. She turned toward Belle's room and saw her lying there pouting. "She'll soon get enough of it," Belle said.

"You better ease up on Charley. You'll drive her away from home."

Belle snorted. "Threatened to move to the tack room and how long did that last? Now she's giving riding lessons." Idly she took up the letter again. "A bust of Clay! What a good idea. A handsomer boy never lived."

"You should of said that to his face while he was still alive to hear it."

Absently, reading the letter, Belle said, "I didn't want to spoil him." She looked up. "I think I'll plan a formal unveiling for the bust when it arrives. We could have a memorial service at the Methodist church. Though I never could stand to sit and listen to that old idiot share his idiocy." She brightened. "And afterwards, a reception! Rum punch!"

Lady pressed her lips together in a firm, hard line.

"I ought to be able to celebrate my own son's unveiling!"

The phone in the dining room rang. They both froze. Belle said, "Don't answer it." It rang again. "What could it be in me," she mused, "a woman approaching middle age, that a man could be after?" The phone rang again. "Never will I understand it. It used to drive Fletcher Burden crazy. Jealous? Just let another man look at me."

Lady put a resigned look on her face. The phone stopped ringing. "If Fletcher Burden had not died in that railroad accident . . ."

"Now it's the railroad."

". . . if he were alive today and could get his hands on this fellow, he'd tear him limb from limb."

Lady moved toward the dining room. Belle snatched up some stiffly strung beads from her bedside table and flipped them into a figure eight looped over the bridge of her nose. "Lady!"

Lady turned.

"How you like me in glasses?"

Lady couldn't help laughing.

Charley swerved off the blacktop into the driveway. Her head-lights picked up the tractor in the field, the tall pole shed, and then the corner of the windbreak. She was driving with one hand and holding a can of beer in the other. ". . . and how they know it's a café, it's got this sign out front says EAT." She found herself turning to look at Juna as she talked. Juna was laughing. They had been laughing all evening. Charley had discovered she could tell Juna funny things the way she saw them and Juna saw them the same way, and they were laughing partly at the comedy and partly with the pleasure of sharing it. "And you go in and Lu-cile—this waitress that looks like she's made out of jerky—she'll come on over to the booth and th'ow outer hip and prop her pad on it—"

Juna laughed so hard Charley had to wait a minute. "And then she'll look at you over the top of her rhinestone spectacles and say, 'Hi,' and she'll give you a minute and then she'll rhyme it with 'Pi?'"

Juna fell forward laughing and caught herself on the dash-board, spilling some beer.

When they drove across the cattle guard, Juna gave in to the impulse and lifted her bottom off the seat and shrieked, and Charley fell over the steering wheel laughing. They skidded to a stop. They got out and slammed doors and came together in front of the pickup and staggered toward the house, exaggerating their tipsiness, and Charley felt drunk on something besides the beer.

KC came trotting toward them with his head down, waggling his whole body from side to side. Juna talked baby talk to him and he threw himself down in ecstasy on the walk and rolled belly-up, pawing the air with pleasure. The locusts were singing their night song. Somewhere a cow was mooing short, desperate-sounding moos.

Juna put up her head, listening. "There's something wrong with that cow," she said.

Charley said, "Yeah. She's getting bred."

Juna wrinkled her glasses back up her nose and said, "Oh." She headed for the swing hanging from one of the low limbs of the sycamore. "What a day!" she said. "My first birth, my first game of pool, my first roadhouse. Smoky's *is* a roadhouse?"

"I never stopped to think is it a roadhouse," Charley said. "I always just thought bar."

"You're an education!" Juna sat down in the swing and Charley leaned against the tree trunk.

"Was this yours and Clay's?"

Charley nodded.

"Do you see much of your sister-in-law?"

"They weren't married."

Juna raised her eyebrows. "What's she like?"

"Reenie? Oh, always mad, face like on a dime. Puts up her nose at the way the world's run. Always into schemes for changing everything."

"She sounds interesting. But Clay sounds like he would have wanted . . . a different type."

"Soft and silly?"

"Something like that."

"That was before Reenie. She might could of done him some good—if she'd liked him well enough. He'd lay out over there mooning, not doing nothing, hanging around. We wouldn't see hide nor hair of him for days at a time."

Juna moved the swing gently back and forth, holding onto the ropes. "You know," she said, "you're a very reckless driver."

"D'I scare you?"

"No-o-o," Juna said tentatively. "You're also a very good driver." Charley was pleased. "If you weren't, you would alas no longer still be with us."

"I never cracked up a car in my life. Only one in this family hasn't."

"Is that how Belle . . . ?"

Charley nodded. "All tanked up in her T-Bird, heading home from Thelma's, those heads sitting on the back seat with their wigs on . . . When she cracked up, there were heads everywhere. First car that stopped, the woman fainted."

Laughing softly, Juna let her head fall onto her breast. "Automobiles!" She shuddered. "It's the deadliest game we've invented, next to war. Red lights, yellow lights, merge! yield! stop! Stripe down the middle, cross it you're out. And all at eighty miles an hour."

She turned the swing till the ropes were twisted together and then lifted her feet and let it spin her around. Lady came out on the side porch, working on a dish with the dish towel. "Supper's dried out. Where you all been?"

"We had a coupla beers up on the highway," Charley said.

"Your momma and me had our supper hours ago."

"She asleep?"

"Tube still going. I reckon she dozing in front of her lineup."

Reluctantly, Juna rose and Charley pushed herself off the tree and they went in.

Belle called, "Juna? Is that you? You're just in time! This show is very educational!"

"Let me get 'em fed!" Lady said. "I want out of this kitchen!"

"Go on to bed, Lady," Charley said. "We can heat ourselves up something."

"It's already heated up. Sit down, both of you."

The other places had been cleared. Only theirs remained. Juna moved her place down next to Charley's. "We shouldn't allow her to do it," she said.

"She likes doing it, don't you, Lady?"

Lady said from the kitchen, "My idea of a real good time."

Juna asked, "Was Smoky's named for the song . . . On top of old—"

"Naw," Charley said. "Smoky, he's named for Smoky the Bear and he just named his bar after hisself."

"Juna!" Belle called.

"Do you really think I can learn to ride a horse?" Juna asked.

"Sure," Charley said. "You just can't let 'em know you're . . . uneasy."

"Well, but I *am*," Juna said. "I took riding in school but that was so long ago. They're *big* when you get up close."

"Yeah," Charley said, "but they don't know it. You take, a horse, when he's face-to-face with you, he sees you're almost as tall as he is. What he don't know is how far he sticks out behind. I mean, a horse don't know how he's made."

"Juna! I was hoping you'd get back in time for this one and now you're missing it!"

Juna called, "Wait a minute!" and said to Charley, "She's a real Leo."

"What am I again?"

Lady came in with their plates dished up. Juna put her head down and her fingers up alongside her temples like horns and gave a long, low bellow.

"I'm a bull!"

"Taurus. And what am I?" She leaned over the table toward Charley, her lips pursed, and made little kissing sounds.

"A fish!"

"Pisces, Cancer rising, moon in Sagittarius."

Lady put their plates down in front of them, shaking her head. "It ain't just the horses don't know how they made."

Juna laughed. "What are you, Lady?"

"Must be a jackass or I wouldn't be staying up till all hours feeding a zoo at the dining room table."

They glanced in at Belle. In the light of the television set they saw her asleep on her pillows. "Shall we turn it off?" Juna whispered.

"Naw," Charley said. "She likes finding it on when she wakes in the night. Anyway, she's got the blab-off." It was there lying beside her among the blankets.

She flicked off the downstairs lights and flicked on the light in the upper hall. They climbed the stairs, Juna in the lead, turning as she talked. "I taught that salad to Lady. Aren't alfalfa sprouts pretty? With all the little lines and dots?" She entered her room and turned on the lights and took off her scarf. Charley had passed her own door and followed Juna down the hall. She leaned against the door frame, her hat on the back of her head, and looked around. The table was piled high with papers and books. Children's crayon drawings decorated the chifforobe doors. Charley walked over with her fingers stuck in her pockets and looked at them. Juna took makings out of a small beaded pouch and began rolling a joint. She lit it and took a long drag, then crossed to Charley, holding her breath as she handed it to her. They stood together looking at a picture of a red pasture with blue trees and an orange sky. Charley took a drag.

"Here, not like that." Juna took it back. "You've got to take some air in with it. Here. Watch." She demonstrated.

"Give it back."

She handed it back.

"Wow," Charley said after a minute. She crossed to the bed and sat, then fell back on it.

"Come on! You can't feel it yet."

"Who-ee!"

"Incredible!" Juna said, sinking back into the rocker. "It must be all that beer."

Charley sat up and reached. She took another long drag, then another, and fell back on the bed again. "I'm going up-up-up . . .

and I'm looking down-down-down on this house, small in the plain—"

Juna leaned forward, excited. "You're hallucinating!"

". . . and the plain is . . . the palm of my hand!"

Juna lapsed back into the rocker and gave it a push with her toes. "I looked up the meaning of your name last night."

"How come?"

"I have the theory that parents try to hand us identities with the names they give us. Do you know what Charlene means?"

Charley felt like she was falling through the bed. She waited till she touched bottom and settled, then she pitched her hat forward over her face and said, "No."

Juna took a drag, held it, and exhaled. "Charlene is the diminutive of Charlotte."

"Ya don't say."

Juna nodded. "Do you see the significance of that?"

"No."

Juna rolled the rocker forward and sat leaning over Charley, "Well," she said in a confidential tone, "Charlotte is the feminine of Charles."

"Well I'll be," Charley said.

"Now do you see?"

"Unh-uh."

Juna handed Charley the joint. Charley inhaled and kept it a minute and inhaled again. She handed it back.

"Well, if Charlene is the diminutive of Charlotte—and Charlotte is the feminine of Charles—to discover the meaning of your name . . ."

Charley rolled onto her side laughing.

"What are you laughing at?"

"You just reminded me of a schoolteacher and then I thought, you *are* a schoolteacher!"

"We must ask ourselves, *what* is the meaning of Charles."

She handed the joint to Charley again, but Charley just lay there with her eyes closed under her hat. "I give up."

"Oh, don't give up!"

Charley giggled and propped her hat off her face with a finger and looked at Juna. "I know!"

"What?"

"Fletcher's brother Charley got kilt when I was on the way—"

"Has no member of this family ever died a natural death?"

". . . so Fletcher named me after him sight unseen. I was supposed to of been a boy. Turned out to be a girl . . . much to everybody's disappointment." She let the hat fall over her face again.

"Including yours?"

"Don't make me no nevermind."

"What *was* your relationship to your father?"

Charley blew her breath out. It sounded like bubbles. "Oh . . . he got a kick out of me when I was little because I could outdo Clay at everything."

"He *wanted* you to outdo Clay? I thought—"

"Oh you know—they say one thing and do another. He wanted Clay to be manly but he didn't want Clay ever to grow up and beat him at anything. He wasn't afraid of that with me. He got a kick out of me like I was some kind of monkey mascot. But when I started to grow up, he wanted me entirely different. He wanted me to put on a dress and forget everything he ever taught me."

"How did your father die? First she'll say one thing, then another . . . hunting accident . . . tractor accident . . ."

"Hell," Charley said, "Fletcher Burden never died. He just roooode into the sunset!" She jackknifed up off the bed, laughing.

Juna said, "Charley is the Teutonic word for man. So Charlene means 'little man.' By naming you Charlene, she told you who you were to be."

"Who was that?"

"A diminutive, for one thing. Less than, you might say."

Charley yawned and pulled the pillow under her head. It crushed her hat up around her ears. "Yeah," she said, "but she don't speak Teutonic."

Juna said, as much to herself as to Charley, working it out with disjointed intricacy, "It's mind-boggling. She named you 'little man.' She gives birth to a girl when they all wanted sons. Why? Because they despised themselves and anything else female. Because of the roles, of course. One of my earliest memories is of a female playschool teacher telling us—imperturbably!—that in China, if they had a girl, they used to just put it out by the road. If anybody wanted it, they could have it. If nobody wanted it, it died. That was before the revolution, of course."

The joint was getting too short to hold. She lifted a turquoise-and-silver roach clip that hung inside her blouse by a chain around her neck. She clipped the roach and took a deep drag while Charley watched. "And I began to scream and scream. She couldn't think what I was carrying on about. I remember the other children looking at me. It didn't bother *them*."

Charley was watching the way her chin worked. Juna could shrug with her chin, pout with her chin, toughen up with her chin. . . .

"So . . . she named you 'less than a man.' Onto you she projected her self-hate while at the same time with this very same name forcing you out of female roles and into freedom, escape from what she is always shoving you toward! The Empress of Double Bind! No wonder she sometimes seems jealous of you. Funny—I like her more and more as I like her less and less." She sighed and slumped back in her chair. "But it's just a different film through the same old projector."

Charley took another drag. The way Juna's mind worked reminded her of her mare Avalanche in a barrel race, lithe and quick, dodging in and out, flying around obstacles. "How you keep all that in that little biddy head?" she said.

Juna rose and walked languidly to the dresser and leaned on her hands toward the mirror. "You think it's unusually small? You make it sound like a pincushion!"

"Naw," Charley laughed, "I mean a little head to hold so much—Teutonic."

Juna turned and sat against the edge of the dresser and peered at Charley over the tops of her glasses. "I'd like to claim etymology," she said, "but I have to confess I looked it all up in a book called *What Shall We Name the Baby*."

———————

———————

Lady still sometimes wondered what she was doing here. Charley had been a small, bristly loner when she came to the ranch a widow with a small child in tow. She was at a point in her life when everything told her to take control in her own hands and make big changes. But numbed by Nap's long illness, still undone by his early death, she was in that state of shock and the blues that makes decisions impossible. She'd seen obstacles to every course of action open to her. She could write for travel money to her brother back in East Texas and simply go on home, but her brother and Nap had hated each other and it seemed disloyal to her dead husband to turn now to his enemy. And travel money home would not solve the larger problem of a job for herself and some way of putting a roof over her own head and Tearl's. Besides, families can be cruel when the stray comes limping home after a brave leave-taking. She might borrow money from Belle Burden, for whom she did weekly housecleaning, and get to California at last. But once out there she would be penniless, friendless, and alone. It was only by way of doing *something* that she went out to see Belle. She hadn't made up her mind to anything.

But Belle was alarmed when Lady talked aimlessly of leaving Tula. She realized suddenly that it was Lady who kept her from going mad on these godforsaken Kansas plains, a Texan in a land of second- and third-generation New Englanders turned Midwestern. She shuddered to think of it. Nobody to laugh at her when she meant to entertain, just all those alien eyes, amazed, and, if she told a good story, suspicious. She realized she couldn't do without Lady and offered her a job on the spot. Lady hesitated—not about the job, though something in her thought maybe she oughtn't settle in a white woman's house—but only because it seemed as if she couldn't make up her mind to anything. So Belle thought to throw in the trailer. Fletcher had just taken it in trade from a fellow who'd bought some breeding stock and couldn't finish paying. She could park it out back and live on the place. And there it was—a job and a roof to shelter her and Tearl. Once she had actually found the job, some women in Tula found her another, as laundress at the hospital, looking stern-mouthed that she'd taken a job as a servant. Midwesterners had strange ideas about what was being a servant and what was not. She had taken Belle's offer partly as Providence providing and partly as a temporary solution till she could get on her feet and deal with things. It had been a temporary solution now for something like eighteen years.

Lady was paring apples. Juan had taught her to dry them, and it saved her days of preserving. She was only half listening to the conversation going on in the dining room. Every month or two the little thing would just appear, always at mealtime. Now she was calling herself Keeta, but they all thought of her as Creep. Clay had called her Creep—"Hi, Creep!"—like it was a name. You couldn't tell who they'd be from one time you saw them to the next. When they'd first laid eyes on her, it was Evening Star. Then she'd gone through Prudence, Tai, and Dimitry Moonbeam. Now it was Keeta, an Indian name, and she spelled it for you. She was always careful to spell it for you. She had a friend

91

out there she frequently referred to named Cera. It sounded just like Sarah till she spelled it.

She was sitting at the table having lunch. Belle always fed her and then, as she was leaving, pressed her to take some money. They had a regular song and dance they went through at the door.

"Oh no, I couldn't . . ."

"But you came all the way out here . . ."

"But I really shouldn't . . ."

Yet she always finally did.

She called herself a friend of Reenie's. When she spoke of Reenie, she drew herself up and called her Irene. "Irene is a wonderful person," she said. "She's the glue. Without her it might all just fall apart."

"It" was an old homestead that had belonged to somebody's grandparents. It had been inherited, or else, Lady suspected, wouldn't a one of them have been in Kansas. What did they do? Why, *everything*. Hogarth could weave and she herself did embroidery, though you couldn't do too much with embroidery. They kept a pig and in the spring the pig had had piglets. They'd thought a little pork would be good in a wok.

"What's a wok?" Belle asked.

Something you th'ow at the cat, Lady thought. She put down her paring knife to serve seconds. The little thing ate like a starveling. "But then," she said, "we gave all the piglets names and now nobody would think of eating them." Instead they had decided to become vegetarians. She spoke in a clear, piping, child's voice. "And of course we meditate." She was thoughtful a minute and then stated it a little differently. "We start out our day in meditation." They had a whole room, she told them, devoted to nothing but meditation. It had pillows on the floor. You had to make your own pillow. Hers was the top of her futon, cut off. She didn't need the whole length of her futon, she explained, because she wasn't very tall. So she had just cut it off and sewed up the

92

ends. Lady was dying to ask what a futon was, but another part of her didn't want to spoil it, she liked it so well as it was.

And Babananda—that was the baby—was *thriving*. Why, he'd just bang away on his tray with his bone—he loved to gnaw on a bone. Irene thought it was because he would soon be cutting teeth—you could feel one or two in his gums and he was so proud of them he'd let you . . .

"Why,"—Belle sounded alarmed—"I'm not sure that's sanitary! Everybody with a finger in that child's mouth!"

But Creep said they thought germs were healthy. "Like, you know, natural immunization." She said she didn't know what they'd do without Baba. He added *schedule* to their lives. She herself would like to have a baby, for the experience. She was thinking of insemination. They had this sperm bank on the West Coast somewhere. You could pick race—though she thought they should leave that out—and height and hair color, eyes. . . . You could pick out whatever you wanted. Of course she wanted a girl. There were ways of telling. "I mean," she said, "like . . . the female sperm either sinks or rises, one . . ." She'd have to find out. It depended on if you shook the tube.

"You could just have one the way Irene did," Belle said with an edge in her voice that she quickly laughed to hide.

Creep said that was of course also a possibility.

What else they did, they took turns at cooking, baking, washing dishes.

Lady thought that was a good idea.

"And we have meetings." They had a lot of meetings. Communication was so important. Sometimes they had several meetings a day. "To talk things out, you know?" It was sometimes hard to get their work done, but nothing was more important than talking things out. Sometimes they had trouble with this person called Petaluma. She spelled it. This Petaluma had had a mystical experience in a place in California called Petaluma,

93

hence the name. Petaluma sometimes needed to lie alone in a room for days.

You never could tell whether "this person" was a boy or a girl. It made asking questions difficult. "Did this person eat?" Lady asked.

Oh, sometimes, but sometimes fasted. At such times they divided Petaluma's chores among them.

"And the child?" The name they had given him Belle refused to utter, and that made it hard to bring the conversation around to where she wanted it. It was like fishing, Lady thought. You put out a little bait and you caught whatever came down the stream. She poured a little coffee to see if it was still hot. It steamed, so she poured herself a cup.

"Irene believes Baba is exceptionally psychic," Creep said. Once they put a crayon in his little fist and sat around for ages to see if he'd do something automatic. She smiled at Lady with her large blue eyes and pink cheeks. "It was just fantastic. He kept waving it around like he does his bone—the crayon, I mean—and sort of gurgling, like he knew what we were after and he was teasing us? Then he put it in his mouth . . . Irene only buys hypoallergenic crayons, he can eat them if he likes. But finally . . . *finally* . . . he put it down on the tablet and drew this single vertical line!" She looked at them expectantly but neither of them knew what to make of it. Belle had pushed back from the table and was sitting with her elbow on her thrust-up knee and her chin propped on her hand, looking at the visitor. "I," Creep said. "See? I! He was proclaiming his selfhood! We were all so thrilled. So Hogarth made some egg rolls. Whenever something like that happens, Hogarth makes these egg rolls. We eat them with Chinese mustard. Hot!" She put out her tongue and rolled up her eyes and panted.

Belle's fingers strummed on her cheek and her jaw was fixed. Lady tried to think what to ask that might give them a little something. "Is Reenie thinking of going back East?"

"Oh no," Creep said. "The air's unbreathable."

That was something.

"She got a job yet?"

Creep smiled with forbearance. She was picking out a potato eye. Though she ate a lot, she picked the food over carefully and always left a little pile of debris on the edge of her plate—a shred of chicken gristle, an apple seed, a scrap of potato skin. "No," she said, "but she's studying a lot."

"What she studying?" Lady asked.

She was studying Baba somebody, the very person the baby was named for, who dressed in robes and wore a spot in the middle of his forehead. Irene was studying because Petaluma was beginning to channel.

Lady nodded her approval. She thought they were irrigating their garden. She had done a little trenching herself so she could just lay out the soak hose if she wanted to instead of sprinkling. It saved a lot of water. This Baba must be a gardener. She was glad they were studying something sensible for a change.

That Petaluma was channeling, Creep said, both thrilled and exasperated Irene. She was afraid it might be a step backward. She'd come to believe the answer lay in politics.

When Creep was leaving, after the song and dance and the bills thrust into her hand, Belle sent Lady into her room to get something for the baby. Lady brought back a small stuffed bear, and Creep couldn't at first make up her mind to take it. "Irene's so particular. . . ." But finally she took it and went off down the drive, dress trailing, listing a little, head to one side as if she were saying farewell to the sunflowers.

"I'd like to see that child," Lady said. "I'd like to lay eyes on a boy of Buddy's."

"So would I," Belle said, watching Creep go, "if it *is* Buddy's."

Lady was dumbfounded. "What you mean, if?"

But Belle just gave her that look that meant don't be stupid.

4

Charley stood in the center of the ring, turning slowly with her hands on her hips, watching Juna in new boots ordered from Shepler's, and a checked blouse, mounted on the big old sorrel gelding with the grizzled muzzle. She sat stiff and uneasy in the saddle, holding the reins across her upturned palm while the horse circled at a walk. KC lay in a patch of shade under the fence, his head up and his tongue out, watching. Maybe you had to be born to it, Charley was thinking. Her own great grandma had come out here from Scotland with her sidesaddle. Down under the willow tree in the draw, in front of the old house, was a boulder with toe holds chiseled in it, long worn smooth, for her to climb up on to mount. Fletcher had been able to remember her. "A little bit of a thing and could outride anybody. Sidesaddle too. She'd of come to about here," striking his arm way below the shoulder.

She cocked her head to see what was wrong. "Uh, okey, let your leg fall straight. Don't hug him with your leg. That's right, just let it fall."

While the big horse circled, she walked over and reached up to turn Juna's hand over so that she held the reins properly. "Oh, right," Juna said. "I knew that. I forgot."

"Drop your heel. Let your weight fall down into your heel. No. Sit up! Sit up! Sit back like that, he'll leave you behind. Sit up over your legs so if you look down you'll just see the tip of your toe. Can you see it? That's better. No, now, what you doing now?"

The horse had broken into a little jog trot. "I'm trying to post!" Juna said. "Like they taught us at school!"

"Well, no, don't do that. We don't do that outchere."

"What do you do, just bounce?"

"Grab aholt of his mane and pull yourself up about an inch out of the saddle. Go on, grab aholt!"

"I don't want to hurt him!"

"You won't hurt him! Go ahead! Do like I tell you!" She was trying hard to be patient.

"How do you know it won't hurt him?"

"I just *know*! You can *tell*! Go *ahead*! *That's* right."

Juna fell back into the saddle.

"No, just hold on till you get your balance and feel like you can keep it. *It won't hurt him*! Your legs'll get some spring in 'em after a while."

"Nice Soldier! I like him!"

"He was Clay's first horse. He learned to ride on Soldier."

"What was your brother like?" They lay in the sun beside the cattle tank in the prairie grass.

"Clay?"

"Clay in her hands? A man of Clay?" Juna tested the name, guessing. Then, with sudden illumination, "Clay Burden!"

Charley was suspicious. "What you so interested in him for?"

"She named him after his own mortality! She named him Death!"

"Wadn' her that named him," Charley said. "It was Fletcher. After *his* daddy."

"Why'd he do it?"

Charley pulled out a weed stem and worked it between her front teeth. "Do what?"

"*You* know . . ."

Charley hiked up her shoulders into what shrug she could manage lying down. "He turned his car over."

"I don't *believe* this!"

"He had a carload of his pals and KC with him. They all got out without a scratch. Car wadn' even hurt, just turned over on its side. They run off the road on a curve. They all climbed out and Clay stood there looking at it and then he said, 'That's it,' and reached in the glove compartment and got his pistol."

Juna sat up and looked down at her. "That was *all*?"

Charley sat up too and hugged her knees and nodded.

"God!" Juna breathed.

The pond just missed being a perfect round. Charley circled it carefully with her eye till she came to the narrow gravel beach at the shallow end that pulled it a little oval. She tried to make the round with her eye. Sometimes she could do it. More often she lost it and had to start over. When she was a child lying out on a hot night in the yard, she used to run her eye that way around the lighted window squares, trying to keep the crisp square lines, tracing them with her eye, but it was hard, especially at the corners. Almost always she had to begin again.

Tracing the round of the pond, losing it, beginning again, she felt herself holding her breath and felt her body rigid. Why did she have to do it? Her eyes were stinging. She had to blink. She made herself look away. She fell back down and looked at the sky. You must be crazy, she told herself. You must be some kind of a nut out of a whole family of nuts. Juna was quiet beside her, waiting, it felt like.

"Fletcher and him kept getting into it, you know. . . . They had these fights."

"You mean . . . fists?"

"Mostly, yeah. Once it was tire chains. Fletcher'd use any excuse to whup Clay. He'd whup him if he did something wrong or just didn't do it the way he thought he should. . . ."

"I see," Juna said, "he'd done something wrong."

Charley looked at her. "Whadaya mean?"

"He'd turned over the car."

"Fletcher was already dead."

Juna weighed some pebbles on her palm.

"Let Clay do something halfway right, why Fletcher'd haul off and do it better, pretending he was showing him how but really just showing him up. I remember when Clay was maybe six years old and Fletcher come home drunk and busted into our room and hung over Clay's bed and whipped off the covers and said, 'Let's see can you get it up.'"

Juna dropped the pebbles. "Oh my God!"

Charley laughed. "Where'd you grow up, anyway? In goosedown? Goosedown, New York, USA."

"I've watched Belle with you," Juna said, "trying not to blame the mother. That was a parlor game of yesteryear. But Fletcher sounds worse than Belle."

Charley crossed her arms under her head and looked at the sky. "He was a pistol ball. Ol' Fletcher was a pistol ball."

KC came padding out of the cottonwoods. She threw him a stick and he plunged into the pond and swam after it and brought it back and dropped it and shook himself. The horses stood with their heads drooping, eyeing the pond. She sighed and got up and led them over to drink. She'd waited for them to cool down first. They stood with their feet in the shallows.

"They're so different," Juna said. "Soldier's so noisy." Soldier blew in the water like a child through a straw. "Avalanche is such a lady." Avalanche had always done it like that, put her muzzle daintily in the pond and sucked soundlessly. Charley laid a hand across the mare's neck, fondling. Avalanche was five years old, silver, almost white, with faint blue rings in her coat.

Juna lay back down on her stomach and propped her head on her hands and looked at the remains of the old sod house that had been built into the side of the little rise. "It must have been hard," she said.

Charley thought she meant Clay till she saw her looking at the melting ruin in the side of the bank. "Homesteading? Hard's not the word for it. I wish I had a been here." She led the horses out of the pond and lay down again beside Juna. "We got some pictures," she said. "You want to see them when we get home?"

"Photographs? Of the place then?"

Charley nodded.

"Oh, wow! Who's in them?"

"Fletcher's great-granddaddy looking like a boy, and his whole family, standing in front of the sod house. Right over there. Looklike there was a rail fence around it—or maybe a kind of hitching post. And a sort of brush corral over yonder." She pointed. "Wadn' any trees then, or any cattle tank. It was just the sod house built into the draw—for protection against the wind."

"It's a lovely spot." Juna shoved her glasses up her nose. Her hair caught the sun and glinted coppery. Charley looked from her to the pastures rising behind her in a heavy ground swell. She looked up toward the old log house at the head of the draw. This was the part of the ranch Belle had promised her. She'd always, since she could remember, had the feeling it was already hers.

"All the homesteads around here were little farms," she said. "They couldn'a thought of ranching. But in one of the panics, a lot of homesteaders gave up and sold out and either went back to Missouri or to the new lands opening up in Oklahoma. Fletcher's great-granddaddy hung on and bought up a lot of land. You could get it for nothing people were so discouraged. His family like to starved. He sold his stock, his cow and horse, he sold the wagon, all but the clothes on their backs, to buy up the land. This is fine pasture, about the best there is."

"Panics? Out here? I connect panics with Wall Street."

"Hell yes, panics. A whole string of them."

"What caused them?"

"Drought. Crop failures. Prices falling just at harvest. They'd have to feed their corn to the pigs, and if pork went for two cents a pound, why you'd need a two-hundred-fifty-pound hog to bring five dollars."

"How awful."

"Yeah, and wadn' nothing to do if you wanted to eat but go out and gather up buffalo bones and sell them for three dollars a ton for fertilizer. Must of been buffalo bones ever'where. Plains must of been littered with them. They'd shoot them from train windows for the sport and leave 'em to rot. Buffalo Bill boasted he'd killed five thou'd'n out here in one year to feed the railroad gangs. They were building the railroads then. Or you could round up wild horses and sell 'em. They was a lot of wild horses in Kansas then. But the droughts and panics weren't all of it. There was also the grasshoppers." She lay looking at the clear, bright sky. "They'd come in hordes till they darkened the sun and the sky'd turn till it'd be like twilight, and where they set down wadn' a blade of grass or a green twig left. They could dispose of a quarter section in an hour and a half, and for dessert they'd eat all the melons and the pumpkins till you couldn't find a scrap of rind. They'd eat the cornfields down to stubs and eat the bark off trees. They'd gnaw on fence posts, shovel handles."

It gave her the willies to think about it, people barricading themselves indoors, some going mad at the whirr and the wind, the locusts a foot thick on the ground. They said people lived in dread ever after, once they'd seen it, the light on the edge of a million wings, coming in like tornadoes, worse than tornadoes.

"No wood to build with, so they cut sod for houses and burned buffalo chips for cooking and raised corn if they could. Wadn' any wheat then. We're selling wheat to the Russians now, but it was from Russia that wheat came to Kansas. The Mennonites brought something called Turkey Red, because of its color. Every family brought a bushel. Handpicked seed grain. Not much wheat had been made to grow out here till then, but this hard

101

Russian wheat grew like crazy. It must be a little like Russia here."

"The steppes," Juna said with a touch of wonder.

Charley couldn't ever remember talking so much. She liked it. With Tearl it was mostly laughing and punching each other and rolling on the ground wrestling and drinking beer. "When I was in high school, we put on a comedy called *Manifest Destiny*."

"A comedy!"

"Yeah. We got to choose our parts. I was Daniel Webster. In a beard and a little goatee." She made a mustache with her fingers and recited. "'What do we want with this vast, worthless land, this region of savages and beasts, of deserts and shifting sands and whirlwinds and cactus and prairie dogs and dust? To what use can we ever hope to put these great deserts, or those endless mountain ranges, impenetrable and covered to their very base with eternal snow? What can we ever hope to do with the western coast, three thousand miles long, rockbound, cheerless, and not a harbor in it? Mr. President, I will never vote one cent from the public treasury to place the Pacific Coast one inch nearer to Boston.'"

Juna rolled onto her back, laughing. Charley looked down at her. "People still feel like that about Kansas. They just use Kansas to drive through."

"You're lucky," Juna said. "Maybe it'll stay like this."

"All this used to be an ocean. Out west of here they found fossils of snakes the size of whales, and birds with teeth, and this big bird six foot tall with little biddy wings that would dive for its food."

"You're making it up."

"There were oyster beds in Kansas! Coronado come th'oo here! He was looking for a city made of gold and this fellow told him it was around here someplace. Of course he didn't find it. So he killed the liar and went on home. He was pretty disappointed after living on buffalo meat all that time. But he said the land was fat and black and he found prune plums like they had in Spain."

The face of the pond was still, a round blue mirror for the sky. Avalanche gave a sleepy snort on a downward scale and dropped her head. Charley threw a rock in the water and watched the circles spread. "That's where the wild horses come from, the ones they rounded up and sold when the going got rough. The Spaniards left them behind when they went lame and they multiplied over the years."

"Why did they move out of the old house?" Juna asked. "It's so lovely."

Charley thought so too but it wasn't a word she'd say. They looked back up the draw at it. "Highway come th'oo. This was too far off the road in winter. If it had a been me, I'd a stayed."

The old weathered roof sloped out to cover the porch with log pillars to hold it up. The porch ran all along the front of the house. The upstairs windows, set into the roof with their own little peaked roofs jutting up over them, looked out over their heads.

"I like it," Juna said.

"The old house?"

"Kansas."

"It's an Indian name," Charley said. "They was a tribe out here called the Kansa. It means people of the wind."

"That's fitting," Juna said, pulling on her sweater. The wind had come up. You could see it bending the grass like hair it ran its fingers through. Charley rolled back over and looked at the sky and felt Juna looking down at her. "Kansas is full of surprises," Juna said. "You're different from any woman I ever knew. You're what a woman should be."

"Me!" Charley laughed and for something to do tossed a pebble in the pond. KC plunged after it and stopped, bewildered, looking for a stick.

"You can do anything," Juna said. "You never let *your* feet be bound. The pioneer women must have been like you. God, they could put you on display at the Smithsonian with a plaque: THIS IS WHAT WOMEN COULD BE." She laughed.

Charley's face heated. Was Juna bragging on her or making fun?

Two horsemen came riding up the draw. They stopped at the old low shed. One was Juan. The other was looking toward them.

"Who's that?" Juna asked.

"Hi, Warren," Charley called.

"Hi're you?" he called back.

She lifted her shoulders. "Awright. Hi 'bout you?"

He lifted his. "Awright I guess."

Charley jumped up and said, "Come on. I'll show you the house."

Juna glanced back at the stranger, but Charley took the horses' reins and started up the draw.

It was dim inside after all the brightness of the draw. The downstairs was one big rectangle with a fireplace at each end and furniture piled up against the back wall with an old patchwork quilt thrown over it. A wagon wheel hung from the ceiling with little cups for candles around the rim.

"What a wonderful house!" Juna said. She put a lot into the wonder. What a *whun*-derful house. Charley was pleased. "I'd love to get my hands on it." Charley was alarmed.

"Whu'd you do to it?"

Juna clasped her hands in front of her. "Oh, I don't know."

They walked up the stairs. The steps came out into a little square upstairs hall with a room to either side. Juna put her head into each room. "It's cozy up under the eaves like this." The rooms had windows opening to the front. "I just love dormers," she exclaimed.

Dormers, Charley thought, dormers, so she would remember. Juna turned in a circle. "Oh, look at the old wood floors!"

"Pine," Charley said.

"They must be a yard wide!"

"Twenty inches."

"It's so snug up here. You could lie in bed and listen to the rain."

They poked around and looked out the windows, then went back down.

"Where's the kitchen?"

"They cooked in the fireplace."

The east fireplace had an iron in it for hanging a pot, and along the edge of the mantel iron pegs shaped like outsize horseshoe nails. "For hanging pans and things," Charley said.

"I just love this house," Juna said, turning, her hands together in front of her lips. "I'd open the back wall and put a kitchen, there."

"A lean-to kitchen," Charley said, pleased. That was where she'd planned it herself. "With a breakfast table at the window."

"Yes!" Juna said. "At the east window! And what about a bath?"

"Up over the kitchen," Charley said. "Off the east bedroom."

"Oh good," Juna said. "And since the plumbing would be there, might as well put a half-bath downstairs."

"That'd be easy."

"But there's no water. What about water?"

"There's plenty of water," Charley said. "There's a well. See the windmill?" It was on the rise behind the house. "That's what waters the pond. There's lots of artesian wells in Kansas."

"Electricity! What about electricity?"

"A wind generator," Charley said. "Enough wind out here to run a factory. And storage batteries."

They looked at each other. For some reason Charley had to look away.

"I'd make gingham curtains for the windows," Juna said.

"One day Lady's gonna braid rugs for the floor."

"She knows how to braid rugs?"

"She braided those in the upstairs hall back at the house. Out of everybody's old clothes. There's clothes of mine in those rugs from when I was eight years old."

"There's enough stored here to furnish it," Juna said, turning over an old wicker chair. "Oh God, that's a pie chest!" She opened the punched tin doors, admiring.

They wandered back out onto the porch and looked down the draw. The sun had dropped over the western swell but it hadn't gone down. It threw long shadows east, over the pasture, and the wind was blowing.

"We better be getting back," Charley said.

They rode slowly, side by side. "But what are you really into?" Juna was saying. "Besides pool and guns and pickups? Like . . . I'm into food . . . and politics. One thing you're into—you're into horses. I get the feeling you and the horses have some kind of metaphysical communication, and all so gentle."

"Well," Charley said, "I don't hold anymore with breaking horses." She thought of the Askews. "That's what they do around here. Then what've you got? Something broken."

They came to the crest of a land swell and stopped a minute for the darkening view. Way off across the fields they could see the windbreak and the red roofs rising above the trees, and the twin silos. The wind whirred in the grass and the horses were restless to get home. Juna patted Soldier's neck and he swiveled his ears toward her.

"C'mon," Charley said, and loped off down the slow slope. She loved loping on Avalanche down a gentle slope. Loping that way the two of them felt like one animal. Juna followed. She could hear her calling, "Wait for me!" And KC ranged off, hunting.

They lay side by side on a Sunday afternoon high in a nest of stacked hay bales, looking up at the corrugated steel roof of the pole shed. The litter of kittens, leggy now, crawled over them. Juna had discovered there were innumerable cats on the place because the outbuildings and the pole shed full of hay were breeding grounds for mice. This litter crawling over them was Mary Jane's. And there was the gray tom Charley'd named Evinrude because, she claimed, you could hear him purring two counties away, and the calico Juan called Flores, with the tip of one ear missing because the winter before she'd got it in the milk and it failed to dry before it froze that night, and then fell off. Cats appeared and disappeared. Some made names for themselves, some were simply "that tiger cat" or "the bobtail Manx." And there was a huge buff-colored tom with violent blue eyes alarmingly crossed and an awful voice, who looked like he could swing from trees by his mink-colored tail. His name was Chinga. It gave Juna a turn to hear Lady at the back door yelling "Chinga!" with a bowl in her hand.

"How on earth did he get a name like that?"

"He showed up one day at Thelma's," Charley said. "And Thelma begged Belle to bring him out here and turn him loose. She said he was Siamese so Belle thinks he's something special. She brings him home and says, Think up an Oriental name, and Lady said, How's Chow Mein? and I said, How 'bout Chinga? And Belle liked it. She wanted to know, What's it mean? But I said, What's the difference?" It was easy to see Charley enjoyed hearing "Chinga!" yelled out the back door at feeding time. Whenever Juan heard it, he still tucked in his chin, shocked in his sense of decency.

Juna liked living with all the animals around. The most she'd had was a furry puppy for a few months, till her father ran over it coming in the driveway one night in his cups, and a few goldfish.

"I never saw horses like yours before," she said.

"Well," Charley said, "the Arabs for a thou'd'n years kept 'em in the tent with them, out of the sandstorms, like one of the family. That's howcome they so smart. You know, the way an animal that lives with people, like a cat or a dog, is different from a wild animal."

"People are like that," Juna said. "People are a little like wild animals till they find somebody they can talk to, who laughs at the same things. I know I was. Wild and shy. Till I found my first friend. I was about twelve."

Charley didn't say anything. That kind of talk embarrassed her. "Out here all you hear is Quarter Horses. Soldier's a Quarter Horse. Want to get fancy, they'll th'ow in a little Thoroughbred to narrow them down at the shoulders."

The wind whistled above them under the eaves where birds fluttered, trying to escape. But where they lay amid the bales, they were out of it and warm in the heat of the sun on the tin roof.

"What else I'm into," Charley said, "I'm into—I like to go out on the range, you know?"

Juna nodded.

"They's plenty of prairie on this ranch where the sod's never been busted. Still like it was for the buffalo. And . . . guess what?"

"What?"

"It's alive."

"Oh wow!"

"One day when I was riding fence I happened to look up. And that's when I saw it and knew it . . . the way you know you like cotton candy. Once I know a thing that way, even afterwards, when I lose it again, I always know it's true."

"De Chardin said once a thing is known that way by one person, it's destined to be known by the whole human race. I guess that's the hundredth-monkey phenomenon."

"Yessir, alive. I like to go out there and lay down on it, and if I'm feeling lousy it'll heal me. You can laugh at that if you want to."

"I don't want to."

"Indians think if you're sick it'll strengthen you to lay down next to a healthy animal. That's what it's like out there . . . a healthy animal that's never been tampered with. And I lay there wondering am I on the belly? the fanny?" She snorted. "Inside the windbreak, I know it's the armpit."

Juna sighed, contented, holding a kitten on top of her and feeling it purr. "It's an air museum," she said. "I dreamed the other night I brought a busload of children from New York City out here and I told them, 'Breathe, children! This is what it was like in the old days!'"

Charley lay on the ground behind the laboring cow, sweat running in her eyes though it was a chilly morning, her sleeve rolled to her shoulder and her arm, streaked with blood, up to the elbow in the cow's hot uterus. Her face slid against the cow's haunch, slippery with blood. She pulled herself closer and inched farther in. The calf was turned wrong. One leg was bent funny. She had to turn it to get it born and the cow couldn't help. She had found her too late and she blamed herself. The calf felt limp and dead. As she turned it gently her eyes met Juna's. Juna stood with her knuckles to her open mouth, biting. The ground was cold and the wind stinging. She got the leg straight. She thought the calf kicked feebly, but she couldn't be sure. She began slowly withdrawing her arm, turning the calf as she pulled, and here it came. She drew it out and it lay there, not moving. The afterbirth never came. She dug the mucus out of the calf's nose with her shirttail, rose, and grabbed a bucket from the wall of the shed and worked frantically at the dying cow's teats till the thick colostrum squirted, rich and yellow like cream. "Oh what are you doing?" Juna cried.

"Run up to the house and look on the mantel and bring me that plastic bottle sitting there. Hurry!"

Juna ran off up the draw toward the old house and Charley milked till the cow was empty and breathing her last, then set the bucket aside and bent over the calf. It moved. It struggled to rise. It got its forelegs up. She circled its belly with her arms and lifted its hind end. It stood wobbly on all four legs. Charley wiped her forehead on the back of her bloody arm.

Juna came running back with the nippled bottle. "What was *wrong*?" she cried.

"I don't know," Charley said. "She was a first-calf heifer."

Juna spied the standing calf and exclaimed. "Oh, the poor little thing! Can it survive?"

Charley was pouring the colostrum into the bottle, trying not to spill. She nippled it and forced it into the calf's mouth, but the calf didn't suck. Charley cursed and tried stroking the neck and squeezing the bottle a little, careful not to squeeze out too much and choke the calf, but it all ran out the corner of the calf's mouth. "Oh, Christ," she muttered.

"What's the matter?"

"She's not savvy."

She took down a length of tube from the wall and handed it to Juna. "I'm going to hold open its mouth for you. You're going to put the tube down its throat."

"Oh, I can't!" Juna cried.

"Yes you can. It's easy. I'll tell you what to do. Just go slow now."

And together they got the tube into the calf and the colostrum in through the tube. The calf was too weak to fight. Once the tube was out, the calf seemed livelier.

"What was that for?" Juna asked.

"The first milk is full of immunizing agents," Charley said. "The calf can only absorb it for a little while after it's born. I mean it could absorb the protein, but not the immunizing stuff. So now it's got a chance."

"But how'll you feed it?"

"I don't know," Charley said. "If I had a mother cow with a dead baby, I could skin the baby and put the skin on this one and

110

try to get her to accept it. But I got no dead babies. This calf's out of season."

Juan came slowly down the draw in the old flatbed. He had a cow tied to the bumper. Her calf frolicked behind.

"We'll try this," Charley said.

Juan untied the cow and she ambled over to the pond, the calf following. She stood while her calf nursed a little, then she snatched at some grass and had a long, slow drink.

Juan caught up the calf and looped a rope around its legs and it lay bawling. Then he grabbed up the newborn and took it over. The cow spun away and looked at it, then snatched another mouthful of grass and raised her tail. Juan grabbed the newborn and got it behind her in time for the yellow stream to shower over it. Juna watched wide-eyed. Then the cow turned, nudged the calf, sniffing it all over, and dropped her head again to eat. The calf nudged at the cow's flanks, hunting. Charley laughed with relief.

"How on earth does it know to do that?" Juna asked, but nobody answered.

"She's an old cow," Charley said. "Maybe it'll work."

The cow ignored what the calf was doing, and it raised its muzzle under her and found her teats and nudged at the udder. The cow raised her head and swung it around and nudged at the calf but then went back to grazing. The calf had a teat in its mouth. It was pulling.

After a while Juan untied the larger calf and the three went off together. "Keep an eye on them," Charley said to Juan.

Juan nodded. "It will be all right," he said, slamming the door of the Ford and pausing to fill his pipe.

A scruffy brown horse walked into the next stall and looked over at them. Juna thought she had met them all. "Who's that?" she asked.

"That's Peanuts," Charley said.

"Hi, Peanuts. He's not like the others. What is he?"

111

"He's a bucking horse."

"What does that mean?"

"It means he bucks."

Juan laughed and Juna looked at Charley, but Charley went over and stood for a minute with her mouth against her arm, looking down at the dead cow. Then she walked over to the pond and squatted and began to wash the blood away.

"It's wonderfully warm," Juna said. "You'd think it would be cold. The air's much colder."

"Water holds the sun," Charley said.

Juna's wet hair parted raggedly in the middle and streamed down alongside her face and then spread out in the pond around her. In the water, darkened by tannin from the trees, their bodies faded away to pale, indeterminate blurs. They had no legs but mermaid nether parts, no feet at all. They were naked, but it was Juna's eyes, so startling, so open-looking without her glasses, that made her seem most naked. They seemed somehow inefficient, and they had that wide, not-quite-focused look of the short-sighted.

"Do you need your glasses to see?" Charley asked.

"I'm blind without them," Juna said. "Well, I see your face, but its outlines are blurry. I see the land swelling up behind you. It's a little surreal. One day I'll turn brave and get contacts."

Charley was relieved that there was such a simple solution. How awful, not to see well, but Juna was smiling.

"It gives you a different perspective, I guess," she said. "But traveling I always carry an extra pair—not in my bag but almost always on my person. I'd be lost . . ."

Charley's eyes kept falling to Juna's breasts. If Juna couldn't see her, was it taking advantage? In the brownish water they seemed to float, round and not at all prey to gravity. Her own were small and close to her body. They weren't a bother.

"Maybe it makes me see more clearly," Juna said. "I once

112

knew a girl who had that awful stammer—you know, the kind where you try to spit the words to get them out, and the head bobs, like they're little darts you try to expel." She tried to demonstrate, but treading water made it hard. She sputtered and laughed and spit out a mouthful. "But this girl was a poet. She wrote such exquisite things. As if the stammer itself made words more precious." She laughed. "And of course Beethoven was deaf. Well, he wasn't always deaf. . . ."

Juna could draw. She had a bright blue pencil case and when they went out together she took a pad with her and in a few strokes made whole pictures. KC was there—in some wavy lines and a couple of smudges—with his rump high and his nose between his paws, about to spring, playing. It made you see KC as if you'd never looked at him before. And Mary Jane and the kittens scattered all over one page, and Chinga looking down from what might be a loft window with his mystically cross-eyed gaze, and some squiggles of birds flying, you'd swear they were butterballs high up, but they couldn't be, could they, already? Charley wondered why Juna didn't fill in all she had left out. But then she thought that would spoil it and make it ordinary. "Maybe you're a—you know—artist or something," Charley said.

Juna laughed. "Oh no," she said. "I'm not an artist. I'm just a fellow traveler. And not just because—well, like, who was it said you are only what you do? That's not true. You can also be whatever you're so assiduously *not* doing."

Though sometimes it sounded like a different language, Charley always knew what Juna was saying, though she couldn't have said it that way herself. She found she could think things she couldn't say. It was as if some edge were always being pushed back, and what was revealed was another part of herself, like rooms you hadn't known were there till you shoved back an old board door at the back of a closet in a dream.

Juna shoved her glasses up into place with that same sideways gesture of her index finger and a sniff. "Do you often feel—you know, like you said—lousy?" They were walking home after sunset along a multiflora rose windbreak. The sky that had burned all day, perfectly clear of cloud, was lavender with a big pale magenta wheel high up over the spot where the sun had set, and all along the horizon the afterglow was bright orange. Juna's pencil case stuck out of her sweater pocket and she had the sketch pad under an arm. She was picking rose hips for rose-hip soup and dropping them into Charley's hat, which Charley held for her.

"Sometimes," Charley said. "Maybe it's more—I'm just mad."

"What at?"

She felt herself flush and almost didn't say. But then she said, "Mad at her for shooting me down. She always shoots me down."

"Maybe she was never beautiful," Juna said. "Who knows? It's hard to say about somebody after a certain age. And here she's got a daughter who is but just won't fix herself up," she laughed, "go dancing, chase men. They like to live through us—you know, immortality through your children?" She laughed. "Sometimes the life they always wanted but couldn't manage themselves. Or sometimes not even wanted but thought they ought to want. And you won't let her."

Of all that, Charley heard only one thing. It had never occurred to her. She wished for a mirror. She tried to imagine her face as if it were someone else's, but it stubbornly remained her own. She was pleased and she wasn't. A part of her thought it was a sissy, foolish thing to be. But to be that in Juna's eyes . . .

"Or maybe she's just jealous," Juna said.

"Jealous!"

"Well, how could they have wanted their lives? Everything hanging on who you marry, and then always to be second, never first, always mate, never captain, always navigator, never pilot."

Charley tried to think of Belle that way but couldn't.

"You never talk about your father."

"I got nothing to say about him."

114

"What was he like?"

"Oh, big, good-looking, you know, with a cleft chin and a slow grin, all that stuff."

"A stereotype?"

"Yeah!" Charley said, like she'd made a discovery. "He was always pulling you one way and then another, one minute showing you off, egging you on to beat the hell out of everybody at everything, and the next growling where's your dress? When he hugged you, it was always in front of people. When he turned on the charm, it was always away from home."

Juna smiled.

"People thought he was wonderful. He had 'em around his little finger. Me, by junior high I'd crowned him the Sleaze King."

Juna laughed. "You're mad at him too."

"And Clay," Charley said. "I might could still be mad at Clay."

"What for?"

"For getting the best pony, best saddle, and then not even wanting it. They always had to make a difference because he was the boy. Everybody cared what become of him. Me, hell, they couldn't a cared less." That sounded like bellyaching so she laughed. "When we were little, we'd play together, fight together. He'd win or I'd win, it didn't matter. But then pretty soon we saw they wanted him to win." It felt good saying it out loud. She'd never been absolutely sure it was true.

Juna laughed softly. "Didn't you learn to let him?"

"Hell no! Wadn' nobody on my side but me! They'd pull for him, I'd knock him winding. Cheer him on, I'd crack him on the jaw!"

"Poor Clay."

"Yeah." She thought about Clay. "He didn't know how to handle himself when he was little. The way he'd run—he'd run

115

like . . . you seen them kids run like they're scared to lift their feet off the ground?"

Juna nodded.

"I could outdo him at everything. But he was the boy, they thought he ought to win. Pretty soon he thought so too. It made him mean."

They faced each other across a carved-up table in one of the booths at Smoky's, an almost empty pitcher of tomato beer between them. It was Saturday night. Two cowboys were playing pool. A drunk middle-aged couple alternately fought and made up, dancing.

"These cousins from East Texas come out here and one day Clay and me were fighting and they took him aside and whispered. Then here he come, suddenly ready for more. I'd been beating the socks off him. But they'd coached him how to beat me. He hit me . . . here." She heard her voice croak and she made a quick, embarrassed jerk toward her breast. Juna gasped. "Hurt like hell, so I banged him in the balls. But Clay and me'd a done better to stick together." She sighed. "No way though. She was scared of him herself by the time he was in high school. He used to shoot the ornaments off the Christmas tree with his BB gun. She's sit there and watch him do it. 'Don't do that, Clay honey,'" she mimicked. "And he'd take and haul off and . . . ping . . . pop." She made the sounds instead of saying them. "Poor old tree. She thought he was really something, but he was crazy." Saying it, she realized it for the first time and sat silent for a minute. Then, "Hey, Smoke!" Smoky looked up. She raised the pitcher for more beer.

Harvey Sears came through the door in a sheepskin vest. He paused and looked around, tipping his hat onto the back of his head, his mouth very red underneath his drooping mustache. Seeing them, he came over and stood at their booth. "Hi. What you two up to?"

116

Charley looked at him coldly, but he began to slide into the booth anyway beside Juna, smiling at her.

"Harvey," Charley said. Harvey looked up. "See them two girls in that booth over yonder?" She pointed, and Harvey looked at the two young women. They looked like receptionists, all dressed up in blouses and earrings and fancy braided vests, looking self-consciously at each other as if they were interested in their conversation and not there at all in hopes of meeting men. But now and then one would sneak a glance around, giving it away. One of them snuck such a look now.

"Yeah?"

"Those girls are just lost without a man around," Charley said. "If you was to go over there, you'd sure be welcome."

Harvey looked at Charley, still smiling, but his eye did its little barely perceptible slide. He looked at Juna, but Juna was weighing the salt and pepper shakers on her palm. He straightened, his set lips belying the smile, and slid out of the booth and walked toward the bar.

Juna laughed across at Charley. "Charley has another meaning," she said. "Charley also means great. You're great, Charleymagne Burden."

Charley laughed. "Charleymane," she repeated. "Charleyhorse more like it. I always been a charleyhorse at home. I always got under their skin. I'm still getting under hers." She looked up. "Here's Reenie."

As Juna turned someone slid in the booth next to Charley, someone with large, dark eyes in a too-large man's white shirt and dark hair that licked at her shoulders like fire tongues.

"Hi, Charley." She leaned a quick cheek against Charley's shoulder and looked across the carved-up wooden tabletop at Juna with eyes full of irony. Charley did the introductions and asked, "What's up?"

"What's always up, if you mean on top? Same old garbage." Her voice laughed but her face seemed angry. Then she smiled

117

and it fractured into planes of light. "Are you the new teach?" she asked Juna, and then asked Charley, "How's Mom?" She laughed again. Juna thought her face was remarkable when she laughed.

"Come see for yourself," Charley said.

"That'll be the day!"

"She wants to see the kid."

"Yeah," Reenie said, the irony back. "Half of her longs to know she's his grandma and the other half's scared to death I'll say he's Clay's and try to make claims."

"Is he?" Charley asked.

She winked. "That's for me to know." She slid out of the booth and stood up. "Maybe his dear old dad was your handsome kinky brother, and maybe he's some young All-American who jerked off in a test tube for the sake of childless maiden ladies everywhere. Toodle-oo." She sauntered toward the booth her friends had taken. Creep leaned out and smiled and waved her fingertips at them.

The middle-aged blonde left her partner on the dance floor and tottered off on her glass-heeled sandals, arms extended for precarious balance, fists and eyes clinched, weeping. "Aw, come on, Gloria," he called after her.

"Kinky how?" Juna asked.

Charley shrugged. "He was good at anguish if he didn't get what he wanted. When he fell in love, he hung himself around her neck and went limp. But she started out liking him."

"I can see why he was so smitten."

"Yeah?"

"She's lively and intense."

"She'd blow up the world and start over."

"Yet I always met her at rallies," Juna said. "One minute it's revolution and the next it's transcendence." She smiled and shrugged. "Has to be one or the other if the world's to be saved."

The couple had made up again and were careening cheek-to-cheek across the floor. Smoky brought another pitcher of red beer.

"I want you to teach me to play pool," Juna said.

Charley laughed.

"I want to learn everything."

"I don't *know* everything."

"You've got *me* fooled."

5

Belle was fit to be tied. "I didn't spend all that money and go through all that excruciating pain just to stay crippled the rest of my life," she said, and then softened a little with self-pity. "Remember when I used to turn on the music and dance?"

"I remember," Lady said.

"You s'pose I'll ever do that again?"

"I 'spect you will."

"But *when*? They promised me I'd soon be dancing."

"Who you gone dance with?"

"That's not the point. The point is, they led me to believe I'd recuperate a whole lot faster."

"We ain't spring chickens anymore," Lady said. "You doing all right. You already off the crutches and onto the cane. I call that progress."

The phone rang. They looked at it.

"You shouldn't of talked back at him. He'd a lost interest."

"That's right," Belle said. "Blame it on me."

"I'm not blaming you. I'm expressing an opinion."

Belle unwrapped a stick of gum and put it in her mouth and got it under control. "You're accumulating a great many opinions."

"They say ever'body's entitled."

"They'll say anything."

"Why don't you turn on your soaps? They'll take you out of yourself."

"I don't want out of myself. I want out of this house."

"Get Charley to take you in town to lunch."

"She's never available to take me anywhere."

Her accounts were scattered across the table in front of her. She shoved them aside and tried to reach the mirror on the buffet and failed, making little whimpering sounds of exasperation. Lady handed her the mirror. "What time is it, anyway?"

Lady glanced at the Coors clock bubbling away over the sink. "Going on four o'clock, but that clock's a little fast."

"It's the only thing around here that is. Time drags." She looked at herself in the mirror, made a face, snapped off the light, and shoved the mirror away.

"I don't know what's got into you. You sure are discontent."

"I've always had it. That divine discontent! What've I got to be content about, I'd like to know?"

"You got your health, you got this place, you got money, and you got us."

"That leaves a lot to be desired."

"Like what?"

Belle pulled her notebook toward her and peered at the page where she'd been sketching a plan of the country kitchen. "Like stimulating companionship, exciting conversation, a variety of interesting friends. Momma had a variety of interesting friends. They were always having luncheons."

"If you want luncheons you can have luncheons."

Belle snorted. "Who would I invite?"

"Make you up a guest list."

"Guest list," Belle scoffed. "Where did you pick up guest list?"

"I been around."

"Well that's more than I can say. When I was younger of course I got out more. It was nothing for me to fly in to KC on a shopping spree and stay overnight at the Muhlbach."

"Get Charley to fly you in. It'd be a treat."

"Don't be silly. How would I get around?"

"You can take a cab."

"When do you suppose the bust will be finished?" She was trying to decide where to put the dishwasher. She'd seen some magazine with little cutouts to scale for room planning. She wondered where she could get some.

"The what?"

"The bust! Clay's bust! Have you forgotten?"

"I haven't, but maybe that hippie has. Maybe he got an idea but didn't do anything with it."

"I hope not. I've got my heart set on it. I've given quite a bit of thought to the memorial, but I can't do a thing till the bust arrives and I know I have it in hand."

KC began to bark.

"Somebody coming up the road," Lady said.

Belle craned her neck to see out the window. "It won't be anybody."

"Trucks don't drive theyselves."

"It won't be anybody who *is* anybody."

"Bound to be *some*body."

The truck crossed the cattle guard and stopped. "Well it's not," Belle said. "It's Charley."

"Whose truck she in?"

"How would *I* know?"

Charley came in and banged the door behind her and started upstairs two at a time.

"Whose truck is that you're driving?" Belle called after her.

"JoJo's. I left mine at the gas station to have an oil change and he loaned me his."

"Where's Junie?" Lady wanted to know. These days when Charley went to town she always brought Juna home after school.

"I don't know where she is," Charley said and slammed the door of her room.

"Uh-oh," Belle said. "*Now* what?"

Lady wondered too. Pretty soon Charley rattled back down the stairs. She had put on her denim jacket.

"Where are you going now?"

"I got work to do. I can't sit around here and jaw. I got to get after the milo." She went out and slammed the door behind her and went to the shed and climbed up into the cab of the combine and started the motor. It wasn't true that she didn't know where Juna was. She had stopped by the school and waited for Juna till the children had all streamed past, either walking home or climbing into the waiting buses, till the janitor came out and brought the flag down and folded it square and took it in. Finally she got out and went up the walk. Mr. Maple stood up when he saw her and hitched his trousers and smiled. "Afternoon, Charlene. How's your momma?"

"Mean as ever," Charley said.

She found Juna bent over a stack of papers at her desk. She looked up and her face was unnaturally smooth and bright. "What you doing?" Charley asked.

"I'm just doing a little homework. I didn't see you."

Charley felt a rush of relief. "I'm in JoJo's truck," she said. "Mine's getting an oil change."

But Juna said, "I thought I'd work here awhile. I've gotten so far behind."

Charley was bewildered. She felt suddenly uncomfortable, too tall standing there in the midst of those little low kids' desks. She wanted to ask how Juna would get home after all the buses were gone, but something in Juna's face didn't encourage questions.

"I can't wait around," she said gruffly. "I got work to do out on the place."

"Oh, I wouldn't dream of letting you wait. Don't worry about me. I'll get home all right."

The artificial brightness in her voice put Charley at a loss. She backed toward the door. "Well," she said. "I guess I'll be going."

"Thank you for stopping," Juna said. "I'm sorry you had to wait."

On the drive home she went over again how Juna'd had too much work last week to go to the movies, and she'd canceled a riding lesson on Saturday. She had believed it all because Juna's eyes had circles under them. Belle had said, "You look bilious!" and urged a purgative. Charley had never got the difference between bilious and peakéd. She herself was always said to be peakéd when she was sick. Now she thought it must have to do with the color of the face, because when she got sick she turned pale but the smudges under Juna's eyes looked like bruises and made her face—tanned apricot in the sun—more colorful than ever. She'd spent all of Sunday afternoon closed in her room— answering letters, she said—and she'd gone to bed the night before right after supper with a migraine.

As she neared the turnoff she grew less puzzled and more angry. She could have kicked herself for stopping by the school. She could have kicked herself for a lot of things.

She grew milo on the irrigated section next to the house. Some years you couldn't harvest till November, but this year was dry enough to go ahead. She had let distractions put off harvesting. She had silage to cut, but she could let that wait awhile. The Askews were baling alfalfa. She'd seen the big, round two-thousand-pounders rolling up along the fence lines. They'd want her combine later, and she'd borrow their big baler.

Juan didn't drive the combine. The milo was all hers. And the truth was, she liked the combine above all other farm machinery, maybe even above the little Skyhawk tethered on the runway. During harvest she felt like she was on a long trip alone, driving all day long, no other vehicles in sight, and she never had to leave home. She got a lot worked out driving the combine.

The milo section lay along the drive, between the house and the blacktop. She was cutting near the highway when the Ranchero turned in toward the house. High up in the closed cab with the tape deck playing, insulated from the world, she tried not to watch the Ranchero, but she was aware that when it crossed the cattle guard and stopped, Juna sat inside awhile talking before she opened the door, and even after opening it she sat a few minutes more, her hand clearly visible on the door handle. Charley imagined Harvey's low, sexy voice saying something, and Juna's tinkling laugh. She turned up the volume on the tape deck. She was glad to get to the turn row. After a while the Ranchero rushed back down the drive and turned toward Tula, and Juna stood talking to Juan. Charley saw that much.

At supper Juna's voice had that fake brightness in it again. Charley wouldn't look at her. She kept her eyes on her plate and got up when she'd finished without saying anything to anybody. "Well, what's got into *her?*" Belle said. Charley was halfway up the stairs by then.

She closed the door of her room behind her and looked around. She'd done nothing but sleep in it since Juna arrived and now it seemed cold and unlived-in. Ordinarily she would have gone to Smoky's and played pool and had a few beers, but tonight she didn't feel like it. She heard Juna come upstairs and then she heard her go back down again. Came up for her books, she thought, and now was working downstairs at the dining room table. She'd done very little of that, but it tickled Belle when she did. Juna said she couldn't work with the television on, and Belle couldn't live without it. She'd soon have one in every room in the house. Charley thought she kept it going because she was scared—of the coming winter, of getting old, scared because now the family was so diminished. Charley suspected that on some deep level Belle knew the meaning of dread. The familiar patter of the television, the familiar voices saying the familiar things, the canned, familiar laughter came between her and her fears like a belt of static and reassured her that nothing changed, that everything stayed the same.

Charley hated waiting worse than anything—probably, she thought, because of all the hours she had spent waiting for Belle in stores, in automobiles, on street corners. She was waiting for Juna to come upstairs. When Juna didn't, she went into the bathroom and ran the tub full and lay in the hot water looking down at her belly. It sank between her hipbones, with the neat brown scar like a frown where they'd cut out her appendix when she was ten and she'd only grown reconciled to losing a part of herself after reading in *National Geographic* that naturalists and explorers often had perfectly good appendixes removed before spending long periods isolated in the wild. As things got worse at home, she'd considered it might be a good thing they'd gone ahead and taken it out. No telling when she'd have to light out. She pinched up the flesh on her belly, her arm, her side. Was she putting on weight? Was she going to take after Belle, who inclined to plumpness? But she couldn't pinch up much. She reached for Juna's bottle of organic bubble bath but put it back down because if she dumped it in the tub Juna might smell it later and know she'd used it. She let in more hot water when it cooled. She dried her hands and reached for the stud book and read a little, keeping her ear cocked, listening. The wastebasket was between the tub and the sink. She glanced into it. It was full of little bits of wadded Kleenex. She reached over and snagged one between her fingers and languidly lifted it to her nose. It had a perfumed smell. She unfolded it and looked at the dark smear inside. It must be what Juna used to take the stuff off her eyes at night. Ordinarily she would have snorted at such a thing, but she secretly liked all Juna did to her eyes, though she would never have done it herself. She read all the labels on Juna's shampoo and conditioner bottles on the edge of the bathtub. Finally she got out and dried herself. She sat naked on the turned-down lid of the toilet and took up one at a time the tubes and jars and bottles from the top of the tank and read their labels, too, and the directions on the back. She opened Juna's body lotion and smeared some on herself and had a time rubbing it in she'd used so much. She picked up the little scissors and the clippers and tweezers and eyebrow pencils, examining them all. She pulled a hair out of one of her own eyebrows and winced with pain. Juna's sissy little razor lay there with the cord wrapped neatly around it. She picked it up and on impulse shaved one of her legs with it. Then she worried that she hadn't cleaned the razor well enough—she cleaned it again—or had dulled it and Juna would know. She unwrapped the cord and wrapped it again, trying to get it exactly as it had been, and worried that she hadn't.

Finally she put on pajamas and went back to her room. It was cold. She turned up the heat and was about to get into bed when she realized there was a visitor downstairs. She opened her door a crack and listened to the voices. Juna laughed. Lady offered another helping of something. They were feeding whoever it was. "Oh, thanks," piped a clear, childlike voice.

"What kind of entity?" Belle demanded.

"You know, somebody from another plane."

"And this . . . entity . . . speaks through . . ." Belle was chubbing. Anything for a bite.

"He speaks through Petaluma."

Charley edged barefoot toward the banisters at the head of the stairs and descended a little way, till she could see Juna's back in her wool poncho. It was pale gray with little orange and purple stripes running through it.

"He says the most interesting things," Creep said.

"I don't know why all these entities channeled by females have to be male," Juna said.

Charley could hear the shrug in Creep's voice. "That's just the way it is, I guess," she said. The entity's name was Nikolayevich. Nikolayevich told them the greatest sin was clutching. They were all afraid, now, that they were clutching. They were trying to detach. Of course he also said it was just a manner of speaking, for actually there was no such thing as sin. "It's all just working things out," Creep said. "Sooner or later we all get through. You get as many chances as you need."

"I hope so," Belle said. "I'd like another time around. I'm getting sick of this one."

"According to physics," Juna said, "time is not what we think. It's just a dimension of space, of the earth and the planets turning."

"Then what's ruining my skin and thinning my hair?" Belle wanted to know. "What's making me old?"

"Maybe it's all this spinning," Juna said. "Maybe friction makes us old."

"Petaluma's a woman?" Lady said.

"Petaluma is androgynous," Creep said.

Nikolayevich said Petaluma came from a yet-to-be-discovered planet and that made for a certain spaciness in the delivery. Because this planet was so far out. So Nikolayevich repeated himself a lot and often begged off because he couldn't explain something to beings on the earth plane.

"Cause we so dumb?" Lady asked. "Howcome he don't just do it like Jesus—just lay it out as best he can and let you mull it over?"

"Well," Creep said apologetically, "Jesus existed on the earth plane too, in a manner of speaking."

"Nikolayevich," she said, "has some interesting information about Baba."

"I hope he says you ought to bring him to see his grandma," Belle said coyly.

Charley had never expected to hear Belle refer to herself as a grandma, coyly or not. It was cold up there in the hall, but she couldn't go down now and let them think she was interested in all this drivel. She sat on the steps with her face to the banisters as she had years ago with Clay, feeling left out and alone, and she felt that it had always been this way. She was peeved at Juna, little more than a stranger and sitting down there big as life.

Creep was telling them that Nikolayevich said Baba—Baba!—must have a careful diet of earth grains. "That's no problem," she said. "Baba loves his oatmeal. And he's to have a certain oil rubbed on his navel every morning because he's still suffering from the shock of re-entry."

Charley rose and went back to her room. She picked up a mystery Lady had loaned her and read a little without knowing what she was reading, going back over things a second and even a third time. Once she heard them all laughing. Finally the bunch of motorized pots and pans that passed as a vehicle for The Family rattled off down the drive. She reread the page she had just read, listening for Juna's footsteps on the stairs. When at last they came, her heart leapt like she was afraid. But they passed her door, and the door to Juna's room closed behind her. Charley scowled at herself in the mirror across the room. She was such a fool. What was she waiting for? Then Juna's door opened again and her heart, like it had a life of its own, gave another leap. But the footsteps passed on the way to the bathroom. She listened to the water gushing into the tub. She took up the book again, but she couldn't read. She now and then heard the water slosh as Juna took her bath. She always took a long time in the bathroom at night. Probably the stuff she wore around her eyes took a long time to come off. She lay there seeing Juna take a little piece of tissue and lean over the sink to the mirror, her eyes open wide. She thought of what she'd done, opening the jars and bottles, sniffing. She squirmed in her twisted sheets and felt her face heat up. She saw herself at a distance, as if she were somebody else performing those creepy acts. She must be some kind of a freak.

As a child she had heard Belle and Lady discussing where

they'd read in the paper about a man in Canada who had killed some people and shrunk their heads and kept them in a row of hatboxes on a shelf in his closet. She heard them discuss another man who killed a woman and skinned her and slipped on her skin at night and danced around in it in his dead mother's bedroom. Belle and Lady dwelt on newspaper items like that. And though she had no shrunken heads in her closet and had never danced around her mother's bedroom even in her own skin, these things had preyed on her mind till she worried was she crazy and told the counselor at school. The counselor had said it meant she was angry and wanted to know what at. But Charley couldn't think what at. She conceived a crush on the counselor and she went back and told her everything she could think of that might interest her. She told her she'd once killed a squirrel with a slingshot. When she saw the counselor's attention wandering, she made up some things. She told the counselor she had a friend named Sollyamo who slept in her shoe at night with his feet in the toe and his head out in the open. He wore a red vest and yellow balloon-type pants and turned-up shoes and carried an umbrella rain or shine. She said they spoke together and he told her the answers to questions on tests so that she never had to study. Then she came to believe it was true about Sollyamo. She could see him and hear his tiny voice. She was relieved when summer came because she was in over her head, and the next fall the counselor was pregnant and looked like she'd swallowed a basketball. Everybody made jokes about that because her husband was the coach. That made Charley feel sick at her stomach and once she cried in the girls' room. But then after a while she pointed and made jokes along with everybody else in the seventh grade, and it was strangely satisfying.

Juna's footsteps padded back down the hall and paused outside the door. Charley cowered in the covers, holding her breath. When the knock came, her traitor heart leapt out toward it as if to abandon her and run to Juna. She lay rigid, with little tremors twitching different parts of her. After a moment Juna went on to her own room. As she closed the door, Charley slammed her fist down on the covers and cursed. She lay awake hoping Juna would come back. Something was rattling outside in the rising wind. Had Juan left a gate open? Was the wind knocking down the corrals? She lay awake another hour, listening.

But Juna was awake a lot longer. She turned up the gas and got into her robe and sat at the table going over second-grade arithmetic papers till mathematics grew bizarre and she couldn't add two and two. It didn't seem reasonable they would always sum up to four. Still not sleepy, she prepared lessons three weeks in advance and made a chart for her schoolroom wall and even read the minutes of the last teachers' meeting. What was *wrong* with her? She always slept like she was plummeting through the bed. Had she been dreaming and was she afraid of her dreams? She opened her dream journal lying on her bedside table and looked at the last entries. She hadn't recorded a dream for some time. When she fell back exhausted on her pillows, it was still hard to get to sleep. When finally she drifted off the alarm rang, but she couldn't wake up. The sky was pearly with dawn when she heard Charley go downstairs. She lay there thinking about Charley. Finally she dragged herself out of bed and went down and phoned Mr. Maple and told him she had a touch of something and he would have to call a substitute. But back upstairs she found she was awake, so she went back down and phoned again and told him to forget it, she'd be there.

The air was nippy. Overnight the water trough had grown a skin of ice, for Charley hadn't yet put in the little windmill that kept the water stirred up so that ice couldn't form and the horses could drink all winter. She was putting the forklift on the tractor when she saw Peanuts. He'd come up to the barn and stood eyeing them. When Juan saw her eyeing him back, he hawked and spit and said, "You going to work out the *niña?*"

She shook her head. "Put a halter on Peanuts," she told him. She turned and ran up the hill toward the house to get her Association saddle and baided bronc bridle and glove, to pull her chaps on over her jeans.

The saddle was in the cupboard upstairs with the chaps lying across it. She took her glove, stiffened with resin, off the buckle where it always hung and buckled on the soft, suede chaps that had once been her prized possession. She shouldered the saddle and went back downstairs and down the draw to where Juan was putting Peanuts in one of the stalls. She didn't look at Juan. She knew his chin would be tucked into his Adam's apple with disapproval.

She climbed the board side and settled the saddle onto Peanuts' back. He shivered noisily, waffling the saddle skirts. Juan was on the other side of the stall. He reached with an old cattle prod for the girth and she passed it under to him and he drew it through the cinch ring, leaving it loose.

She knew every trick in Peanuts' twisted brain, but she hadn't bucked in a long time. She climbed up the side of the stall and straddled it. She came down easy in the saddle and hooked her braided bridle onto the halter and got the cinch tucked under her thigh while she pulled on her glove. Juan had moved to the makeshift gate. He was waiting. She pulled the cinch tight and fixed it. She put her toes out over the points of the horse's shoulders and said, "Okey!"

Juan yanked open the gate and she came out spurring. Peanuts was mad. Nobody had submitted him to the indignity of being mounted for so long he thought they'd learned their lesson. He came out of the stall in a leftward twist, and he came out of the twist with his hind feet all but over his head. Then instead of bucking he sunfished. That ought to show her.

Charley, with her left hand high behind her, whooped and

hollered. The old bronc bucked in place, thundering down on the soft dirt of the corral. In an arena it would have shaken Charley's teeth. She spurred till her heels caught the saddle skirt in back of her. It was frustrating to Peanuts. She could read his mind by watching his head. She knew what he was going to do before he did it and she was hard to unseat. But Peanuts came up with a new one. He reared straight up. She hung on and stuck like chewing gum to the saddle. But then instead of coming down again or threatening to go over backward, he gave a leap on his hind legs, humped double, and bucked her off into the dirt and ran kicking like a mule at the corners of the corral.

Charley picked herself up and stood looking after him, working her shoulders to loosen them. "He's a rank old bastard," she said to Juan, but Juan was having none of it. He'd already gone to putting the sides up on the old Ford flatbed.

When she turned Peanuts out to pasture, Juan reappeared and walked over to the fence and nodded in the direction of the dark colt, Saud, and breathed, "Negrito." To humor him Charley looked. Juan had this thing about that colt. She felt she ought to try getting back his approval after bucking the bronc. She followed him over to the fence. The colt was lively in the autumn air. Just for the fun of it, he was running hard as he could run along the fence to a corner, wheeling around crouched on his haunches, forelegs in the air, and running back toward them with his black mane flying.

Juan had been strange ever since he got back from Ruidoso. He'd begun telling her something, talking always in Spanish, as if only Spanish suited the subject, whatever it was. At first she couldn't make it out. It was continuous. It went on from one day to the next, disjointed, in snatches. It seemed to be about a person. She made out this person's name to be Maggie. He was telling her about a girl? He grew eloquent and strained her command of the language. It turned out that this Maggie was not a woman at all, but a boy named Marguerito Martinez, called

133

Maggie, and that this Maggie was a genius of some kind. It turned out that his genius was horses and Maggie Martinez was a jockey. He rode the horses of one particular rich man, and the rich man had seen to it that he was never to be sent back across, that he was never to come up against the border patrol. He had been made a citizen. Juan said it firmly: Maggie Martinez was a Yank. And he had red hair. Juan pointed out this detail about the boy more than once. She saw that it had significance for him. It meant that Maggie-the-Jockey Martinez was a true descendant of the conquistadores. You could only be sure of that in the case of Mexican boys if they had this certain kind of hair. It was red, almost the red of cherries when they are overripe. No, of cedar wood when it starts to rot. This red hair has Spanish blood in it, Juan said. And Maggie Martinez had it.

Some days he stayed away from it altogether, like a fast, like an abstinence, but he always came back again. It accrued like money in the bank, a little at a time. And when he returned to it, his eyes strayed from her face to look into some middle distance where there was nothing to see, and then they came back, anxious, insistent. She had begun to listen when Juan talked about the jockey. Not knowing why, she nevertheless understood that it was a solemn, weighty subject. This morning he made her understand that it was connected with Negrito—Saud.

After they'd filled the feeder banks they saddled up and rode out past the pit silos to the herd. Charley began to feel good. The pastures lay like a quilt over the rumpled plains. The herd grazed out of the wind in low places. It was so still you could hear them munching when you got close.

She stopped on a rise and lifted herself in the stirrups, stretching her muscles. With Juan so quiet, you could feel alone out there. Looking at the horses excited her. The cows gave her another feeling, a feeling of calm, as if this were still an ocean and the cows were grazing it like small rusty boats, becalmed. In the sky big onion-shaped clouds stacked up on top of one another, mountains of cloud, showing how high the sky was. Without looking at Juan she spurred Avalanche and loped down among the cattle and right away saw the heifer with its hoof torn almost off. It must have tangled with barbed wire and panicked. It panicked again when she tried to get close. She had to rope it before Juan could catch it and examine the damage. She liked roping— the sudden burst of speed, the precision of the loop snaking out, Avalanche's expertise. They said mares were no good at working. They could say what they wanted. She worked this mare daily. She was the best cutting horse Charley had ever ridden. And she worked when she was in season.

"No chance of that healing," she said, kneeling over the heifer.

"She heal," Juan said. "You see."

Maybe, Charley thought. But she might heal a cripple and hobble around the place on three legs.

"Where did we leave barb wire lying around?"

Juan shook his head.

"She had to get in it somewhere." She might have the choice of a cripple on her hands or killing the heifer for meat. She didn't want to decide. For now she could give it a booster. She'd have to drive into Tula to get the serum.

They drove the heifers into the pasture near the old house and closed the gate. They had to put them down the chute and into the cattle dip. But that could wait till tomorrow early. Charley hated the cattle dip, hated working with the bullwhip while Juan used a prod, and the heifers coming out the shallow end shaking themselves, bawling their discontent. But even the cattle dip was better than branding.

Juan stayed behind at the barn to nail boards back in place on the calving pens so they wouldn't have to do it in the spring, and she rode up the draw toward the old house, where she'd left her truck. She was about to dismount and unsaddle Avalanche when she saw up above her on the edge of the coulee a silhouette in the

135

midday glare. Then she recognized its shape and wheeled Avalanche around.

"Hey! Wait!"

"I'm *busy*, Warren!"

"So the hell am I."

So she waited while he came sliding in his boots down the side of the draw. "Whatchoo want?"

He took hold of the reins under Avalanche's chin and stroked her dark gray nose. He looked up, his blue eyes squinting in the light. "I was just passing by," he said.

"Oh, Warren," she said, exasperated. She sighed and blew it out like a bubble and slumped in the saddle, looking off toward the horizon.

"I just happened to think as I was passing—there's a dance over in Dade this Sat'day."

"Oh, Warren . . ." The sound rose at the end. She pulled Avalanche's head and spun half around. "Why don't you listen to me?"

"But Charley, we always been friends. You and me and Clay and Tearl. Always. Don't you ever think of that time we—"

"I don't want to talk about that!"

"I just can't hep—"

"Warren Hubble, don't you ever talk to me again if you can't pay attention to my feelings!"

"I'm sorry, Charley, I—"

"You're sorry! You're sorry! But you keep on and keep on and keep on."

"Oh, hell, Charley."

"*Please*, Hub, get off my case, will you?"

His smile faded. His jaw set. "Awright," he said. "I will. Forget it. Just forget it. Hell, you don't even know you're a girl. Goddammit! Look at you! Feeling like this about somebody like you makes me feel downright queer."

He looked so mad and anguished she laughed and threw up her free hand. "What am I supposed to do about you?"

"Nothing! I told you! Forget it! Just forget it!" He turned and started back up the sand hill, his arms out, waving for balance, and his boots sank in the sand.

Charley sat watching him climb back out of the draw. She really didn't know what to do about him.

"Where are you going?" Belle wanted to know when she got back to the house.

"I got to go to the vet's. There's a calf with a torn-off hoof that needs a shot."

"I'll ride in with you."

"I got to come straight back. I hadn' got time to fool around." She ran upstairs two at a time to get her billfold.

"I need to get out of this house," Belle said when she came back down.

"Get her out of here," Lady said. "I need a little peace."

"If it's just a ride you want, you don't need to change your clothes," Charley said.

"Well, you certainly ought to change yours. I don't want you going in town with me looking like that."

"All the clothes I got are just like the ones I got on."

"Get out my car. I'm not riding to town in any truck."

"The T-Bird's out of gas."

"Then gas it up at the pump."

"The pump's out of gas."

"*Why* do I have to tell everybody what to do when they know perfectly well what to do? Siphon some out of the tractor! Honestly!"

But Charley headed for the truck, got in, and drove it to the ramp while Lady, slanting backward, wheeled Belle down. "You know better than to let this happen," Belle said to Charley, and to

Lady, "Phone in and make sure they get a delivery out here today."

Lady got Belle into her coat and put her cane in back of the seat.

"She don't need that," Charley said. "She's not getting out."

"Well, you got it, just in case," Lady said.

"In case of what?" Charley gunned the motor and Lady slammed the door.

"In case of emergency!" Belle said.

"Please slow down," she whimpered. They were rushing toward the blacktop. As it was the truck and not the T-Bird, and as they were alone without an audience, Charley slowed down. "Honestly! The way you dress nobody'd dream the state of Texas sent your granddaddy to Washington."

"Anything to get shut of him," Charley said. The fields were turning. The flat land to either side of the road was already tawny.

"You say things like that just to hurt me. You've lived out here so long you're like the natives."

"I *am* a native. I was *born* here."

"I know where you were born. I was there. I'm your mother, remember? I'm trying to tell you who you are."

"Nobody has to tell me who I am. I know who I am."

"No you don't, and you don't care. On my side you didn't come from your ordinary immigrants like the ones that settled out here. Those came for a scrap of land and a mule. On my side they had plenty of land already, over there. They had a large estate. They crossed first-class, not steerage."

"Why didn't they just walk over?"

But Belle wouldn't laugh. She pouted a minute and then said, "They came for political principles."

"What political principles?"

Charley had asked this question before. Belle didn't see that it mattered. And she wasn't sure she'd ever heard. It had something

138

to do with one of the wars they'd had over there. She was silent while they passed the rodeo grounds, reading all the new billboards going up. "Sometimes I think you might be a quitter, Charlene." It wasn't the non sequitur it sounded like. Charley held her foot steady on the gas and looked straight ahead, as if she hadn't heard, and Belle added, "Both my children." When they had passed the rodeo grounds, Belle said, "You needn't pretend you're interested in *my* side of the family."

But Charley had what, had Belle known, she would have called a morbid interest. For Belle had a picture of her own grandmother taken in the Old Country that could have been Charley in costume. Though this great-grandmother was wearing a black dress and had long hair done up in braids wound around her head, Charley's own eyes stared back at her out of that old picture. It was so startling she never understood how Belle could fail to see it at a glance. And she'd known at once that it's not true that no two people are alike. She'd realized in a flash there aren't all that many molds to go around and the only reason it works is simply because the identical ones are not alive at the same time. As if that wasn't staggering enough, it was followed by: If they weren't alive at the same time, what kept them from actually *being* her, Charley, by some other name? This great-grandmother's name had been Frederica. Sometimes she imagined a sonorous voice calling "Frederica!" suddenly, out of some indeterminate space behind her, to see if she could surprise herself into a start of recognition.

"All I know is what Grandma Slaughter told me," Belle said. "She said she could remember the coat of arms in the stone fireplace—that proves they were *some*body—and a house on a hill, and it took twenty-two horse teams to work the land. It must have been extensive. But it all belonged in the family and had to be left behind."

Charley had heard all this before but she listened every time, hoping for some new detail. She knew that land intimately. She had often taken the place of her little five-year-old great-grandma and sat in a rocker on the porch of that house on that hill with the cherry tree beside it—Belle had left out the cherry tree this time—and watched the rockets' red glare of some bygone war over a distant swell of land that looked a lot like Kansas.

"Grandma Slaughter's daddy was a gentleman farmer," Belle said. She turned and Charley felt those bright eyes studying her. She braced herself for another inane remark about her clothes or her hair, but Belle said, "You'd be a pretty girl if you just let yourself."

Charley snorted.

"Sometimes I see a little of Momma in you." Belle reached over and Charley knew she was about to try to do something with her hair. She jerked away, ducking over the wheel, and said, "For crissake!" and Belle snatched her hand back as if she'd touched a hot stove and sat there small in the seat beside Charley. Charley said something profane under her breath. She glanced out the window on her side of the pickup. She felt guilty and feeling guilty infuriated her. It infuriated her to realize the bleak, hopeless tenderness she sometimes unaccountably felt for Belle. She imagined Belle there next to her, so low in the seat that if she looked over at her she would have to look down, imagined the hair that was never right though it showed all the scars of having been endlessly teased and twisted and tortured out of whatever would have been its natural shape, the wide, thin-lipped mouth, a comedian's mouth, with its dry crumbs of lipstick clinging around the edges, the plump mole pressing sweetly up under the edge of one nostril of her little round nose like a biddy under a hen, the eyes that squinted and frequently blinked. It gave her the feeling somewhere in the bridge of her nose that she had breathed some pungent effervescence to think that for all the powders and lotions and ointments, the tints and dyes and wigs, in spite of the dressmaker, masseuse, and Thelma, Belle had never once been satisfied with the way she looked, and in spite of all her pains she never looked anything but outrageous, wild, unkempt. For her true self was irrepressible. It kept escaping the ideal one, which never existed anyway except as a torment in her mind or in *her* momma's imagination.

It nagged at Charley now and then, but she didn't know what she could do about it. She saw herself grabbing Belle by the shoulders and shaking her till her teeth rattled and shouting into her deafness, "Look, goddammit, don't you see?" Or yelling after her as she drifted over a rise toward the sunset and threatened to disappear, "Listen, goddammit! Can't you hear?" And she had the fear that Belle would grow old and disappear over that rise forever and it would never be resolved between them. If that happened, she would be left with a bleak and unremitting anguish. Nothing for her would ever be finished. Yet the thought of a moment of sweetness between them filled her with dread.

Belle had been silent too long. Charley steeled herself and glanced over to see if she might be crying.

Just then Belle exclaimed, "Look! There's Newton Thorp!" They were passing the Ford dealership. "Stop the car!"

The sound of Belle's voice erased everything else and the old anger rushed in to fill the vacuum. "I told you I want to make a quick trip!"

"Do as I say! Stop this truck! I won't be a minute!"

Charley leaned against the front fender of the silver Lincoln in the showroom while Belle sat inside the car with Newton, a handsome, graying man who was vain about keeping his hair and went to Thelma once a week. His hair got longer and longer and fluffier and fluffier, and he had taken to wearing Western shirts with ruffled fronts and string ties. He was showing Belle all the gadgets. Belle tried everything, poking in the glove compartment, shifting the backrest back and forth.

"And that's the air conditioning," Newton said.

"Well, we don't need it today," Belle said with a little flirty shiver. "Don't you dare turn it on."

."And this is the cruise control."

"Think of it! Just set the speed and sit back and enjoy the scenery!"

Newton laughed.

"What's that you've got on, Newton?" Belle asked. "The women won't leave you alone if you don't watch out, wearing a cologne like that."

Newton said it was after-shave lotion called Steak 'n Ale, but Belle giggled, sniffing his ear, and said it smelled like Attar of Roses to her.

"I just love the appointments," Belle said. "Charley, don't you just love the appointments?"

"Come here, Charley. Poke your head in here and take a look. That's not Naugahyde. That's the real camille—genu-wine twenty-four-carat cowhide. Lemme take you girls for a spin."

"My daughter's in a terrible hurry," Belle said.

"Naw she's not. You got time, hadn' you, Charley."

Charley scowled out the plate-glass windows at the highway and ignored the two behind her.

"I don't dare," Belle said in a stage whisper. "She might skin me alive."

"Aw, lemme prep 'er up and bring her out."

"Maybe next year, Newton. Soon as my ship comes in."

Charley caught sight of Harvey's Ranchero turning the curve toward town. She watched it till it was out of sight.

"I can give you a real good trade for your T-Bird," Newton said. "What year is it, anyway? Hell, I bet it's a classic by now."

"Well, I'm not sure I *want* to trade it. I don't think I could bear to part with it. The T-Bird was a gift from Fletcher. You sold it to him yourself! When I saw it, I said, 'Why it looks like a great big Easter egg.' Hardly has any mileage on it, old as it is. I love that car. They don't make cars like that anymore. I was reading in *Time* magazine where people are like that over in Germany. They spend their Sunday afternoons shining their cars and clean-

142

ing them inside out. *Time* magazine said it was called auto-eroticism, and I think I've got it when it comes to that old T-Bird."

Charley groaned and Newton shouted a laugh. "I'll make you a real good trade."

Belle's voice struck a gentle note of regret. "Oh, Newton, I know you would. But I'll have to think about it."

Charley thought they were about to get away, but Belle stopped to peer into the big RV parked next to the Lincoln. The step had to be put down, and she had to be helped inside where she stood looking around in amazement. "My, just look at this. Why, I've never seen anything like this. Why, I can't get over it. I could live in this. Who needs a big old house to look after?" She sat on the edge of the couch that made into a queen-size bed and bounced a little, then shrieked with laughter. "I could leave you all behind and be off to see the world!"

When they drove past the school, the schoolyard was full of children out for lunch and the sidewalks were crowded with the older ones who went home or went into town to eat. The Ranchero had pulled in to the curb. Charley slowed to pass. She took a good look at Harvey inside. He was bent, fiddling with his radio.

"Well, look at that," Belle said, swiveling her head to keep an eye on the Ranchero. Charley kept having to glance at the rear-view mirror. Juna came down the walk and got in, and the Ranchero headed after them into town.

"Looks like Juna's got a boyfriend." Belle said, glancing at Charley. "It's almost noon," she added. "We might as well have lunch."

"I told you I'm in a hurry," Charley snapped.

"Well you needn't bite my head off."

Charley had just gotten her steakburger and Belle her prime rib when Juna and Harvey walked in, Juna with a chalk smear on her nose and a little chalk dust in her hair. Charley turned her back on them and went to the salad bar, but when they passed the table Belle pretended surprise. "Why, looky who's here! Won't you all join Charlene and me?"

———

Juna was aware that the meal was not a success. Charley scowled into her plate and Belle was maddeningly arch. Harvey was miffed that she had accepted Belle's invitation and frustrated at not being able to show it because, with his dream of gas leases, he had to be polite. It was all somehow false. Juna could not say precisely where the falseness lay, but there it was, some misrepresentation of which she was herself the principle. She felt uncomfortable, as if caught in some cosmic lie. She wanted to escape. The smile on her face felt plastic. She no longer found Belle funny. She resented her innuendos. She disliked Harvey's hand falling now and then on her arm as if claiming her, something he'd never do if they were alone. She couldn't raise her eyes to Charley's, though she wanted urgently to see Charley's face. Though she was doing nothing, she was aware of doing something—she didn't know what—that made her feel diminished in her own eyes. She longed for the meal to be over. She measured the time it would take to get through it, to claim the check, to retrieve coats and jackets and cover the distance to the door, all of which had to be accomplished before she could breathe clean Kansas air and somehow—she hadn't figured out how—walk back alone toward the school.

It was on that walk that realizations began breaking in upon her which she found not exactly frightening but unsettling. She had taken pride in her self-knowledge, and here the floor had dropped out from under her to reveal yet another staircase down. You ought to be pleased when that happened. She might even *be* pleased. She didn't know what she was. It was a strange, dark, troubled feeling. She went over details of her friendship with

Muriel Gebberfield, looking for signs and portents. She was too old, she thought, to be going through a phase.

On the sidewalk outside the school, children converged on her and clung. She smiled and let herself be moved forward like a papier-mâché giant in a carnival of little people. She would just forget about it, work harder, give up all these learning experiences.

At the school door she stopped and, wiping her glasses, gazed nearsightedly out toward the row of trees along the street. They blurred mystically at the edges against the sky that blue hardly described, at the clouds that were never just white but magenta, lavender, purple, and a plaintive voice inside her said, But I don't want to give up anything.

"Miss Evins kin I . . ."

"Miss Evins kin I . . ."

She wrote EVERS across the blackboard in sweeping letters and said, "Now, who can say it?"

"EVERS!" they chorused.

"Right, and Miss Evers skin *you* if we don't have some peace and quiet in here."

Rollicking laughter. They weren't afraid of her. She loved it that they thought she was funny. A homely, bespectacled, plump little girl sidled under her arm. "Yesterday Ferrel he promised—"

"She's lying, Miss Evins. I never no such of a thing!"

They were rowdy after lunch. It took them time to settle. Oh she needed some space in which to think.

"Melissa's takin her socks off!"

"Walter's got him a toad!"

It's a frog!"

"It's a garten snake!"

Once they'd settled, it would be time for siesta, with heads down on desks. She would have a breathing spell. But that time hadn't arrived.

"Peter's writin nasty on the blackboard!"

"Phew! Somebody made a . . ."

"Miss Evers may I leave the room?"

"Ferrel, pass out the spelling books."

Out in the hall Mrs. Jenkins was talking to Mr. Maple. Discipline, she was saying. A firm hand. There's entirely too much noise in that classroom.

"Miss Evers!"

"What?"

"Miss Evers may I . . ."

"May you what?"

"I got to go! I got to go!"

She had to think. Above all, she had to think.

The door of the school bus opened and Juna welcomed the rush of fresh air. She stepped out and the vacuum door whooshed to behind her, closing off the wild, excited voices of the children. She waved back at all the disembodied hands waving at the windows. She laughed in appreciation of all the goblin faces practicing at the back window for her benefit. She didn't breathe till she had walked a little way and the bus exhaust had dissipated. Then she stood still and took a deep breath and let the horizon swell toward her. Her heart gave the flop she recognized as the one a heart will give when you see the person you love walk through a door. The whole of Kansas spread out—before her, behind her, around her. She turned in a circle to take it in, and her heart soared like a fledging that had to get a running start and she recalled a line by Hopkins but couldn't get it right. The wind was strong and soft like a large hand in a furry mitt, like a presence, like a touch, and the sky was pale behind an unfolding layer of cloud. She was thinking about something without really thinking about it, letting it lie there unaware of her. She kept quiet not to startle it lying there more endangered by her than she by it. Suddenly she needed to see Charley the way she needed air when she'd been under water.

The grain whispered around her like the rustle of silk. Beyond the red-gold milo so thick and perfect it might have been painted on the landscape, the combine moved toward her. The cab came into sight. She lifted her arm and hesitated, then waved vigorously, waited, and waved again. The combine churned forward, growing louder, the cab riding above the grain like a square green boat, and Charley, high up inside, glassed in, taller than the grain, moved majestically toward her against a sky where, north, gunmetal-colored clouds were massing.

She walked into the turn row. The combine bore down on her, huge when its hull suddenly broke through the grain, but she didn't move out of the way. She was smiling, but her smile glazed, and she thought for one paralyzed moment that Charley might keep on going and run right over her. She realized with surprise that Charley was angry. She stood her ground. The big motor shifted to a lower pitch and the combine stopped.

She ran around to the door, but as soon as she moved out of the way the gears growled and the motor roared and the combine lurched on into the turn row like a big green tank. She ran alongside, waving, trying to make Charley look at her. When Charley wouldn't, she ran ahead of the combine and stumbled backward, waving, in front of the milo Charley meant to cut. Charley had to stop. She leaned over and opened the door and looked down, her eyes as cold as winter.

"You want something?"

Juna clutched her books to her breast with one hand while the other fluttered upward. "Help me in, Charley."

But another Charley sat looking down at her, not the one she had come to love. She had to hold all the books in one arm and pull herself up. When the door closed behind her, the noise of the engine instantly cut out, replaced by Crystal Gayle on the tape deck singing, "Don't it make my brown eyes blue." The contrast was startling. She stood in the step well, her head just clearing the bottom of the window. "Oh wow," she said, peering around at Charley. "You're so elevated."

Charley didn't say anything. Her eyes had never looked so pale. "My," she said, "I've missed this. It's a mistake to concentrate too much on work. There *is* such a thing as diminishing returns." Why did she have to chatter? She bit her lip.

Charley threw a lever and the combine moved. It was very quiet but for the voice of Crystal Gayle. The music spread out around them. Juna clutched the under edge of the dashboard. She wanted to look at Charley again but instead she held her books tighter and looked out over the headed grain. The light was strange. It was almost the color of the milo. She wanted to say something, wanted again the eager flow of words between them. Most of all, she wanted to hear Charley's voice. She turned and tried to read her profile, the high checkbone, the flamboyant stubborn curl of mouth, the wide-winged brow. She heard her own voice like someone else's. "I've never ridden a combine before. It's so . . . quiet in here, so . . . detached. You'd hardly know we're threshing grain. That *is* what we're doing? Threshing grain? It's like a golden sea," she laughed, "the sea of waving grain. It's like that painting by Brueghel." Except in the painting no storm was brewing.

Charley wouldn't look at her. They were coming to the far edge of the field. They nosed into the turn row. A few drops of rain spattered on the big square windshield. "Oh, Charley," she pleaded to the fringe of bangs, the curled edge of mouth. "I'm sorry. I'm so sorry . . . I . . ." She released her hold on the panel to free a hand and lay it on Charley's knee. The combine lurched a little, not much, but enough to throw her against Charley's leg. Charley turned and looked at her, her eyebrows doing an exercise Juna had never seen them perform, her eyes like something live dropped in a fire. Charley reached out and switched off the motor

148

and, in a whirl of motion that spun Juna around, swarmed past her out the door.

Startled, speechless, Juna hung onto the door and watched Charley fly down the turn row, her arms flailing like bees were after her, her shirttails flapping. She shouted, "Wait!" but the wind blew the words back upon her. Charley disappeared where the turn row curved around the grain. The grain, bent by the wind, broke over her head like a wave, like high surf breaking, and swallowed her up.

Juna dropped down on the bottom step of the combine. Her books and papers scattered around her in the stubble. She picked up a spiral notebook and dropped it again. She realized she was crying. "Oh damn," she said. "Oh damn, *damn*, DAMN!"

———

Running full-tilt, hard as she could run, Charley felt the moment approach when her lungs would burst, and then it came, piercing as a knife in her chest, and when it passed she was in slow motion, like the man on the moon, running in those slow bounds that eat up ground and put everything behind you. She and Tearl used to run like this, down the road, over the broken field, breaking left or right, eluding the tackle, a knotted jacket underarm like a football, her shirt out behind her, loose, the wind at her back. She dodged around stubble, bounded off clods, the tallest thing in the landscape, in the ring of the horizon, like dodging lightning. As a child she'd been terrified of lightning. Abner had said never to be the tallest thing—in a field, in a pasture—and never *ever* get under the tallest thing, like a tree. It'll bring you down for getting so high. It'll strike the tallest thing and nothing to do but lie down flat and make yourself small. But lightning had struck and she had reached for it to propel her. She was using its energy, turning on. She was crowned, lit up. She could all but see herself shining. She had run in terror, but what-

149

ever she was afraid of hadn't killed her, it had set her free. Where the land began to swell toward the draw and the prairie grass started, she threw herself down on her stomach with her arms spread and pressed herself to the ground and felt the fine rain on her back. She rolled over and laughed and stood up and looked down over the roof of the old house, over the pond, the cottonwoods, the sprawling, tumbledown, weather-gray shed and corral and the mares grazing with their foals. Saud—Negrito—had seen her. He was running wild. It was almost feeding time. She leapt with her arms loose down the hill, shouting, seeing how loud she could yell. The mares, grazing with one foot out in front of them, pulled it in and raised their heads toward her, like cows with their tails to the wind, like sailboats, they say, face into it on their tethers, all turned in the same direction.

She loped down to the shed and bucked down a bale from the fenced-off stack and broke it on her knee and pulled off the wire. Outside, the rain was slanting down. Behind it, the pasture looked like a watercolor. She threw around cakes and chips, and the mares ambled in, Peanuts coming behind them, nosing the hay but not much interested, waiting for grain. She opened one of the garbage cans she kept it in and scooped up a bucketful and dropped a cup or two in each of the feed dishes. They clumped up softly and buried their muzzles, the foals nosing around, interested in the oats. The mares nipped at them gently, making them wait. She put her arms around Avalanche's neck and hugged the mare, her cheek in the damp, silky coat. Saud hadn't come in but, excited by the rain, kept running, running. She was cold. She grabbed a piece of whang leather off a nail and looped it over Avalanche's nose Indian-fashion. The mare lifted her face and leapt toward the rain, Charley alongside, running, then swinging up. They loped up the hill, the rain now splinters of ice, to the old house, where she let go the whang and it fell off in her hand and the mare, her wet coat dark silver, spun around, tossing the rain off her mane, and flew back down to her dinner.

Inside Charley pulled off her boots and, propelled by some energy she couldn't dissipate, flew up the stairs and knelt on the window seat. She pried up the window with its old, soft wood and wavy glass and inched her way out and, crouching, climbed the roof. Then, straddling the peak, getting her feet under her, she slowly stood, arms out, balancing, hugging on with her toes. Her face in the rain, hair molding her head, she walked the peak from one end to the other and back again, as she'd done as a child to prove herself, while the pastures blurred and ran and a semi gearing down in the distance supplied a drumroll of fanfare. She walked back down to the dormer, mouthing it to herself, and walked its little peak, then went over the side back in, shivering and spent and satisfied.

The rain came harder. Inside, it was cold and the rain noisy on the roof. She padded downstairs and knelt and wadded newspaper and struck a match and fed in chips. When they caught, she put on some small wood. She took off her shirt and dried her hair with it, then hung it close to the fireplace on the back of a chair. She pulled on an old canvas hunting jacket somebody had forgotten and drew up the wicker rocker and watched the fire catch and burn. She rocked, staring into the fire. She felt like she used to feel at Christmas. Clay was always feeling up the presents, guessing what was inside. Not her. Unwrapped presents turned into socks and underwear. Once you knew, you knew, and all that feeling of hope and longing disappeared. She didn't want to know what was in it. It was enough to know it was hers and it was not socks or underwear, it was something she had wanted all her life.

6

"Level her out! You're tilting!" Charley yelled over the engine noise. "A plane is like a horse. It's like it's in your hands but you're a part of it, you know?"

Juna, frozen at the controls, thought she did know, but she was scared with that thrilling fear she'd got as a child on a Ferris wheel. She was laughing but she didn't know what at. The sky was clear and intensely blue overhead where the wing cut out above them. Below them, Kansas spread out like a gigantic map of itself, and their wing-spread shadow, gigantic, moved over it. The fields were a broom and brown and winter-wheat-green geometry cut out by section roads with here and there rectangles enclosing huge circles like the remains, seen from the air, of the outer circle at Stonehenge, or those parade avenues in the deserts of . . . she couldn't recall which deserts. These were the fields watered by the giant, circling sprinklers. "When they land from outer space, they'll see those," she shouted. "They'll think they had some mythical significance to the race that once peopled Kansas."

Charley laughed and Juna glanced at her. Though her hands were frozen to the wheel, she had a dangerous impulse. She wanted to reach out and brush the fringe back off Charley's forehead. She gripped the wheel till her fingers ached. It wasn't at all like flying in a jet. It was more like sailing, like being a bird.

"You're doing fine," Charley yelled. "Just wait! You're going to fly!"

Belle was watching the Miss Kansas pageant. She favored the rollerskating trombone player, though playing a trombone on roller skates wasn't a very ladylike thing to do. But the girl had—what was that new word?—*charisma*. The announcer slobbered every time he put his arm around her. He kept having to give her little fatherly kisses that didn't fool Belle one bit.

How she would have loved to glide across a stage like that, just once. She'd always wanted to. But what chance had she, marrying so young? In those days you *had* to marry. Nowadays they'd just go to some quack. Not even a quack, a reputable physician. Or *have* it, for all anybody cared, like that hippie girl Buddy took up with. She'd been so peeved at Fletcher. He was so careless. They were at school together, she a serious student of the drama, Fletcher just playing around. She'd gone to her Aunt Sofie, Sofa behind her back, who put a Slipper Elm splinter up her to try to get rid of it but it hadn't worked. And once her daddy knew, there was no getting around it. He'd threatened to kill Fletcher and he would have, too. Nobody'd known but the four of them, not even her momma. Her momma would have died. So the only lead she'd ever had was walking down that aisle.

Charley stuck her head in to see if Belle wanted anything before she went up, and she had to see that hair. If she couldn't walk across a stage like that, she might at least have had a daughter who . . . There, the announcer was doing it again. Fletcher hadn't wanted a daughter. He'd thought he wanted a son till he took one look at Clay sucking away contented at her breast. He'd growled and stomped out of the house. He wouldn't have anything to do with her or the baby—except, of course, in the middle of the night when, tired as she was, he'd be at her again. She could have sworn he was jealous of the very babe at her breast, and that child his own doing. She herself had adored Clay from the minute he kicked inside her, and then she'd tried to make up for his daddy's neglect. She'd spoiled him rotten but she didn't care. No, none of that was entirely true. A girl in an antebellum dress was playing a violin. She hated violins. The truth was, she'd resented that pregnancy. With Sofie's help she'd tried to do away with Clay. She'd felt guilty toward him ever after and that's why she spoiled him so.

Eighteen months later Charley came. Fletcher was crazy about Charley, couldn't do enough for her, riding her on the saddle in front of him, as soon as she was walking putting her in pants. It was Fletcher cut off her hair, Belle thought. That like to killed me. And that little thing setting her face when her momma came near, or hiding it against her daddy's leg and refusing to budge, and Fletcher egging her into it. So Clay had been hers, and Charley her daddy's boy. How long did *that* last? When she got to be twelve or so, he wanted her in skirts with her hair curled and he'd taken another look at Clay. He'd growled again, but he thought he could twist and bend him into the shape of whatever he wanted him to be—that or else break him, one. But, shoot, he didn't *know* what he wanted him to be. Let Clay even begin to look manly, Fletcher'd find some way to shame him. Poor Buddy—damned if he did and damned if he didn't.

It was late. The contest was over. The rollerskating trombone player didn't win. It went to a sweet girl soprano from Wichita instead. She wasn't much, Belle thought, but her dress was perfectly beautiful and she had dimples. She knew why the trombone player lost. It was because she was too tall, too cocky, gliding around, sliding that trombone out and in. They'd pick the helpless ones every time. Now *she'd* have picked the trombone player there smiling at the end of the lineup, trying to look like it mattered not. Belle watched her instead of the new Miss Kansas. The crowd was clapping their heads off. The new Sunflower Queen stepped shyly out and they piled up roses in her arms. The crowd went wild. She loved all that—crowds clapping, praise, applause. She began composing a speech of acceptance in her head. Oh I'm proud, I'm so proud, this is the proudest day of my life. . . . She could hardly get it out they were shouting and clapping so. So she paused and threw them kisses. She wanted to throw them kisses lavishly with both hands, but the roses weighed her down.

Juna lay with her head aside, looking out the tall window at the night. The moon was out and the sky fumed with clouds passing quickly on their way west, to the mountains. It was like the earth cooling after Creation. Tomorrow would be as blue-and-gold as ever.

Her hand rose languidly and touched her nipple and all of her drew into that single point. She shivered and closed her eyes and saw the herd lying down or grazing, the cows with their sturdy calves and the milling mares with their foals. Then light, pale on the horizon. The house inside the windbreak still slept in a dawn like the lining of a shell. KC barked at something and stopped. She imagined him tucking his nose inside his folded paws to doze again. The kittens were burrowing in the hay, and only Chinga on the prowl stirred the stillness like the webbed feet of waterfowl under the surface of a pond.

She touched her stomach, aware of the warmth in the bed beside her, and all of her drew in to that point.

And Charley is having a dream of danger. Slow motion she rides a bronc. The world reels—the arena, the crowd. She's coming off! She's sailing! The crowd roars. Still asleep she thrashes with her arms and legs like trying to swim backward in air to undo it and break her fall. An arm circles her and saves her, plucking her out of the dream. She relaxes and calms and turns into the circling arm and, startled, begins to wake. She opens her eyes and sees the brass of the bedstead and, across the room, the library table stacked with books, then Juna smiling at her. She remembers the night before they each had a number of beers at Smoky's, happy that things between them were right again, and later back home they flopped down here on Juna's bed. She'd felt so good, so relaxed, but then, as she lay there, that strange twitching started that would grab any part of her suddenly, then let go. She'd heard her own laugh, staccato with breathlessness. And Juna said, "I'm cold. I'm getting under the covers." She lay watching while Juna sat up and removed her blouse. All pink and white in the lamplight, she'd lifted her bottom and dragged off her jeans. She had on little pants like a handkerchief on a string. She got under the covers while Charley lay there fully clothed and now and then twitching.

"Well," Charley said. "I guess I'll go on to bed."

Juna said softly, "Stay."

Charley looked at her to see if she were saying what she thought she was saying, and she thought she was. She lay there confused but resisting the questions that tried to formulate in her consciousness. But she couldn't take her clothes off, could she? And she couldn't get under the covers with her boots on.

"Stay," Juna said. "Sleep here, with me."

She didn't look at Juna. She lay there another moment, but she wasn't thinking it over. Then she sat up and took off her boots. She dropped one, and then sat with the other one in her hand. She looked down at Juna, at the shadow that fell in the large dimple like a thumbprint on her chin. She pulled off one sock and then another and let them fall across her boots. They hung there in the shape of her feet.

Juna moved on the bed and lay on the pillow still indented from her own head. Charley undid her silver-and-turquoise belt buckle and turned, hesitating. Silently Juna unzipped her jeans. She fumbled at a button on her flannel shirt and Juna reached up and, beginning at the top, worked her way down till all the buttons were undone. Her shirt falling open down the front, she still couldn't bring herself to take it off. When Juna reached out and opened it and looked, Charley stared at the rails of the brass bed. Then, amazed at what was happening, she felt her eyes go blind and she was off somewhere else besides eyes and ears, someplace she hadn't been before, where senses were not for seeing or hearing. She collapsed over Juna and felt Juna's arms surround her. Then Juna's face came up and they looked at one another, surprised, Charley holding her breath. Her jeans were very tight. She rolled over and lifted her rump and dredged them down, and then they bound her legs together at the ankles. She had to kick to get her feet out. She lay there twitching again till Juna pulled out the covers and she was lying on the sheet. Juna's eyes swept all the way down. Charley thought she was dying. She closed her eyes. But she opened them and Juna was pink in the light. Then she closed them again and reached. She'd thought it couldn't be done and it was easy. She had never felt another body all down the length of her own. There were no words to think the feeling. It was right that it couldn't be thought or said. She'd had intimations before that there were things that couldn't be said or could only be said at peril, like catching a butterfly and ruining the color of its wings. It was right that it had to exist only as this, as itself, entirely on its own.

She wanted to look at Juna and she didn't want to move. But she rolled over and looked down. She had never seen this face before, so delicate and lovely. She whispered, "I've never done this. Have you?" Her voice was hoarse. It didn't even sound like hers.

"Yes—no—not like this."

She was watching Juna's lips. They were a little open and pinkly striated. She studied them like a chapter of natural history, amazed, then touched them with her finger, and then, in stages, lowered her own to touch them, lightly, then draw back, then touch them again, lightly. It took several bobs before she could let them stay—for one thing, it was hard to get her breath—then she kissed the upper lip, then the lower, and only after a while could she manage both at once. Juna's opened, and they both lay still, testing that. Then Juna's tongue came up to her lips and lay there plump and limp, a small thing afraid, and she brought up her own to meet it, and they lay together like their bodies, testing, till finally she had to fall away and learn to breathe again.

"Oh, Charley," Juna whispered, as if she had to say Charley. "Where did you learn to kiss like that?"

"I just this minute learned," Charley gasped, with a laugh.

"Other people . . . are not like that," Juna said. "They're— very intrusive."

Charley wondered what other people. She put up her hand and touched Juna's breast and Juna froze like a dogie you come up to in a draw, the minute before you put out your hand. She put her lips to the full underside of it and then, gaining courage, moved higher. The nipple was soft and undefined, then gradually puckery and hard. And Juna made a small sound. Charley thought she'd hurt her and pulled away. Juna's hand came up alongside her cheek and guided her face back. Charley's hand found Juna's belly and jerked away, shocked at itself. But it went right back again to Juna's belly, which sank like her own between her hips, so it was easy to let her hand slide till it encountered the crispness of fur and rested. The heel of her hand seemed to want to knead a little. When it did, Juna opened and gasped.

Charley yanked her hand away and looked up and was so relieved when she saw Juna's face that she fell across her, limp and smiling, and she lay there stunned again at the feel of their bodies touching. Juna's arms held her and she lay in the magic of bodies touching till Juna reached for her hand and moved aside

158

to put it back and they lay like that, not moving. Anything more would be too much. Finally Juna said, "I don't know what to do."

But Charley knew. She felt she had known forever.

———

Juna lay with her eyes closed to see more clearly what was passing before them, a scene more real than the room or the sun falling in an elongated rectangle across the old flowered rug the way it did in the morning. They were in a private place. She couldn't tell if it were made private by trees or by the walls of an arroyo, or what the shadows came from. Charley had brought her here. She was showing her something. She bent, sat, squatted—Juna couldn't tell. She was looking down. Perhaps she had dug into the earth. Or had she lifted a lid? Whatever, she turned then, her head bent over, and looked sideways up at Juna, to see her face when she looked down and saw whatever marvel was there. But Juna didn't look down. She kept looking at Charley, at the pale eyes so darkly set. Charley looked down again. Her lashes swept down over her eyes and made them secret. Then she looked up again to watch Juna's face when she looked down to see what it was she had brought her here to see.

She grew aware that Charley was awake beside her and it vanished, but she would always see it now, if she wanted to—one of those memorable dreams you sometimes have in the hypnogogic state, etched into your memory, that you never forget. She wished now she had looked down as Charley had meant her to, to see what it was Charley had wanted her to see.

Silly, she said to herself. It was your dream. So what was it? That was why she hadn't looked! She didn't know what it was. How strange. It was so real she wanted to turn to Charley and ask:

"What was it?" But how could Charley tell? No, it was gone, lost. She felt desolate.

Charley, meanwhile, had an impulse she acted upon. She rolled up out of bed and pulled on her jeans and swaggered across the room, rolling from side to side like a sailor on deck, zipping her zipper, shaking herself down in the jeans like you'd shake something down in a paper sack. She knocked a cigarette out of her pack on the dresser and hung it in the corner of her mouth and lit it and shook out the match. She stood there barefoot, bigger than life, inhaling, and looked up to see herself in the mirror but instead saw Juna behind her, laughing soundlessly. She dropped the match. Her face burned. She snubbed out the cigarette and turned. Juna held out her arms and she took a running leap onto the bed and buried her face in the pillows.

Then tremors again. Mortifying! But slowly she got her arm out from under her and turned, and there was Juna's face, the new face, close up, and they collapsed together laughing.

———

After school let out in the afternoon, they drove all over four counties for the sake of being alone together. They went to Charley's favorite haunts. One was a café in a town hardly more than a crossroads, where a motherly-looking waitress named Myrna slid into the booth next to Charley and teased, "Charley dudn' come to see me, she comes to eat New Mexico chili," and rumpled Charley's hair, and Charley, smiling at Juna, said, "Naw, I come to get my hair messed up," and Myrna said, "Aw, Charley, you don't have enough hair for any real honest-to-goodness messing."

Another was a bar in the next county different from Smoky's because there was no jukebox and no pool table and people drifted in from fifty miles away and, though recognizing faces, didn't really know each other. You brought your own liquor in a paper bag and huddled over it in your booth while the barman looked away, and the only accompanying sound was the popcorn machine continually popping. They drank pitchers of tomato beer and put away big salad bowls of popcorn. It was on the house because the proprietor grew his own and it didn't cost him anything. "It's what everybody comes for," he was always ready to explain to the room at large. "Why else would anybody drive all the way to hell and gone just to drink?" He said it was his philosophy people would go to any length to get something for nothing. "Tell me why," he'd urge with a narrowed eye. "What do you ever get for nothing?"

When nobody could think of the answer, he'd polish a glass on his apron and hold it up to the light and say, "Love." It was this desire for love that made people gamble at cards and horse races, that made housewives sit at their kitchen tables and enter sweepstakes by the hundreds, that turned honest men into thieves. It was this desire for something for nothing—that is, for love—that brought him customers from so far afield without so much as a two-dollar ad in a local paper. Yes-sir-ee-bob, free popcorn was a substitute for love. He said to make a go of business you had to understand human nature. He had a scoop-shaped chin and limestone-colored eyes, one of them practical, looking directly at whatever he was talking about, the other romantic, looking off at an angle, taking no part whatever in the conversation. While he talked he slipped into the booth beside you and ate big fistfuls of popcorn. "Go ahead, try it," he said to Juna. "Good for you! They's plenty more where that come from." And he added, "If the mice ain't got it." Then the laugh at her surprise.

Joyce, his wife, kept giving him looks and little laughs meant to suggest to their customers that they had some secrets, but her husband's romantic eye seemed to miss these looks entirely. She had a narrow face with blond hair piled up on top of it in a bouquet of curls and at the bottom a set-back chin that made her cheeks look plump and her teeth in front a little crowded. She had once been a nurse. She was getting the good out of her white nurse's uniforms and oxfords by waiting tables and tending bar in them. She had quit nursing, she said, because she got sick and tired of the selfishness of The Sick. "You never saw nothing like it," she said. "No consideration!" And the hospital was way over in the next county, too far to be traveling to and from on section roads at all hours of the day and night, you never knew what might happen. So she retired from nursing and they'd been doing this ever since. *This* meant the bar. It was, she said, an ideal life.

She looked at every customer who came in with bright, expectant eyes, dreaming of movie stars or millionaires or TV personalities who marched to a different drum and liked taking byways to out-of-the-way places to check on what the country was really like. She longed for framed photographs covering the walls, with autographs—To Vic, To Joyce, With Love. All they had so far was a photograph of a dog in a hat whose owner and trainer stopped in one day bragging his dog was a television commercial star, and another of a young woman dressed in the style of the thirties who claimed to have been in movies and, now that she was older, taught in the drama department at Lawrence.

Charley kept her eyes on Juna's face to catch her reactions. It all seemed wildly exotic to Juna.

They bowled in the Tula bowling alley where Charley kept a bag under the counter with her ball and shoes. They shopped at the hardware store and outfitted Juna with a sleeping bag and a casting rod and various other items suitable for her new pursuits. Every time the movie changed, they sat in the back row of the Majestic where now and then their hands touched under the armrest. They flew all over Kansas on sunny Saturdays and once, without planning to, landed in Topeka and toured the capital. They inspected the memorial to The Pioneer Woman and the statue of Abraham Lincoln. They laid their heads back and turned in circles looking up at the underside of the dome, and Juna said, "Why, it's a mandala." They rode in the old cage elevator and looked a long time at the John Steuart Curry murals on the second floor. Charley liked the cattle—the bull looked like a bull she knew—and next to that the swell of the horizon. Juna liked the sky but she shivered at the portrayal of John Brown. He looked entirely too fanatical against what was either a battle scene or a prairie fire. They stood together in front of the statue in its niche of Amelia Earhart. They ate dinner in a steak house whose dark, private booths had open spool screens to the ceiling and plenty of dark red leather, and spent the night in a motel where they never went to sleep.

One weekend Charley put the camper shell on her pickup and unrolled her foam mattress in the truck bed and tossed in her camp stove and icebox and they drove ninety miles to a Corps of Engineers lake where they sat out of the wind with their rods, pretending to fish, making one cast last, and told each other new chapters in their personal histories.

"But what are you really like?" Juna asked, leaning against the bank, the sky behind her. "Maybe I've made you up. I could, you know. It would be easy. With your horses and combines and trucks and airplanes, you're very exotic to me. We're from such different worlds. You seem to me so . . . brave."

"You've been all over the world," Charley said. "All by yourself. I haven't done anything. I've just stayed home."

"Well," Juna said, watching the drama taking place in the sky, "I guess there's all kinds of courage." She pointed to a big, heavy cloud the color of a bad bruise roiling along toward them with so much going on inside it might have been pregnant with wrestling giants. Charley thought *twister* and tried to remember the last overpass they'd seen on the highway, just in case, but Juna, looking up, the wind stirring the soft wisps alongside her face, said, "Kansas is Oz."

Charley said, "*Your* Kansas is."

They threw back the two fish they caught, both of them Juna's though she'd never been fishing before, and ate in a Howard Johnson and went to bed in the camper shell as soon as it got dark. It rained all night and most of the next day, so they kept the curtains pulled and lay propped against the back of the cab drinking tepid tea out of a thermos and eating egg salad sandwiches side by side under the lumpy contour map that was the fiberglass ceiling.

Juna had brought along her sketchbook. She got it out and propped it across their knees and turned the pages slowly, letting Charley see. She had gone sketching through all those countries, but she hadn't sketched those landmark towers—the Eiffel Tower or the Tower of London or The Leaning Tower of Pisa. She had sketched a wavy line of shore with a large rock coming up out of the sea, or a bird standing on one leg on top of a post, or a line of rooftops white against the dark water with something far out that might be a sail or might be a gull. "They aren't very good," she said thoughtfully, turning a page, shoving her glasses back up her nose. She didn't say it as if prompting Charley to argue, so Charley didn't say anything. She didn't know if they were good or not, but they filled her with longing, not for faraway places, but for all of Juna's life that had been lived without her in it. She tried to retrieve some of it by looking hard, getting all of it she could out of the pictures. She was jealous of that rock, that one-legged bird, of even the rooftops and the white thing far out that might be a sail or a gull. She wanted to put herself in that place, to go back in a time machine and be there with Juna. But she hated to travel. The sight of a bus or a train made her lonesome. The only traveling she could enjoy was what traveling she did in her truck, pulling a stock trailer, or in the little Skyhawk, herself at the controls, or in the combine.

"Listen to it rain!" she said.

"I like the fall," Juna said. "Something happens to the light out here." She closed the sketchbook and stretched out and looked at Charley. "What's your favorite season?"

Charley had never stopped to think if she had a favorite. "Well," she said, "it's not winter."

Juna smiled and rolled onto her stomach to look at her. She traced the line of her cheek with a lazy finger, from the high cheekbone to the stubborn chin. "You don't like being indoors," she said. She had taken off her glasses and Charley was studying her eyes. They slanted up at the corners. "Think what's your favorite," Juna prompted. "I can tell a lot about people by their favorite things."

Charley tackled it again. "I guess it's the changes," she said. "You know, like when spring's coming, or summer or fall. Even winter. There gets to be a kind of excitement in the air and the sky, and in the light." She could say things like that now.

Juna's finger stopped tracing. She looked stunned. Charley, alarmed, thought it was a foolish answer, but then Juna reached out and with her forefinger moved back the fringe on her forehead and she knew Juna had just wanted to touch her again. "We must never," she said, "come to believe we *know* each other completely. We have to know the mystery is always there. We must never"—she shuddered—"come to feel like we're one person. How lonely!"

The rain stopped about three o'clock and they put on the rest of their clothes and got out and built a fire on the shingle beach. It had gotten a little chilly in the truck. Most of the other campers had gone, discouraged by the weather, but an old man with a two-day stubble sat in a chair leaned against the back bumper of his old pickup camper and grinned and waved. He had his generator going. His boat, pulled up on the shingle, was ready to go fishing, and when he invited them to go along, they toured the lake and trolled for an hour and brought in a nice-size bass and some crappie, which Charley gutted and scaled and put on ice to take home to Lady for supper. "It'll prove we really went fishing," she said, and Juna put a hand under her arm and huddled close for warmth.

Sometimes Juna woke at night with the startled thought: What am I *do*ing? She didn't take relationship lightly, and she'd begun to wonder what this one meant—in terms, as she put it to herself, of the rest of her life. But a look at Charley's sleeping face was enough distraction to make her forget all that and hang on an elbow tracing the elegant scroll of Charley's lips, then putting her face up close enough to wake her with her breath. Then she'd say, "Close your eyes," and Charley would, and she'd close her own and they'd put their foreheads and noses together and Juna would say, "Now!" and they'd open their eyes at the same instant and see only one large cyclops eye in the other's face and fall away laughing. It was called Wowl, after Owl, and she'd played it as a child with her father.

Charley never thought at all, she daydreamed. After all these years her old habit had returned. Driving the long, straight roads in her pickup or lounging in her saddle atop Avalanche on a rise of pasture overlooking the herd, she daydreamed. The dreams weren't totally formulated. They were cloudy at the edges, contained in their own bubbles like the dialogue in comic strips. They all included Juna and the old house in the draw, complete in the dreams with kitchen and baths and wind generator with a backup gasoline motor. There'd be a table at a window and the two of them sitting across from each other over cups of coffee on a checked tablecloth, or the bedroom under the eaves with an old pegged bedstead—she knew where she could get one—and Lady's braided rugs on the wide-board floors, or Juna in one of the dormer window seats sketching and herself, Charley, waving as she walked up from the barn at suppertime.

———

Coming out of her trailer, Lady looked up as she pulled the door to behind her and saw them on the south side roof over the porch. In they underwear, bless 'em. Juna's were something catlike—leopards?—with feets like a baby's snuggies. They were purple, and over them, on her legs below the knees, some long woolly lavender leggings. Charley was in a union suit from the dry goods store that Juna had dyed forest green using her biggest kitchen pot. Next time Belle wanted spaghetti, she'd probably get it green.

She walked down the flagstone path among her dead flowers, watching. It was like something she'd watched with Belle on the tube, young people dancing in tights and he'd pick her up over his head and turn, slow, and her lying on looklike the air. She could just hear the music—slow and glidy from one place to another. As she moved, gliding a little, up the walk to the back door, she heard Juna say now and then something mysterious. Salute to the Sun. That was nice! King Dancer. A fitting name for a king! She paused before the corner of the house cut them off. They were standing on their heads, their toes—Juna's purple and Charley's in gray wool socks with red-and-green Christmas cuffs—pointing to the sky, and Lady was suddenly propelled to a great distance out, rising fast, like a saucer, like a ship, and she saw the world as a spinning top leaning toward the floor of the firmament and for the first time understood with a thorough and mystical knowledge that Juna was right, there couldn't be any such thing as time, and the two of them on the pole of it in a slow spin of their own, their whole selves pointing out, sticking up out of the world like the whatchacallits sticking up out of space fliers, out of the big heads of the little people from out yonder, beaming it in, beaming it all in.

"Beaming what in?" the voice of the skeptic inside her scoffed.

She shook her head, smiling as she opened the back door. Good vibes she thought they called it.

7

"Weather's changed," she said to Belle's back as she banged the kitchen door open and let it slam behind her. "You can feel it in the air. I turned up my blanket last night." Something in the shape of Belle's back this morning was bad news. She decided to ignore it, to jolly her along. Sometimes it worked. She took off her old gray sweater stretched all out of shape. A shame to be seen in it. But she couldn't give it up. She needed the pockets. Juna called it her Virginia Woolf sweater. She hung it on the back of the door.

The coffee was already made. That was unusual. "How long you been up?" she asked, but Belle didn't answer. "Ain' slept well again?" Belle hadn't been sleeping well for some time. Claimed she heard noises in the night.

"What's that?" Belle said, starting, then cursing because, Lady guessed, she'd got an eyebrow on wrong.

"What's what?"

"That noise!"

"I didn't hear nothing."

Belle gave a little shiver and hissed an intake of breath. "I can't get warm in here. Turn up the heat."

"You got it on high as it'll go. You don't want to blow up the boiler." The workings of the heat in the house was a mystery to Lady, but she'd had a horror of a blowing up the boiler ever since she'd heard of such an accident blowing a family out in the street. She took out the bacon and put it on low.

Belle said, "I'm not sure a country kitchen is a good idea."

"You the one wanting the walls down, not me."

"It might be too big and barny. Everything too open."

"Well, change your mind. You can, you know. I don't want to go through nothing like that. Leave me out. I'll take a trip to Florida and get warm if you go tearing us up again."

"I wish I could get some sleep. I'm a nervous wreck."

"Let me get something hot inside us and I'll put you down and give you a massage. Tearl always said I had healing hands and it's true. These hands got a life of they own." She looked at her hands and turned them over, then poured two cups of coffee and brought them to the table and sat down.

"I don't know what gets into them. Sometime I can't get them to do a thing right. Just won't do what I want. And sometime they won't rest. *They'll* fidget. And—you might not believe this—but now and then they'll come out of a spell like that knowing how to do something they couldn't do before."

But Belle wasn't listening. She was thinking about something else. "You ought to think a long time before you go making radical changes," she said. "I'm always too quick. When I want a thing, I want it now."

"You always been that way."

"It gets things done!" She sipped her coffee and then her hand jerked and she spilled a little. "What was that?"

"Remember the time we took up that . . . whatchamacallit? With all the twine? And hung up the flowerpots with it?"

"Macramé," Belle said absently.

"These hands didn't have to learn. They just up and did it. You ever have anything like that happen to you?" Belle didn't answer. She was somewhere else. Lady got up to turn the bacon. "Like some part of you's got a life of its own, separate from the rest?"

169

Belle gave another little shiver and when she spoke Lady couldn't tell if she was taking part in the conversation or starting another of her own. "Sometimes an outlandish notion comes into my head," Belle said. She paused a moment, thinking about whatever she was thinking about. Then she shrugged off the outlandish notion. "Why, it's perfectly outlandish."

"That's different," Lady said, bringing the coffeepot over for refills. "The head's the operations center. You can expect things to pop up there. What I mean is more like—they's a tiny little *head* in the tip of your *thumb*, and *you* don't know what's going on in it but there's where your *hand* is getting its briefing."

"Well, *something's* keeping me awake," Belle said.

They both heard it this time. Lady thought she knew what it was, but for some reason she didn't question or try to understand, she kept it to herself. "It's the bacon spitting," she said.

"It was not! It was something else!"

"*I* know what's bothering you."

For the first time since she'd come in, Lady had Belle's full attention. "What?"

"It's them phone calls."

Belle immediately lost interest, but Lady pressed on, conscious she was into a game but unconscious of why. "Put them out of your mind. They just some creep's launchpad. Nothing to lie awake about. Report him to the phone company. Change your number."

But again Belle wasn't listening. "I get the feeling," she said, "lying there in the middle of the night—there's something hanging over me."

Lady went to the stove to take up the bacon. "Ain' nothing over you but your old bedroom. Takes time to get used to sleeping in another room after all those years upstairs."

A sound came from the porch roof that could not be ignored. It resounded through the house. Lady thought it was Charley, hitting the yoga mat. She glanced up at the ceiling. "Does my heart good to see them two hitting it off so well," she said. "Swimming in the pond . . . romping in the hay . . . And Junie learning to ride a horse and Charley learning to yoga. Early every morning I see them out on the roof in they underwear."

"That's it!" Belle said. "That's what I've been hearing!" But she didn't seem pleased to have the mystery solved. "I shouldn't have been so quick to take in a stranger."

"Why, what's got into you!" Lady said.

"What do I need with boarders?"

"Aw, come on . . ."

"I'm not sure she's a good influence."

"Why, you couldn't th'ow her up to Charley enough! A wonder Charley dudn' hate her."

"An Eastern feminist radical vegetarian!"

Lady laughed. "Charley needs a friend. She always been too alone. How you want 'em, scrambled or fried?"

Lady looked up when Charley and Juna came down the stairs. Used to be, Charley was up and long gone by six, but now she came down at a normal hour and had breakfast with the rest of them. She was dressing different, too, almost a little natty. Where did that plaid vest come from? You'd think Belle would be pleased but she wasn't.

Juna was saying, "See, Leo is a fire sign, and Gemini is air. They're compatible."

Charley seemed not entirely convinced. What on earth was it all about? Juna could tell you things unheard of, outlandish things, and she believed in them—about food and the stars and your own digestion. Belle looked at them sourly. Charley sat down at her place and picked up the newspaper. Juna joined Lady at the stove.

"Can I do anything?"

"You can check the biscuits." Wadn' it nice to have somebody else take an interest in the cooking.

"Where've you got the cows?" Belle asked.

"Still in the north pasture," Charley said without looking out from behind her paper.

"Couldn't be anything left over there."

"They're finding enough," Charley said, rustling a page straight and turning it. "Soon as it frosts good, I'll let them clean up the alfalfa."

"No telling when that'll be! It could be weeks!"

"Days!" Charley said. "I'm keeping an eye on them. I'm th'owing 'em a little hay."

"You go light on the hay! This could be a long winter."

"Since when did we ever run short of hay?"

"What about the steers?"

"They're on the feed banks."

"Have you given them their shipping shots?"

One edge of the paper collapsed and Charley glared out from behind it. "I spend a whole week with a cattle prod in the goddam squeeze chute, green shit all over me, and you don't even notice!"

"Move the whole herd south," Belle said. "Do it today!"

"I got a trip to make today!"

"I don't care what you've got to do. You'll move them when I say move them."

Charley threw down her paper. "If you want to run this ranch, run it. If you want me to run it, leave me the hell alone."

"Alone. You're never alone."

Juna turned from the stove. "Will it take you long to hitch up the trailer?"

Lady brought a platter of eggs and bacon to the table and Juna came behind her with the biscuits.

"I hitched up the trailer last night."

"Where," Belle asked, "are you taking my stock trailer?"

Lady handed her the platter. "Here, have some eggs." Belle neither answered nor looked at her, but she slid two fried eggs onto Belle's plate anyway.

"I *told* you," Charley said. "I'm taking a mare over to Sego's to leave her till she's bred."

Juna rolled her eyes heavenward and closed them. "I never tasted eggs till I tasted these."

"If you raised Quarter Horses like everybody else, you could just run them down the road, not over half the state. You needn't think I'm handing out any stud fees."

Charley said in a voice that Lady disliked, a small, wheedling voice, "I don't need the whole thing right now."

Juna said, "They're so versatile." Still on the eggs.

Belle said, "I don't want to discuss it."

Charley said, in that same awful voice, "I don't have *time* to discuss it. When a mare's in season, she's in season."

Lady picked up the coffeepot and poured seconds all around. "Yawl sure are cranky this morning."

"Imagine the emotions of the first woman who discovered if she beat them they would stiffen! And stand up!"

Belle looked at Juna with a shocked face. "What on earth is she talking about?"

"I can pay 'im half now and half when I go back to get 'er."

Belle glanced irritably at Juna. "Oh, *why* can't we carry on an intelligent conversation!"

"It'd be great to carry on an intelligent conversation," Charley said.

"If it's not conversations," Belle snapped, "what *are* you carrying on up there till all hours of the night?"

Without looking directly at anybody, Lady was aware that Charley looked like she'd sat down in something and Juna was suddenly listening and Belle fidgeted like she'd let something slip that she'd like to take back.

"Look at you," Belle said. "You don't have to run all over the country looking like that." Back on familiar ground. But it was strange. Belle never neglected nailing a point once she'd won it. "The way you get yourself up, no man will ever look at you." A

173

long time since she'd played that tune. Bound to be some exploding.

But Charley said quietly, "I don't want them looking at me."

"Then something's the matter with you," Belle said, then shied again. "Poppa used to say to me from the time I was a little girl, 'Knock 'em dead, honey!' And I did. They didn't name me Belle for nothing." Lady got up to get more preserves. Belle turned her attention to Juna. "Where did they get a name like Juna?"

"Juna is not the name they gave me," Juna said in a small, prissy voice. "It is the name I gave myself. I chose it because it is without associations. I chose it as a sign of my own freedom."

Belle brightened and Lady thought, Here we go.

"It's not your real name?"

"Oh, but it is . . . my real name."

"But what was the name they gave you?"

"Saying it would put energy into it. I don't even allow myself to think it. I don't know how women survive the names of . . . of flowers." Lady could see she had almost said something else.

"Daisy?" Belle said eagerly. "Violet? Rose?"

"Of soft summer months," Juna said with contempt.

"April?" Belle said. "May? June? June!"

But Juna smiled, superior, and Charley said, "I known a sissy once named August."

"See," Juna said. "A sissy!"

Lady laughed. "You think they named me for a bug? They named my sisters after play pretties. Pearl. Opal. Ruby."

Juna shivered. "That's better than small, cuddly, vulnerable animals."

Belle picked up on that shiver. "Kitty?" Juna recoiled. Belle laughed triumphantly. "Kitty? Kitty-kitty, here kitty-kitty!"

Juna flushed. "How can women take themselves seriously with names like that?"

"I never wanted to be taken seriously," Belle said. "I wanted to

174

be a woman and have men wait on me." The phone rang. Lady picked it up off the buffet and put it on the table by Belle. It rang again. Belle lifted the receiver and listened and said, "There's nobody here named Clyde," and hung up.

"Look at that," Charley said. "She's disappointed. She thought it was her boyfriend."

"Maybe we shut of him," Lady said.

Charley said, "He's two-timing you. He's found him a pretty little heifer in some out-of-the-way pasture somewhere. Some sweet little yearling cow. That's what they do around here."

"I won't have perversions discussed at the breakfast table!" Belle snapped.

Charley flushed and Juna said quickly, "Why don't you load up the mare while I put the lunch together?"

"No school today?" Belle asked.

"I'm just hitching a ride as far as town," Juna said. And to Charley, "Will you be warm enough? You didn't get the heater fixed yet."

Belle's eyebrows shot up.

"I'm *fine*." Charley grabbed her sheepskin coat. "Let's get going."

"You needn't think you're getting any money out of me and that's final."

"I won't be a minute!" Juna said, busy at the counter.

"Plenty of places to stop for a hamburger," Belle said. "What's wrong with a hamburger?"

"The beef's full of hormones and the bread's embalmed," Juna said.

"All I need's a thermos of coffee!" Charley said. "Slow driving makes me sleepy."

"You drink too much coffee," Juna said. "It kills your enzymes. I made you a thermos of rose-hip soup."

Charley went to the sink and downed some pills with a cup of water. "You wouldn't have those migraines," Belle said, "if you got some sleep at night."

"I don't have a headache," Charley said. "These are vitamin pills."

"Lady gave us these two spice shelves for our vitamins," Juna said. "I took the top one." She pointed. "This one's yours." She laughed. "We can label them! Hers—and hers!"

Lady laughed. Belle's eyebrows sprang higher. "Come on!" Charley said, "I gotta hit the road if I'moan get back today." She went out and slammed the door after her.

Belle said archly to Juna, "You're going to make some man a good little wife."

Juna grabbed up the lunch and hurried into the hall, "Not on your life!" She put on her coat, took up her books, and hurried after Charley. Mary Jane appeared at the door and asked to be let in. Lady opened the door for her and Belle sang out, "Kitty-kitty, here kitty-kitty!"

Lady ran water for the dishes. Belle said, "*Will* you come back in here and sit down? I hate all this rush-rush in the morning."

Lady sighed. It was going to be a long day.

There was a gunshot outside. Belle jerked, startled. There was a second shot, then another. A horse whinnied, frightened. Several shots followed in quick succession. Lady rushed to the window and looked out. Juna was stumbling, sobbing, toward the house. Charley, rifle in hand, hurried after her. They mounted the steps, Juna in front, and crossed the porch, Charley gesturing, talking excitedly, her hat on the back of her head.

"Look! Will you listen a minute? Wait! It usually takes me one shot!"

Juna entered the house, Charley behind her. The door slammed. Belle and Lady faced the hall as Juna ran through, handkerchief to her face, toward the stairs, Charley close behind.

"One shot! That's all. It's the gun sights. I never should of let Harvey touch it. They're way off."

Juna gained the stairs and whirled around. "I don't believe it! You think *that's* what's upsetting me? That it took you too many shots to kill it? I'd never have pointed if I thought—" She burst into tears and ran up a few steps.

"I . . . I thought . . . You said Look! So I grabbed my gun and—"

"It never occurred to me you'd do such a thing!"

Charley looked rattled. "But jackrabbits are pests, like the mice. We always—" She stopped.

"Kill them?" Juna said. "I wanted you to *see* it! I didn't want you to *miss* it!"

"She didn't!" Belle chortled.

"You gentle horses. You don't hold with brutality. My God! You're schizophrenic! Half one thing, half another." Juna ran on up the stairs. A door slammed above. Charley threw down her hat. She paced the hall, running her hand desperately through her hair. She moved back to the foot of the stairs and called, "The mare's already loaded!" She waited. There was no response. She paced again.

"Just a jackrabbit," Belle said.

"You stay out of this!" Charley said. She stopped dead-still in the hall and looked at the rifle in her hand, then moved purposefully toward the gun case near the front door. Belle pulled her plate back in front of her and began to eat her breakfast. She gave a little laugh and said in a low aside to Lady, "It never could have worked."

Charley stood at the gun case, handling her rifle fondly. Then with decision she opened the glass door and put the rifle inside next to her father and brother's guns. Turning, she walked determinedly toward the stairs. She didn't look at Belle or Lady sitting at the table.

Belle's mood was much improved. "They don't have a thing in common. Where's my oatmeal? I didn't eat my oatmeal."

"I th'ew it in the slop for the hogs," Lady said.

"Those hogs'll soon have to be cut," Belle said. "Remind Juan." She held her cup for a refill. Lady sighed and went to get the coffeepot.

"If she can't stand to see a rabbit hit the dust, what'll she do when she hears the hogs screaming?" She laughed. "Tell Juan to do it this afternoon." Lady refilled her cup. She was on her second round of biscuits. "I think when this bust arrives I'll have the memorial unveiling at the Majestic. It seats more people than the church and there'll be a crowd. They're always eager for a look at us." Lady shook her head and moved back to the sink. "And we can have the spotlight on the bust." She sipped her coffee, made a face, and put it down. It was too hot. "I wonder what they'd charge me for the Majestic? Probably try to hold me up but I won't let them."

"Well," Lady said, "Buddy never set foot in the Methodist church if he could help it, but he sure didn't miss nothing at the Majestic."

"I could still ask the minister. . . ."

She shoved her empty plate away, wheeled herself to the buffet, took down her mirror, and wheeled back to the table with it. She set it down and turned on the light and looked in it at herself. "But why trust him to do it, doddering old fool. I can do it myself. In my new pantsuit!" But she grew thoughtful. "How do you do an unveiling?"

"You th'ow a flag over it and when the time comes whip it off."

Belle shook her head. "That wouldn't work. The colors don't go with pink."

Upstairs, a door opened. They looked toward the hall. Charley's voice was saying, "You're right. I never even give it a thought."

Their footsteps descended the stairs.

"It dudn' make a lick of sense," Charley said. "Just something they do out here."

They came into view in the hallway and paused. Juna turned to Charley and laid a hand on her arm and said, "We've just got to turn all this ancient shit into fertilizer."

They walked together out of the house. Belle's mood reverted. "I want that herd moved today!" she shouted. Then she said to Lady, "You're right."

Lady couldn't think what about.

"It's no wonder I've been uneasy. These phone calls so upsetting and me lying down here . . . a helpless invalid . . . on the ground floor . . . alone. Well, there's a simple solution."

"What solution?" Lady said, full of misgivings.

"I don't have to be alone."

Juan had seen the whole thing from his perch high up on the narrowing tip of the fruit tree ladder. He wasn't sure what to make of it. Charley had not killed clean. It must be the gun sights. But it was just a rabbit.

He dropped a MacIntosh into his apple sack. He was in no hurry. He could stay up there all morning with his head in the sun and think. He was thinking of the jockey, Maggie—Marguerito—Martinez. He was thinking of him *here*. He had sent a picture postcard of the courthouse to the downs at Ruidoso. The jockey would arrive on the bus and he, Juan, would drive in himself in the flatbed Ford to meet him and bring him home. They would sit at the table and be waited on and he would be gruff and masterful with the women—pass this, pass that. The two of them would lean on the fence and chew grass stems and look at the horses together. When Maggie Martinez saw Negrito, his eyes would narrow with knowledge. He would turn to Juan with new respect and nod, seeing him for the aficionado that he was.

After that, all would be different. Just how wasn't clear. He would have to work that out. But he, Juan, would make the woman rich. Richer. He admired this woman though she was a woman, for she never had to work at anything and she kept her fingernails long and blood-red and she didn't even wear her own hair. But even so, it would come to pass that she would depend on him, Juan, for money to pay her taxes. They must be terrible, those taxes. She would depend on him for money to keep the rancho going. And Charley would be much in the winner's circle. And he, Juan, would dress in new boots and a new hat and he would smoke dollar cigars whenever he liked. A regular path would be beaten between Tula, Ruidoso, Raton, and Santa Fe. He would discard his yellow suitcase and travel in style. How would he travel? Not on the bus. Would Charley fly him in the airplane? Charley would fly him to Ruidoso!

Charley drove slowly, pulling the stock trailer. It peeved her to think Belle wouldn't buy her a proper horse trailer. She was still feeling chastised and she longed to put things right again. "She'll make me crawl for that stud fee." She heard the hint of a whine in her voice but she couldn't help herself.

"You run that huge ranch single-handed and you do it for handouts," Juna said, sounding cold and critical.

"I've owed Smoke hunderds of dollars just for beers and games of pool. She'll let me sweat. . . ."

"Why have you put up with it?"

The question startled her. She had never asked herself why. She had never considered she had a choice. "Aw hell," she said, "I'm just bellyaching. How many have a new pickup every year, hunderd dollar boots . . . I don't have it so bad."

The yellow school bus crept along in front of them, filled and rowdy. A boy in the rear window made a face at them. A girl raised her lunch bag and hit him over the head and he ducked and disappeared.

They had to crawl past the rodeo grounds. The bus stopped outside the gates to pick up children from down the road. Preparations for the rodeo were almost finished. There was the big stock truck, GILMAN'S RODEO STOCK in big letters along its side. Horse trailers were parked in the lot. They could hear hammering. Booths were going up, for hot dogs and cotton candy and beer. Cows for the roping event mooed in the field. You could see the bulls through the walls of the stockade. They were unloading the broncs. Juna watched all this while they idled there behind the bus, but Charley looked determinedly ahead. The boy bobbed up like a jack-in-the-box and stuck out his tongue. Charley put a thumb in an ear and waggled at him, scowling, and he ducked behind the emergency exit door. A young cowboy yelled from the top of one of the chutes. "Hey, Charley!"

"Who's that?" Juna asked.

"JoJo," Charley muttered.

"I thought he worked at the gas station."

"Hell, they'll all goof off for days. They all think they're cowboys this time of year."

The bus began to move. They followed it to the school, where they left it behind, and drove up Main Street. It was lined with pickups. There wasn't an empty parking place anywhere. The sidewalks were full of schoolchildren, men talking in groups, tradesmen standing in front of their doors. It was rodeo time. Eveybody had gone Western. The kids had on neckerchiefs and toy guns in holsters. Bunting flew over the street. They could hear the band practicing in the sports field at the high school.

They pulled into the filling station. A line of cars waited at the gas pumps. The whole county was streaming in. Charley pulled the pickup and trailer in alongside the walk so she could drive it on through without having to back up. An attendant fitting the gas hose into the side tank of a pickup lifted his chin in greeting. Juna got out.

"Hey, Billy," Charley yelled. "Can you change all the filters when you get a chance? I got to make a trip."

"If I *get* a chance," Billy said. "I got the place alone today. No sign of JoJo all morning. It's more'n I can handle."

They walked up the block together. An aging rancher turned away from the group where he'd stood listening and smiled at Charley. "How's your momma?" he said.

"She's fine, Nate, fine."

"'At's good."

A woman dragging a small child by the hand smiled at Juna. "How's 'at kid behaving hisself?"

"Wendell is settling down, Mrs. Mayhew," Juna said.

"If he gives you any more trouble just knock a wart on his head and I'll give 'im one to match when he gets home."

They entered a coffee shop and slid into a booth. The waitress gave them menus.

"Just bring us some tea, Frances," Charley said.

Juna dropped her menu and looked down at her hands on the table. "I think you accept Belle's presents because you want something from her."

"Dang right I want something from her," Charley said. Then she tried to think what.

The waitress put down two glasses of water and went away.

"I wanted to go to Manhattan, learn about crops, 'quipment, breeding, vet medicine . . ."

A pretty high school girl paused at their booth and handed them each a card, smiling. She rattled off a speech. "My name is Gloria Linderman and I would appreciate your votes for rodeo queen. You'll see the ballot box near the door as you go out. The contest ends at noon. Thank you very much."

Charley looked at her blankly, but Juna smiled. The girl moved on to the next booth. They could hear her repeating her speech to the people behind them.

"Why didn't you go to school, if you wanted to?" Juna asked.

"Fletcher wouldn't send me. Haven't you heard? Girls don't need an education."

Juna smiled. "Fix yourself up, you might catch a husband?"

182

A drunk cowboy reeled over the table, catching himself on it, and tried to kiss Juna. "Honey," he said, "I'm willing, you sweet pretty l'il ol' thing you."

His friend caught him by the arm and swung him away. "He don't mean nothing, lady. He's a good ol' boy. He just celebrating, ain't you, Lester?"

The waitress brought the tea.

"Did you try for a scholarship?" Juna asked.

Charley fiddled with her water glass. "Hell," she said, "you think they'd give *me* a scholarship? Fletcher Burden's kid? They thought he owned half the state. He had a finger in lots of pies."

Harvey Sears, on his way out, paused at their booth with his smile in place. "You riding broncs tomorrow, Charley?"

Charley looked up. "Naw, Harvey. Are you?"

His smile never faltered, but his eye did its barely perceptible slide. He nodded to Juna and lagged a bit as if he wanted to stay but then went on toward the cash register by the door.

They sauntered along side by side toward the school.

"You're just another deprived child from a wealthy family," Juna said.

Charley didn't like the sound of it. "Me? They might not a given me a scholarship in Kansas, but they offered me one in California." She was bragging and she knew it, but she had a lot of bitching to make up for.

Juna stopped dead in the middle of the sidewalk and looked at her. "A scholarship in California!"

Charley nodded, tossing her hat in front of her and catching it.

"In what?"

"Gymnastics."

"Well, why in heaven's name didn't you grab it?"

She caught her hat and looked at Juna, dumbfounded. "*California?*"

But Juna just looked at her. Charley tried to laugh. "My God,"

183

Juna said, "you're bound to her!" She looked stricken. She turned and walked slowly on.

Something flared in Charley, part anger, part dread. "I'm not bound to nobody!" But that didn't come out right. Juna looked at her. Charley laughed a short spurt of laughter. "Hell," she said. "What do I need with scholarships? I coulda gone on my own if I'da wanted to. You know them horses of mine? I bought the foundation mare at an auction with birthday money when I was fourteen. Nobody else knew what she was. They just saw she wadn' no Quarter Horse and she had that outsize muscle they'll get on their neck when they been foundered. They all thought I was a fool. But I parlayed that foundered mare into a herd. Ever' last one of them horses is worth at least five thou'd'n."

Juna stopped dead on the sidewalk and looked at Charley. The children in the playground ran toward them, calling.

"Miss Evins!"

"Miss Evins kin I . . ."

"You promised! Yesterday you said . . ."

"She did not!"

"It's Harold's turn to feed the gerbil!"

"*Dollars*?"

Charley nodded, proud of herself.

"Then you could do anything you wanted! You don't *need* her!"

Something had backfired. The children converged on Juna, tugging at her, noisy and fond, knocking each other out of the way for the privilege of being next to her. They began moving Juna toward the school. Laughing and fond in the midst of the chaos, she allowed herself to be carried along. Charley, alone on the sidewalk, looked after her, bewildered, touched by some new, unwelcome glimmering of knowledge. She turned and walked slowly back toward town.

"Charley!"

She turned. Juna was standing with her hand up. She smiled and waved. "School lets out early today for the parade!"

"I'll be back in time!" Charley yelled, restored. "I'll pick you up!"

———

Belle was watching her favorite soap but it seemed to her that she'd lost track of what was going on and, worse, that it didn't matter. She was sick and tired of the hospital atmosphere on that show. Lady's footsteps descended the stairs, but Belle didn't turn around.

"You're making a mistake," Lady said.

"I don't intend to argue."

"Wait and discuss it with her first."

Honestly, sometimes it was like living with a pack of children. She had all the responsibility, all the decisions. But let her ask for a little consideration . . .

She forgot and looked at Lady. Lady stood there with an armload of clothes on hangers and a pair of rough-out chaps buckled on over her dress. Snowshoes stuck up like wings over her shoulders. At a rakish angle on her head sat a white Stetson hat. But Belle was determined not to laugh.

"I don't know what you got against that girl," Lady said.

"What girl do you mean?"

"You know what girl."

"I haven't the faintest idea what you're talking about."

"Sometimes a couple will each grab a child and square off against one another. That what happened?"

"If you want to talk Greek don't talk to me."

"He grabbed her and you grabbed him? Then he jealous of him and you jealous of her ever after? Was that it?"

"You're speaking in riddles."

Lady sighed and walked off down the hall toward the new den, talking to herself as she went. "Sometimes I get to feeling heartsick. I could pull up stakes and start to wander."

"That's the most stationary mobile home in the State of Kansas!" Belle said. "Not even any wheels."

"Tearl said when there's motion in the soul, wheels not hard to come by."

"I doubt Tearl said half of what's attributed to him." She was watching the soap again.

Lady reappeared empty-handed in the door, but Belle kept her eyes determinedly on the screen. She didn't intend to budge. Where would they all be without her? It wouldn't hurt them to sacrifice a little for a change. "He's the sweetest, most considerate thing, this young doctor," she said. "All my doctors were like that, just wonderful." When she said it, it seemed like the truth. Then she thought, these gallant young doctors weren't doctors at all but just actors got up to look respectable. It seemed suddenly diabolical, like a plot to lull you. And her doctor in the hospital hadn't been at all like that. He'd been short and bald with a pouch under his belt and two more under his eyes. He'd looked a lot like Raymond.

The phone rang. She stared at it. It rang again and she snatched it up. "Hello!" she said angrily. "Oh"—she trilled a little flustered laugh—"Mr. Thigpen. I wasn't expecting to hear from you. You're at the bar! Why, Mr. Thigpen!" She watched a little of her soap. "Why, certainly, bring them by. I appreciate your remembering to put them in your car. You'll save me a trip to town." She hung up and watched the soap till a commercial came on.

Lady's slow footsteps headed back down the hall toward the stairs.

"Mr. Thigpen's stopping by," Belle said. "He's on his way home for lunch and he's bringing some papers for me to sign." She sighed. "He claims I can save money by giving money away.

I told him I don't know anybody I want to give it to. He'll be after me again to contribute to the Presbyterians. He's an active Presbyterian."

"You can contribute it to me," Lady said, starting up the stairs.

Belle watched the ancient Chrysler come up the drive, slower than most vehicles came up it. She waited till his footsteps crossed the porch to switch off the television by remote control and arrange her face. "Come on in, Mr. Thigpen. Excuse me for not getting up. I don't get around like I used to."

He came in smiling, his wisps of gray crown hair spun out by the wind, and spread the papers before her, uncapping his ancient fountain pen and pointing. She took the pen and signed and he folded the papers and put them in an inner coat pocket.

"You're amassing quite a little fortune, Mrs. Burden," he said.

"Yes, Mr. Thigpen. I have put to work all my daddy taught me. If my father'd had Fletcher Burden's resources, he'd of died a very wealthy man."

"Well, I reckon you come by it naturally."

She laughed. "It was our little game. We'd decide when to buy, then watch the columns of figures go up, up, up. Decide to sell, and they'd drop down, down, down. Then buy again. It was all a game but it seemed so real. Now it's all real but it seems like a game. I'm playing Monopoly, Mr. Thigpen, with real money, and I keep on landing on Park Place. Poppa would be so proud of me. But what good does it do, I ask you, Mr. Thigpen? What can I do with it?"

"You can make all your dreams come true."

"Then what would I do for dreams?"

He chuckled, rocking back and forth on feet planted close together.

"I could of course give up the game, but what would I do with my time?"

"I have learned, Mrs. Burden, you don't deal with time. Time deals with you."

She couldn't get along without him, but she hadn't asked him to sit down because he made her gloomy. He was doing it again. She was reminded of all the times when, providing him with the record of her earnings—she thought of them as winnings—for the quarterly returns, she tried to halt at some halfway point and he looked up at her with that sweet, expectant smile of the almost deaf, waiting innocently, implacably, for more, and inevitably she disclosed and disclosed till at the exact moment when she had no more to disclose he sat back in his ancient oak swivel chair and laced his hands together over his small, high belly, satisfied, and she told him he was her conscience.

"The operation you run out here is too efficient," he was saying. "I need more in the expense column or it'll all just go to the government."

"We'll be stringing new fence along the section roads this fall, and enlarging a couple of tanks and digging another pit silo," she said.

"Fine," he said, "but I'll have to depreciate all that. I need some straight expenses—like salaries, for instance."

She didn't like the way he was looking at her. She laughed. "Oh, good," she said. "I can give Lady a raise."

"It's either put Charley on the payroll or give it to the government," he said.

"Government! Government! What do I get for all I give, I'd like to know! Potholes and bombs!"

"And I wouldn't be doing my job if I didn't remind you again of what I've told you already about estate taxes." He was relentless, turning his hat chest-high in his hands.

"I'm not old yet, Mr. Thigpen. I'm still a young woman."

"Yes, ma'am, so much the better, if I may say so. You're entitled to move ten thousand yearly out of your estate."

"You know how I feel about giving money away, Mr. Thigpen."

"It's not a question of that, ma'am. It's a question of do you

188

want to give it to the government or do you want to give it to somebody. Perhaps some worthy cause—"

"I intend to live to be a hundred, Mr. Thigpen."

"Yes, ma'am," he said, "and that means you could move out, why, something like four hundred thousand before—uh—that time. You can't start on a thing like this a day too soon."

Belle was looking out the window north, across the irrigated sections. "And this gift-estate-tax business, could that be in real property?"

"Yes, ma'am, it could."

"I mean in real estate."

"Yes ma'am." He nodded.

"I mean like—say—in land."

"Yes ma'am."

"I see. Thank you, Mr. Thigpen. You are like a good dentist. You do your job well and never mind the pain."

He smiled and bowed a little. "Why, thank you, ma'am."

She watched him down the walk, tall and gray and stooped between the flowers. She was thinking she could give ten thousand a year on top of wages to Lady and Lady could give it right back to her. But Mr. Thigpen's voice in her head said, "Ma'am, that wouldn't qualify. It wouldn't be a gift, now would it, if there were strings attached? Also, I must warn you, it is illegal and could bring you to grief at some point down the road. And, too, if the money went back into your coffers it would be a roundabout maneuver to no purpose whatsoever." She often used Darrel Thigpen's voice to tell herself what she would just as soon not hear. It was not such a boon that she'd taken Fletcher Burden's wealth and doubled it. It took her beyond where she wanted to go. She wasn't making money to enrich the government, but if she gave it away where would she be? They'd all be gone.

The phone rang. She stared at it but let it ring till finally it quit. She gazed absently at the screen. "I wonder what they see in me?" she said, loud enough for Lady to hear, and absently picked up her hand mirror and eyed herself in it.

"They see in your pocketbook," Lady said down the stairwell.

"You're just jealous you're not white," Belle said.

"Unh-unh," Lady said. "I'm jealous I ain't red-headed."

"I realize that remark was meant to sound smart," Belle said. "But frankly I find it offensive." She took off her wig and eyed it. "Thelma dudn' have it anymore," she muttered. "She's losing her touch. You know?" She raised her voice. "I woke up this morning not knowing where I was."

"I thought you said you ain' slept a wink."

"Sometimes I wake up and think—I'm seventeen and visiting Big Momma on the farm, and I'm just waking up and that's a little bird I hear, chirping in the scuppernongs. That ever happen to you?"

"Naw," Lady said. "It dudn't."

"And as I began to wake, I thought—why, no, I'm twenty-some-odd and I'm lying next to young Fletcher Burden and . . ." She no longer saw what she was looking at. Her gaze had wandered back through some foliage of time but couldn't get through to the clearing. "Then I realize I am *not* twenty-some-odd. Why, I'm thirty-five and my children are in school. And then, all in a rush as I'm surfacing, I know I'm forty, forty-five, fifty, and time is flying, like one of those old movies where everything's speeded up. . . ."

Lady's footsteps descended again. She appeared in the door bearing a double armload of boots of all varieties and, beneath the boots, in her hands, a pair of muscle-building weights. On her head was a black flat-crowned flamenco hat with little colored balls dangling from the brim that Charley had won at the state fair. Belle took it all in with a kind of wonder and said, "Didn't we have us some good times when we were children on the Palo Verde?"

Lady said, "I didn't know you when we were children, Scarlet honey."

Belle saw her then, and laughed. The phone rang. They both turned and stared at it. Lady said, "Why don't you answer the phone?" She started back down the hall.

Belle sat staring at it. "I'm not expecting any calls."

It rang again.

"Maybe you won a church raffle," Lady said.

"I haven't bought tickets to any raffle."

"It's Mother Bell, checking on the service."

"That'll be the day."

"It's Monkey Ward," Lady said, coming back empty-handed, "saying your order's in."

"But I haven't ordered anything!"

Lady stood in the door. They waited. The phone rang again. Belle reached tentatively and picked it up and listened a minute and said, "Hello?" Then, in the relief she felt, she realized her stomach muscles were sore from being knotted. "Ben! Why, I'd about given you up. You must be the most sought-after man in this county." She laughed. "When are you coming out?"

Lady sighed and headed back up the stairs.

"But I don't *know* what I want," Belle said. "I need to talk to you about it, get your ideas. If I took a vote out here, the kitchen would stay put. Sure, this afternoon will be fine." She glanced toward the hall and lowered her voice. "And Ben—have you been to the state line lately?" She laughed again. "I knew I could count on you. How many can you let me have? All righty. Whatever dudn' have somebody else's name on it."

She felt so cheered when she hung up that she switched impatiently from channel to channel with her blab-off, turning off her favorite soap in the middle, and when the phone rang again she picked it up immediately, without thinking. "Marlon! Where on earth have you been? I've tried calling you every day this week

191

and you're never in your office. Where do you get to like that in the middle of the day when you're supposed to be managing my money?" She sat listening. "You've what?" She picked up a pencil and beat its eraser head rapidly on the table. "I told you to leave those Ginny Mays alone!" The eraser drummed faster. "You don't know what you're talking about, young man. Or maybe you do but you think I don't. I don't need you to tell me about margins. I knew about margins before you were born. If you're entertaining notions of trying a little churning, put it out of your mind, it's an idle fantasy. You're not dealing with any sweet innocent little old lady, you know." She hung up before he could say anything and suddenly felt her sweet tooth. That was a good sign. She wondered if there was any pie in the house.

"Who *is* this Ginny May?" Lady asked, descending the stairs.

"Never mind," Belle said, "it's not a person. Honestly, Marlon's more trouble than he's worth. If you want something done, do it yourself." She turned around.

Lady stood in the hall wearing the stuffed elk's head on top of her own. Belle guffawed and flung herself back in her chair. Lady went deadpan down the hall.

Belle's spirits had revived. She wheeled herself over to her desk and rolled up the top and put on her green eyeshade.

Over the desk on the wall hung the framed photographs of the old sod house with Fletcher's ancestors lined up out front looking seedy. She yanked the eyeshade down and got to work.

Charley squatted on the ground beside Ralph Sego just inside the white board fence. They each chewed a grass stem and eyed Charley's mare cavorting in the strange enclosure.

"What changed your mind?" the rancher asked. "Grassfire, now he's a nice stud, it don't make a whole lot of difference, but I thought you were set on Trigger Happy."

Charley pulled out the grass stem and threw it away, casting around for words. She pulled up another grass stem and poked it between her teeth. "Well, see," she said, "Princess there—she's a Leo." Her face heated. "That's a fire sign." Ralph Sego slowly turned and looked at her but she looked determinedly at the mare trotting along the fence, then turning and trotting along it in the opposite direction. "And Grassfire—May—he's Gemini. Air."

She turned. They faced each other.

"But you take Trigger Happy—according to the stud book he'd be a Pisces. Water."

He stared at her. She made herself meet his whiskey-colored gaze till finally he turned and gave a slow nod, as if, she thought, he realized she had lost her mind and he'd better humor her.

On the way back to Tula she saw sticking out of the fence-line brush the unmistakable tail of a coyote, long and low, not up and wagging like a dog, curving just as it reached the ground. She saw more than one hawk riding on the air, looking for field mice, and some doves and red-winged blackbirds, and after a long stretch of empty road she scared up a cock pheasant that lifted, iridescent, over the roadside fence and sank on spread wings out of sight. She left the section roads and drove fast with the empty trailer on the Interstate.

Main Street was littered after the parade. She pulled in to the curb in front of the school. She'd made it back in record time. The playground was deserted. The janitor had taken in the flag. She honked her horn.

Juna looked up from her desk and gathered her things. The room was empty except for Billy John Etheridge, who was dropping food into the cage where the gerbil ran on his exercise wheel. Billy John had followed her at a distance all day, hollow-eyed and wan, with something on his eight-year-old mind, she couldn't imagine what. He must be turning over a new leaf if he'd asked to take the gerbil for the weekend. She watched him, puzzled, as he tapped on the wire and then turned, pushing the hair out of his eyes.

"Finished, Billy John?"

But he didn't answer. A tawny shock fell down to his eyebrows. One cheek was pale with chalk dust. The other was pink with a bubble gum blow-out. He brought his eyes up to hers and took a deep breath. "Do you think I'm sexy?"

So that was it. She smiled. "Incredibly."

To keep his pleasure from showing, he hitched up his pants by the belt and turned to get the gerbil cage. "I can carry those too," he said as they started out, reaching for her books.

Outside, Charley fiddled with the radio dial. She brought in country western, then a preacher, then crop prices. They were down but beef was up. She'd been holding the steers back. Maybe they'd soon be shipping. If she could get the trucks.

Juna came down the walk with the Etheridge boy, who was carrying a cage with a mouse in it. They lingered at the intersection with the sidewalk, then parted, waving, and Juna got in the truck. "What a day!" she said. "We didn't get a thing done. I might as well have gone with you. What's it like over there?"

Charley shrugged. "The mares enjoy it."

Juna laughed. Charley shifted and pulled into the line of traffic.

"We had the best fish salad for lunch—yesterday's leftovers they would ordinarily throw to the cats. The lunchroom ladies are learning."

Charley pulled to the curb outside the post office and went in. The box was crammed. The tip of a pink slip showed among the handful of bills and circulars. She handed it to the clerk at the window.

"Hi're you, Charley?"

"Pretty good, Mac."

He turned to look for the package. It was squarish, larger than a hatbox.

"Yo' Momma into the mail orders again."

"I reckon."

She slid behind the wheel and put the mail and the box on Juna's lap and slammed the door. She nosed the pickup back into the parade traffic bound for the opening of the rodeo.

"They made the salad with sprouts we sprouted in Science," Juna said.

"I hope I'm doing the right thing," Charley said. "Grassfire, he's got a nice dished face, but he slopes a little in the crupper."

"The children were so thrilled. Poor Billy John's in the throes of his first crush."

"Good face—good eyes. Set way out. You could knock 'em off with a stick."

Juna shuddered.

"Just a saying."

As they edged out of town Juna laid a hand on Charley's thigh, absently. It gave Charley a pleasurable shiver down her back.

"Why is it again that Pisces and Leo don't mix?"

"Well, we can't say that unequivocally. We'd have to go into the entire chart. But August—Leo—is fire, and Pisces is water. Mutually destructive elements."

"And Grassfire . . . he's late May. . . ."

"Unless, of course, kept in perfect balance. Then you get lots of energy. But it would be a terrible chance to take."

"Yeah, well, when we get home, I'moan go over my stud books again. If I want to change my mind, I can get Ralph on the phone."

They were passing the rodeo grounds, creeping in the traffic. The band was playing. The MC's voice rode out over it. "Ladies and gentlemen, Selma Mackey, the rodeo queen . . ." The stands went wild for a minute, then a girl's voice, small, unintelligible. And the MC again. ". . . and tomorrow, the bucking events, the bull riding and the bareback, and the saddle bronc contest."

195

Charley looked stolidly ahead and waited for the moment they'd break free of the cars and pickups and she could step on the gas. She could feel Juna looking at her.

"He's gone up on his stud fees," she said. "She'll make me crawl."

"You don't have to crawl," Juna said. "You know, maybe you lost confidence that time you were thrown in the rodeo. Maybe that's why you knuckle under to her."

"I don't knuckle under to her."

"*Sometimes* you knuckle under to her. And you have a certain kind of self-destructive pride, Charley. Oh, yes, you do. You don't have to be ashamed of flying off a bucking bronc. How many stay on, after all?"

They were free of the traffic. The blacktop stretched straight before them, hazy where it ran into the horizon, for it was beginning to give up the heat of the day. Charley felt the force inside her building, and then it exploded. "I might coulda stayed! I never had a chance! The dirty bastards!"

"I don't understand."

"You draw your horse, see, for the bucking events. And ever'body's ever rode that bronc before yells out telling you how he bucks and where to take the reins. You need that. Twisters all do that for one another."

"They wouldn't tell you?"

"Oh, they told me all right. Ride 'em long! He bucks with his nose in his frog! So I rode 'em long and got caught out and like to got kilt. They thought it was about the funniest thing they ever did. Fucking bronc was a stargazer!"

"What does that mean?"

"What do you think? Looks at the sky! Bucks with his nose in the air! With long reins I come outa the chute off-balance. I couldn't do a thing after that."

"They lied? But why?"

"Why do you think? I was a girl!"

"Oh Charley."

"Yeah, oh Charley," Charley laughed bitterly.

"That was so unfair."

"*Tell* me!"

"And Belle's unfair. You should figure out what you ought to get for running the ranch and present it to her."

"She'd laugh in my face."

"Then tell her you'll look for another job."

"What kind of a job? All I know is what I do around the place."

"But you do everything! You raise beef catttle, you make crops, you operate heavy equipment, you act as a vet, you breed and train horses, and in your spare time pilot her around the country in an airplane."

Charley snorted. "They hire cowboys, not cowpersons."

"You've got to realize it's not you who need Belle but Belle who needs you."

"How could I ever leave her? A helpless cripple!"

"Helpless! Belle?" Juna laughed. "You just don't value yourself, Charley."

"If she had to hire somebody, she'd put a man in over me."

"She won't hire a man. That's just a threat. She likes being top dog." Charley looked at her skeptically, and she added, "The spectator sees more of the game."

"Nah," Charley said. "She'd still be top dog. She owns the place."

"No she wouldn't. She has a conditioned response to men. She doesn't have to go into that song and dance with you."

"If she was to say no, where'd that leave me?"

"Right where you are now. So what have you got to lose?"

They turned off the blacktop onto the ranch road. Charley didn't say anything.

"Have you got the nerve?"

197

She turned and looked at Juna. "You think I'm scared of her?"

"When are you going to stand up to her?"

"When I need to stand up to her."

———

Lady had been canning all afternoon. The kitchen was hot and fruity and she needed to get out to her trailer and put herself under the shower, but she was scared she'd miss Charley. She didn't know what she could do for Charley but she had to be there when she came home. She felt bad about everything but the row of jars cooling on the windowsill, twelve quarts of apple-sauce. She made applesauce but she dried her pie apples. She already had the cored and sliced rounds ready to string up. They kept their sweetness best that way. She'd learned it from Juan. Thank God for the bumper crop of apples. How would she have got through this day without them?

She had a casserole to make. Just a washday supper, she thought, but won't nobody have any appetite anyway. Belle had been at it all afternoon, starting with Ben Bunsen's visit. She was pretending to work at the desk, but she had the open bottle on the floor beside her and a half-full tumbler on the desk. She'd been acting goofy, humming a little, keeping time with her head, and once rolling herself to the window and swearing she saw some-body hiding behind the old limestone fence posts she'd stuck out there as antiques. It scared Lady to think she could so easily start seeing things again. They were in for it. It was starting all over.

Belle hummed a little and then sang. "The starrrs—are gonna twinkle and shiiiine—tomorrrrrow—about a quarter to niiiine."

She laughed a shrill, little-girl laugh. "That's an old one, Lady. Before our time. Poppa used to sing that. He was sooooo handsome. He'd take me by the hands and I'd step up on his two-tone shoes—I was just a little thing in an organdy dress—organdy was soooo scratchy—and we'd dance." She was singing again, keeping time with her head and rolling her eyes. "*Let* me put my arms a-bout-you. *I* could never live with-out-you. Oh. You. Beautiful doll, you great big beautiful doll. If you ever leave me how my heart will ache. I'd love to hold you but I'm 'fraid you'd break." She laughed. "I always thought that last was for Momma." She sobered. "Momma was a little fragile thing." She rolled her eyes up and dropped a hand on her breast, clowning. "She was ladylike and delicate, given to vapors in the afternoon." Then she stopped guiltily. "But I wasn't a thing like her. I never suited her. I could never do a thing to please her."

"Kinda like Charley," Lady said.

"I was not! I wasn't a thing like Charley."

"I 'spect you was. Just hid yourself under a bushel and got confused."

"Oh, you can be such a bore." She turned back to the desk. "These books are a mess. Turn your back for a week and everything falls apart." She sipped from the glass and put it down and picked up her pencil and poked at her old-fashioned adding machine that trailed a long paper tapeworm to the floor.

Lady heard the trailer before she heard the truck. Empty, it rattled down the road toward the house. Belle, in her wheelchair, pretended to go on working. Lady glanced at the Coors clock. It was after three. She didn't turn around when they came in the door, but Juna headed straight for the kitchen.

"Lady! What's that I smell? Applesauce!"

Charley dropped the mail on the desk and set a large, square box down beside Belle. "I'moan go get my stud book," she said. She had missed the glass of booze.

"Yeah, applesauce," Lady said. "I was at it all afternoon but they's still a bushel out there on the ground for the hogs."

"I think I'll make a pie!" Juna said.

"Make half a dozen," Lady said. "We can freeze them." Out of the corner of her eye she saw Belle replenish her drink and set the bottle unsteadily down in plain sight on the desk. Lady was

199

listening for Charley's footsteps descending. When they came, they were slow down the steps and slow across the hall. They stopped in the dining room door. The strange, slow steps, so unlike Charley's usual rout, got to Juna too. She turned.

Charley stood looking across the room at Belle, her hands in her pockets jingling loose change as if to keep themselves occupied and out of trouble, as if to keep from hitting something. "Okey," she said. "What's the joke?"

"What's the matter?" Juna asked.

Charley gave her a quick, white-eyed glare and looked back at Belle. "All my stuff's gone. Nothing left up there in my room but the bed and the chiff'robe. It's picked clean. So who's the grasshopper?"

Belle was flipping through her mail. She picked up the box. "What's this?" She tore off the string and pulled at the wrapping.

Charley turned toward the kitchen door. "Had to be you, Lady. *She* couldn't of managed."

"I just do as I'm told around here," Lady said.

Charley looked back at Belle and whistled a little tuneless whisper between her teeth. She walked slowly across the room to the desk, her hands still in her pockets, still jingling, as if she couldn't trust them to be let out.

Belle took the lid off the box and looked up. "I haven't had a good night's sleep since I don't know when," she said accusingly. "What with these menacing phone calls and me downstairs by myself. I'm not used to it."

But Charley had spotted the bottle and the glass of bourbon. She took her hands out of her pockets and gave a long, low whistle. She reached for the glass but Belle deftly lifted it off the desk and swung it away. "I'm a nervous wreck," she said.

"Where'd you get hold of that?" Charley said. "Goddammit, Lady!" She turned. "We not going through that again."

"Don't look at me," Lady said.

"I don't get any sleep at all anymore," Belle said. "And today I thought I saw somebody hanging around the place."

"You two had one busy day," Charley said. "Where the hell's my stuff? What's this all about?"

"I don't intend to spend another night down here alone," Belle said. "You'll find your things in the new den. From now on that can be your bedroom. You ought to appreciate it but you won't. Everything in there is new. The couch makes into a bed—I paid a fortune for that hideaway—and all carpeted, private bath, private entry . . . You'll have plenty of room. Why, you could hold a dance in there if you wanted to. And Juna can spread out. She can have the whole upstairs."

Charley lunged for the glass but Belle snatched it out of reach and wheeled her chair back away from Charley and sat with both hands up, one holding the bottle, the other the glass. "You leave me alone!" she said. "This is *my* house! I can do as I like."

"No wonder you hadda get pickled." Charley whirled on Lady. "And you! Honkey says move, you got to shuffle? I thought you were a friend!" She spun back to Belle. "You act like we're checkers and it's always your move! Don't even bother to ask!" She turned on Lady again. "She's a cripple! A helpless cripple! Look at her!"

And Charley hung there frozen for a moment, looking, Lady thought, as if something had threatened to break through but didn't quite make it. Lady looked back, wanting her to hear what she herself had said. Juna, beside her, had grown very quiet.

Charley stood for a moment confused, looking at the two of them in the kitchen door. But then she whirled on Belle and grabbed the wheelchair and spun it around. Belle rocked like a dummy, hit the backrest hard, and looked at Charley with large, round eyes. She wanted to clutch at the chair arms but she was caught with both hands full. She hung onto the bottle and the glass. Her mouth opened as round as her eyes, but she didn't make a sound, just looked up at Charley.

Charley felt a surge of exhilaration. She put her hands on the arms of the wheelchair and leaned over Belle till Belle had to rear back away from her. "Look at you! A cripple! A helpless cripple! And think you're queen bee around here." She laughed. She grabbed the chair and spun it on one wheel in a circle. Belle's frightened face came around again. Charlie switched on the wheelchair's motor and sent Belle riding off toward the hall, swaying like a mannequin, the motor whirring like a hoarse, whispered plea.

"I been a fool!" Charley ranted behind her. "Let you tell me what to do, treat me any old way. . . ." She grabbed the chair just before it hit the stairs and swung it around toward the dining room. The motor purred its soft little plea. Lady started forward but Juna, beside her, breathed, "Wait!"

"I do all the work!" Charley said. "It's *me* runs this ranch, all ten thou'd'n acres."

She caught the chair before it collided with the table and spun it toward her and for a moment hung her face in Belle's. "And think I got to do it for handouts . . . from this old red-headed dominecker!"

"Charley . . ." Lady said.

"And listen to her bellyache morning to night . . . and think that's the way it's got to be. Well, it don't *have* to be that way." She spun the chair around and laughed, sending it back toward the desk in the corner, following it and raging. "From now on it's gonna be different. I'moan have some say around here. I'moan have the old place. You gonna give it to me. And money ever' month, like most people get for the work they do. And if you don't, try running this place without me."

"Charley!" Lady said. She left Juna and ran to Belle and caught the chair before it hit the desk. She turned off the motor, and after all the noise the room was very still.

Belle drew herself up. First she set the bottle and the glass carefully down on the desk. "Are you finished?" she asked Charley.

Charley smiled down at her. "Naw," she said. "I'm not. I'm just getting started. I been saving up. I got a lot to say. You might have to listen to me all night."

Belle reached for her cane and rose to stand royally. "I *have* been listening to you all night."

Charley's grin slowly froze and then turned foolish. She glanced at Juna.

"And I've had enough!" Belle said. She looked from Charley to Juna and back at Charley. Charley's expression had turned sheepish. Juna steadily met Charley's eyes, but right before her own Charley began to shrink and cast about, confused. Her hands went back in her pockets. They bounced the keys and change they found there while Belle moved on her cane toward her with intimidating slowness. Charley stood her ground for a moment, then backed and turned aside.

"I've had enough!" Belle said. "I thought I'd have some company . . . but no! Night after night . . . heaven knows what goes on up there. Right over my head! Under my roof! In my bed!"

Juna stared calmly back, but in the corner of her eye Charley began to fold, to turn toward the wall and reach out to brace herself against it, leaning over, her head hanging below her arm.

Belle moved closer. "My daughter!" She laughed harshly. "Some daughter!"

Juna thought she heard Charley moan.

"I'll leave everything to Clay's baby," Belle said. "It'd only end with you . . . like a mule."

Charley sagged toward the wall and Belle seemed to tower. "What are you, anyway? Answer me!"

Juna thought she heard a sob. The phone rang. Belle turned and looked at it. It rang again. She picked it up and listened. She laughed. "Sure," she said. "Come on out. I've been wanting to see your face." She put down the receiver and laughed again. "I'll give you the reception you deserve." She walked majestically toward the hall and crossed it to enter her room. Lady sighed and went over to the desk and bent to pick up the wrapping paper and string off the floor.

Juna hesitated, then crossed to Charley, who looked as if she had been struck and left wounded and bleeding, still leaning on her arm against the wall. Her face looking out from under her arm was both drawn and open, pale and flushed in different places, and her eyes had turned to glass. Juna reached out and touched her shoulder. "Oh, Charley."

Charley turned in an instant from a wrung-out mop leaning there to something wild. She flew into the corner and looked out at Juna with eyes hardly recognizable, bruised-looking, pushed back in her head. "Leave me alone!" she said. "Get away! Get back. Look what you've done!"

Juna stopped and stood looking at Charley. Her hands, waist high in front of her, bit at each other like kittens on their hind legs fighting. She backed and turned and walked into the hall. She paused and swung on the newel post and looked back at the dining room, her eyes ranging around, not settling on anything, and then she went upstairs.

Lady, at the desk, didn't look at Charley. It would be a shame to look at Charley. Charley ought to be left alone. She reached in the box, a tall, white box like a square hatbox, and took out the bust and held it up and stood eyeing it, turning it this way and that to get at different angles. It did look a little bit like Clay.

8

A storm had hit, silent and raging, leaving the bedroom in tatters, the closet door open, drawers hanging out, suitcases strewn across the floor, the bed hidden beneath piles of clothes. Already near the door a duffel bag, a portable typewriter, a sewing machine in its case, and an exercise mat huddled against the wall. Juna had been at it for some time. Lady, despondent, sat at the old library table drinking coffee and playing solitaire.

"You were going to make them pies," she said, slapping a black jack on a red queen.

"Sugar speeds up your processes and shortens your life."

"Where'll you go?" It didn't look hopeful. She only had one of her aces out.

"I don't know. I don't know what I'll do but I'll do *some*thing. I've always, since I was a kid, had the feeling I ought to *do* something, you know? The world is such a terrible place. I mean, the world isn't terrible, but there are such terrible things in it . . . I always felt I had to do something."

"Do good, you mean," Lady said.

Juna nodded.

"Try to fix something, you got to be awful careful. It can backfire. Like, once when she was a child Charley brought home a horny toad from Manitou and put it in the garden. That toad loved that garden. You'd talk to him, he'd cock his little flat head back at you, listening. Them little reddish eyes! That toad got fat. It's sides just sat down on the ground from all the insects it ate out there. And I'd swear it changed its colors from what fit The Garden of the Gods to what fit here. But Charley worried herself sick that she'd brought him here where there weren't any other horny toads, so she sent off for one, mail order, so he could have a friend. And it came and all and . . . you know what? The first horny toad disappeared. She always wondered did he feel like she didn't like him and got herself a new horny toad? Did he hate sharing his territory? Did they just plain not get along? And she felt so bad. She was trying to do the right thing."

Juna waited to see if there was more, but there wasn't. "I guess I'll go to the Siesta Motel."

"You won't get a room at rodeo time," Lady said. "And you won't like the Siesta Motel anyway. It's mostly just local hot pillow trade."

"I can tell them at school I was too far out," Juna said, and disappeared into the closet to emerge with an armful of sweaters. "That's probably the truth."

Did Charley think it was something to hide in the dark, to creep around, to accept in shame? She returned to her packing with the kind of anger that longs to confront, engage in combat, or, at the very least, to win an argument, to pommel her opponent into pleas of mercy.

How could you!

Have you no self-respect?

Who are you and where is the Charley I thought I loved?

Her breast rose. She breathed rapidly and yet with a depth that expanded her sense of herself as a young woman of principle, dignity. She would never creep. Never. She caught sight of herself in the mirror, all but pigeon-breasted with pride. She laughed but it came out a sob.

She paced to the window with a nightgown in her arms, grieving for the compact, perfect, physical Charley. But that was irrational. You can't take this body, that consciousness, another psyche, a different sensibility and assemble them into whatever you think you want. That would be Frankenstein.

But what cowardice!

She turned to the dresser. She pulled out a drawer and stood facing herself again in the mirror. Easy for you to say, she said. It's not your home, your town, your mother.

And if it had been?

Her mother was not Belle Burden. Her mother would just get books from the library on psychology and resign herself. She saw her parents. The two of them sat across the room from each other, he with his paper and his glass of straight vodka they pretended was ice water, she knitting with her glasses slipping down her nose. And once, at the country club, sitting with them like that out on the terrace overlooking the golf course, Juna had risen in her dress and hose and heels and walked sedately to the pool and jumped in.

Her family wasn't a bit like Charley's. What was it like to be Charley? She hadn't the least idea. She had made a hero of Charley and now she was angry that that wasn't who Charley was. Was that Charley's fault?

She cut short that train of thought. It was as if they had fought and Charley had won a round and that left her more upset than ever. She slammed the drawer shut and flung open a suitcase on the bed.

Lady was fighting the urge to go through the deck one at a time but keeping herself honest. She could have told Juna, You don't have to leave. But she knew better than to say anything. The young got to learn for themselves, she knew. They got to try to invent the world. But she said, "You learning to ride a horse and Charley learning to stand on her head . . . don't th'ow all that away. Pity poor Charley."

"I do," Juna said. "I pity poor Charley."

Lady gave up and, with a sigh, put her arms down on the table around the solitaire and swept all the cards into a heap in front of her. "If you leave," she said, "what'll become of her?"

"Just what would have become of her if I'd never come here." She'd drink more beer. She'd begin to watch football on television as she grew older. She'd grow a paunch.

The coffee in her cup was cold but Lady drank it anyway. "That ain't true," she said. "It ain't the same. It's different now."

"She was right. It was all my fault. It was all a mistake. I don't belong here." Her voice caught. She sobbed, suddenly sorry for herself. "And I . . . what a fool I've been, ready to change, throw up all my—" She heard herself and stopped. She sounded Victorian.

Lady had been aware for some minutes of the sound of a plane approaching. She was listening with one ear to the plane and one to Juna, now silent at the window, looking out, forgetting about her packing. If only the year were over, but it had barely begun. If the year was almost over perhaps she could think of it as An Adventure and put it on a shelf to look at sometime together with her artifacts of Greece and Nigeria, or, not exactly look at, let her eye pass over with a faint trace of recognition. But what she saw out the window was not Greece or Nigeria. In this short time it had become the ample country of her heart.

The plane was climbing. Lady waited for that moment when at the end of the climb the motor seemed to cut out. Then here it came, spiraling down over the house as if attacking it. Juna looked up, clutching one of her new boots to her breast. At the bottom of the dive the plane whined, then thundered. Juna bent double with her arms over her head and the boot on the floor, but Lady just leaned on her elbows on the table.

The plane pulled out of the dive and began to climb. Juna looked at Lady. Lady gathered all the cards in a pile and turned them till their edges lined up. She broke the deck in two and shuffled.

Juna stood up. She turned to the window and looked up into

208

the cloudless, late-afternoon sky. "It's Charley! What's she doing?"

"She driving the cows."

"In an *airplane*?"

The sound of the plane was rising again. Cows bellowed. You could hear them beginning to stampede in the pasture. Juna watched as the plane soared straight up, flipped over, and seemed for a moment to hover, then fell headlong, turning slowly as it came, twisting like a straw in a vortex, directly overhead. She was halfway out the window. At the moment when it looked as if the plane would crash into the house, when it was a fight to keep from wrapping her arms around her head, it straightened and skimmed and dipped out low over the corn stubble, then began to climb again, the sound fading a little.

"She'll kill herself!"

"Naw she won't."

Juna looked at Lady. Lady was laying out another game of solitaire. "Her daddy used to get drunk and run them poor cows all over kingdom come."

Juna stared at her. "How *did* he die, Lady?"

"Fletcher Burden?" Lady shrugged. "Charley was notified. But it had to be some mistake. She thought they got the plane numbers mixed up or something 'cause Belle was right here at home. Then it come over the tube from Topeka in the evening news. Mr. and Mrs. Fletcher Burden, killed in the crash of their private plane outside of Vegas. See, that's how they'd signed themselves at the Sands."

The sound of the plane was rising again.

Juna asked after a minute. "Who was she?"

"Some little oil company secretary from Tulsa. Took 'em some time to identify her. All they had to go on was rings and bridgework."

Juna shuddered. "Poor Belle."

Lady had to raise her voice over the noise of the diving plane.

"She tied one on that time! That's when she first ended up in the drying-out place."

They couldn't talk anymore. Juna put her hands over her ears and clinched her eyes tight but she couldn't close it out. The plane plunged, its engine whining. Juna ran into the hall and dropped at the head of the stairs against the banisters with her arms around her head.

Below her, Belle emerged from her room looking up, her eyes bright, a small, satisfied smile on her face.

"She'll kill herself!" Juna cried.

But Belle was looking up and around with that little smile of pride. Without looking at Juna, as if to herself she said, "She should have been a man!"

Juna couldn't believe it.

Belle looked at her for the first time. "She knows what she's doing! She's just like her father. She's Fletcher Burden all over again."

————

The only light came from the fire roaring in the fireplace at the west end of the long log room, and Charley ranged, her fist clinching a can of beer, her shadow hulking around the walls. Another fist had clinched inside her, not a physical fist or even a physical sensation. Its fingers were her arms and legs and its thumb was her head, and though not physical, it drew her tightly in upon herself. It wasn't a bashing fist like the one clutching the beer can. It was a hiding fist, closing upon a shameful kernel, small but corrosive, radioactive. She could never get rid of it because it hurt too much to open up where she might have to look at it, and also she didn't know where she could throw it if she tried to throw it away. It was full of contamination that nobody would want and everybody would run from. She was stuck with it.

Dive-bombing the house hadn't helped. Running the mischief out of the poor dumb cows hadn't helped. She called herself Judas but that didn't make it. She was more like Peter, denying. Yet who she had failed had not been Juna so much as herself. She had prided herself on her courage only to find she didn't have any. She had trained all her life and come in last. She wanted to go away and find some place, some featureless landscape without another human face.

She reeled back to her rage and kicked the fender around the fire. She hunched over, hands in pockets, in front of the picture still hanging on the wall of an upright, grim old couple with a pitchfork and a white frame house behind them. It seemed clear to her they were to blame. She hauled off and hit it with her fist, the real, physical one, and the glass broke and the picture crashed to the floor. She sucked her raw knuckles, wiped the blood on her shirtfront, and took another swig of beer. There were several six-packs on the floor by the door. She couldn't risk running dry.

She sucked in her breath and laid back her head and found herself staring at the wagon wheel hanging overhead with its candle stubs still in their tin cups around the rim. She set the beer down and leapt up and grabbed hold and swung. Eerie shadows, huge and grotesque, spun around her on the walls, something in chains with an old ship's wheel and a body bound upon it. She kicked out at everything in reach, sending chairs, an old flower stand, and a ragged quilt flying, making a racket oddly satisfying.

She dropped down and reared back and drank, emptying the beer can, and threw it away to clatter in a corner. She liked the noise. She went to the front door and opened it and looked out. The moon was scudding behind some ragged clouds. She returned to the fireplace and took out a torch and went back to the door and out into the night, leaving the door open behind her. Holding the flame high, she advanced into the draw till the shape of her truck, iced in silver, loomed before her, its door hanging open. She lowered the torch and inspected again the flat tire from

211

which, an hour ago, she had extracted a five-inch strand of old barbed wire. She had inspected the wire with a practiced eye. The brave pioneers had reached out and done her in. Her ancestors had lain in wait to punish her shame. It was very old barbed wire. She could sell it to the fool barbed-wire collectors for enough to buy herself a new tire, but instead she hurled it in the pond. Give it a decent burial, she told herself. The pond was silver and, beyond, the pasture was empty. But she could hear the mares farther down, snuffling, clumping on the side of the draw as they grazed.

The firelight glinted through chinks in the old log walls. She went back in and threw her torch toward the fireplace. It missed and landed on the floor. She stared at it absently and turned to kneel and pry another can of beer from a plastic ring. She felt suddenly woozy. She didn't dare pass out. It was bad enough awake. On that edge between awake and asleep, demons lay waiting, like the hundred-year-old barbed wire.

She got up off the floor. The torch lying in front of the fire had turned to smoldering. She kicked it gently into the fireplace and leaned her head against the big smoked mantel beam and looked into the flames and flicked with a finger the metal tab on her fly zipper, remembering how Tearl had put out the fires on nights when they'd been drinking there together. She shook the beer can vigorously, then held it low in front of her, pointed down. She pulled the tab and let the beer spurt out all over the fire. The flames went out and a single pillar of smoke went up the chimney. She stood for a while in the light of the dying embers and the moon at the windows, thinking of Tearl. She could see his face. "Quit kicking yourself," he said. "They's always plenty be happy to do that for you." She heard a sob. It felt like a sneeze high up inside her nose. "Goddammit!" she said in a loud, hoarse, argumentative voice. Clay lounged on the old wicker couch with its must-smelling pillows, his beer can sitting on the swell in his jeans. He'd always been big on pocket pool. She was glad to see him in his jeans and T-shirt, looking like himself. The last time she'd seen him he was in a satin-lined box with his head wrapped in opaque plastic, all dressed up by Belle in a sport jacket and a pale silk tie. "Serves you right," he said. "Do you good. Just a long overdue comeuppance." She threw the can in her hand at the empty couch. It spewed beer, hit the back, rolled off the seat, and clattered on the floor.

"Pay him no nevermind," Tearl said. "He's always been jealous."

"I'm the one shoulda been jealous!" But instead she had this little, soft, nagging guilt.

"You didn't do nothing to Clay," Tearl said.

"I beat him at everything."

"They give him the best horse he couldn't ride it, best saddle and he couldn't stay in it."

"I ought to've let him win."

"Like you let Belle win? Like you let them lying twisters at the rodeo win? Like you folded up and stayed home and didn't go off to California to school so you wouldn't win?"

"Wadn' Clay's fault he was a mess."

"Wadn' yours, either."

"He was my brother. You were my soul brother and he was my blood brother. There was something I might coulda give him."

"Yeah, right. Give him Juna, why don't you? You don't deserve her, do you. You're just a girl."

She laughed. "Where are you, anyway? Where've you got off to now?"

"What diff'unce it make? You don't need me. You know what you got to do."

He was right.

She pulled the fire screen across the hearth, picked up what was left of the six-pack she'd been working on, and weaved unsteadily around the room till she found her jacket on the floor. She swooped it up with her toe and caught it and shrugged into

213

it, shifting the beer in its plastic rings from one hand to the other. Then she turned and stumbled out the door.

She walked past her truck, but twenty feet beyond, without a break in rhythm, she circled back and hauled off and kicked it. Then she hiked up and over the rise and into the brightening moonlight.

The house was dark except for the light in Juna's window, and bathed with moonlight strong enough to cast shadows. Off to the south, over at Askews', some cattle were lowing, and some of their own, restless in all that brightness, answered. A dog barked in the distance but KC was not around. He didn't answer. He liked to range all over the countryside when the moon was out.

She stopped inside the windbreak and stood dangling the two cans of beer from her pinkie by one of the plastic rings. She squatted and looked up at Juna's window and opened one of them and drank and shook her head to clear it. She left the unopened can on the ground and rose and drank again and spit it out. Then she took off her hat and emptied the can of beer into it and put it back on and closed her eyes as the cold beer ran down her face. She shook her head again.

Intent on Juna's window, she tossed the empty can up and caught it and weighed it in her hands. Then, holding it out in front of her, she drop-kicked it toward the back of the house.

Inside, Belle had been dreaming. She dreamed she was balancing with one foot on top of a wobbly stool and the other on the windowsill. She knew she had to make up her mind which way to go, but she couldn't. She felt awkward and heavy, and neither hold was certain, both began to give. Then something disturbed her dream, a sound outside, and she grabbed at the edge of the windowsill, which turned into the sides of her bed. She shot up and called, "Who's out there?"

Charley breathed a muffled curse. She circled, her hands in her pockets, looking up now and then at Juna's window. She toed

214

a rock out of the sand, then scooped it up and threw it at the square of light. It struck the second-story wall, bounced back across the roof of the porch, and fell to the ground.

A window on the front of the house flew open. Belle's voice called, "Who's out there I say!"

Charley ducked into the shadow of the trees and fell to one knee and drew an imaginary gun from an imaginary holster and fired toward the sound of Belle's voice, not by pulling the imaginary trigger but by dusting the palm of her left hand across the hammer. She'd seen either Johnny Mack Brown or Hopalong Cassidy do it many times.

Belle picked up her glass off the bedside table and searched with her feet for her slippers. She emerged stealthily into the hall, weaving a little. She took a long drink to fortify herself, then approached the gun case and stood listening. She heard running footsteps outside and her heart rose in her chest and clapped excitedly. She set the glass on top of the case, then changed her mind and had another swig and set it down again. She let her hand linger on it for courage.

Charley ran lightly up the ramp and stepped out onto the banisters. She balanced there precariously for a few steps and leapt down into the yard. To keep from falling she grabbed Juan's fruit ladder propped against the porch roof and swung around it like a child around a pole. Losing her nerve, she crossed the yard and absently picked up the last can of beer. She stood looking at it and dropped to her knees and dug a grave and buried it and patted the little mound humped over it. She ran her hand behind her over the ground till she found a stone. She set it at the head of the beer can's grave. Maybe she'd leave it buried for all time, and maybe she'd have to dig it up again sometime, like a dog with a bone. No telling. Then she sat on the ground and traced with her eye the square of light that was Juna's window, missing the angle at the corner, tracing it again.

Inside, in the moonlight coming through the windows, Belle

steadied herself on the gun case, holding her breath to keep from making a sound, and waited for her head to quit turning. Then she went to the front door and, speaking almost as if afraid to speak, said, "Who's out there?" and waited, and gathered her courage and said, "So it's you, is it!" Nobody answered, so she opened the gun case and reached in and lifted out Charley's rifle. The barrel glinted in the moonlight. It looked so cold she shivered. It was a nicely balanced rifle and she held it hanging at the length of her arm where it helped her move across the bare, polished hardwood floor the way the pole helps a tightrope walker across the pit.

At the foot of the ladder Charley hesitated. She climbed a few rungs, hesitated again, and dropped back in the yard and stood with her hands in her pockets and toed the ground. Then she backed away from the shadow of the house till she could see Juna's lighted window over the porch roof. It was the point her whole self yearned toward and the sight of it gave her courage.

The light went out. She slumped. She heard the breath go out of her. She jammed her hands in her pockets again and walked in a circle. There was Tearl's face. The mouth was moving. She tried to read his lips. "Go on," he said. "Go ahead." With Tearl prompting from the shadows of the windbreak, she approached the ladder again and took her hands out of her pockets in time to grasp the uprights. Slowly she began to climb. The rungs of the homemade fruit ladder narrowing toward the top were far apart. She had to pull herself up as she ascended, finding them with her toes.

Watching, Belle grasped the door frame with her free hand and had a palpitation. The nerve! The very nerve! So he'd taken her up on her invitation! Nasty pervert! "Come down off that ladder! Come down from there this instant or you'll answer to me!" She stepped out on the porch and raised the gun and sighted down the silver streak that was the top of the barrel. She felt her heart banging to be let out to go about some urgent business of its own. "Stay right where you are!" she said, but he was scrambling up the ladder. He would soon fall over the edge of the porch roof and disappear. "Stop!" she said. "Stop right where you are or I'll shoot! I mean it!" The response was a final burst of speed.

Just like her poppa had taught her, holding her breath, Belle squeezed the trigger. She didn't hear anything, but the gun thrust itself into her shoulder, almost shyly, the way a child kicks in the womb to remind you of something.

The figure on the ladder stopped. Juna's light came back on and laid a bright outline of the window across the yard, elongated like a shrunken garment somebody had taken in hand and stretched.

Belle closed her eyes and squeezed again, then opened them to see the figure on the ladder let go and dangle out over the yard, holding by one hand. She continued to aim till the hand let go and the figure fell and crumpled and lay there like an old winter coat somebody had thrown out. She lowered the gun slowly and stood frozen in awe of herself. Then, purposefully, holding the gun by the stock, she used it as a cane and thumped across the porch and descended the steps one at a time—thump-halt, thump-halt. Juna, at her window, heard it clearly. The footsteps sounded like the halting gait of some awful Quasimodo. Her hand rose to her throat. A light came on out in Lady's trailer and the door opened, silhouetting Lady in her nightgown.

"Who's out there doing all that shooting?"

Juna tried to answer "I don't know," but the chords in her throat had petrified.

Belle reached the bottom step and then the ground and stood peering over at the fallen figure. He didn't move. She limped toward the crumpled body and bent in dread, for she couldn't stand the sight of blood, and the thought that she had killed both thrilled and nauseated her. For a moment she denied that she saw a fringe of bangs, a long curl of lip, and a single, long stroke of eyebrow, but then she realized that was what she was bound to see, what had lain in wait for years, ready to spring out laughing. She let go of the gun and it arced slowly over and slapped the ground and sent up a puff of dust she smelled but didn't see. She dropped on a knee and heard a moan. It took a while to adjust her ear and know it came from her. Her hands in front of her grabbed hold of each other for comfort. She made herself reach out. She tried to lift Charley but Charley was a frightening dead weight, so she took her head and held it. She began to rock. She rocked stroking Charley's hair, her whole head. She buried Charley's face against her breast, rocking.

Lady halted abruptly a few steps away. Juna, where she'd stopped on the steps, gasped aloud and stood motionless while Belle, rocking Charley, moaned and looked up from the dark at the bright sky. Turning, searching, she said, "Fletcher?" And getting no answer, turning again, she said, "Clay?" And still getting no response, turning, looking up, she said, "Momma!"

Charley was hearing organ music. She thought she recognized the hymn, and a choir sang somewhere in the background, maybe on a cloud. An oily gentleman stood with exact replicas of himself on either side while people in pews hid their faces behind kleenex and a slow line moved toward a platform to the front where a box banked by candles and sickly-smelling lilies stood open, its pink, satin-tufted lining, the exact color of Belle's new pantsuit, showing inside the lid. Belle, in her new hat and wig, sat in the front row holding a hanky to her face. Women viewed the remains and left the platform and bent over Belle and patted her shoulder and said pretty . . . so pretty . . . idn' she pretty . . . I never saw her looking so pretty . . . And the old maid saleslady from the millinery department at the dry goods store murmured, "Health is wealth. That's what I always say." Lady, dressed all in black, moved in the line toward the bier, looked, gasped, and cried out, "No!" Juna approached with her ravaged face and looked down and gasped, exclaiming, "No!" Then Charley, curious, wafted toward the coffin and saw the body lying there on pink satin. The hair had been done by Thelma. It had been eased slowly out of the skull till it was long enough to be curled. The cheeks were red with rouge, and the mouth was drawn with lipstick, and a single strand of little pearls circled the neck above a sleeveless dress with a tight bodice and a full skirt. Below the skirt a pair of legs in hose stuck out, the feet in little black patent-leather pumps. It looked like a vaguely familiar thirteen-year-old that Belle had got hold of and fixed up to suit herself, a poor done-up dummy with its hands crossed over a prayer book, the bitten nails all polished.

Her nether limbs spun under her and backed her away, and when she turned she saw a way out and took it. As she emerged she forgot where she had been, and though she meant to keep on going, she didn't want to move. Lying there rocked, cradled in Belle's arms, aching, still a little drunk, she felt something come over her like a scent, soft and aromatic. She cracked her eyelids and in the light from Juna's upstairs window saw Belle's throat up close, full of those crinkles you see in old tissue paper that has lain for years wrapping something precious in the cedar chest. The fall from the ladder had jarred her insides and done something awful to her shoulder. Her head swam and the shadows inside it lengthened, chasing out the moonlight. She wanted just to lie there on the cold, sobering ground and let go, dim out, but she had to hold onto herself. Otherwise her hand might reach up and clutch Belle's breast or a finger hook itself over Belle's lip and the rest of her melt down into something small and helpless against the plush bosom of Belle's thick plum-colored robe. As she watched she saw herself diminishing till she threatened to disappear. She began to flail before she could even feel if she had any limbs. She struck out with wrists and elbows and scrambled up, and Belle sprawled gape-legged in the yard. She backed away, turned to run, then, half turning back, for part of her didn't dare lose sight of her mother's face, limped into the dark beyond the ring the porch light made, looking for all the world, Juna thought, like some barely remembered portrayal of John Wilkes Booth limping off the stage before the stunned audience could make a move, shouting, "*Sic semper tyrannis!*"

"Charley!" Lady cried and in her felt house slippers started after her.

"Charley!" Juna cried and ran barefoot toward the edge of the light.

Belle paddled like a shored seal but could not rise. They bent over her and each took hold of one arm. She cast around for her cane. They all looked at the rifle lying there on the ground where she had dropped it, but they left it where it was, nobody wanting to touch it. They let her pull on them and she nearly pulled them over, but that way she got herself to her feet. Her eyes were wild and her own hair stood out in straight, sparse shocks from her head, and she tried to back away from them, looking from one to the other, but as soon as she let go, she began to topple and grabbed onto them and said, "I didn't know it was her!" She turned from Juna to Lady. "It was dark!" And back to Juna, "Why didn't she answer me? What was she doing on that ladder?" And back to Lady, "It was an accident!" And Lady said with a bitter-tasting laugh, "You didn't know the gun was loaded." Belle looked at them with her mouth open, then turned and tottered toward the house like a mechanical toy going downhill.

When they got her up the steps and inside, Juna came back out on the porch and squinted into the dark, but Charley was gone. Then a motor gunned rapidly several times and roared. She ran down the steps toward the row of sheds. She thought it was the

T-Bird, but whatever came tearing past her toward the cattle guard trailed a huge, dark, billowing cloud behind and up above, in the air. The plastic tarp caught on one of the old limestone fence posts by the gate and subsided, but the sports car with none of its landing lights on raced away from her down the drive.

9

Belle slumped into her pillows. She was hiding—the pillows came up around her head like blinders on a mule—and pouting at the same time, looking at the television set across the room. She was watching it but she didn't know what she was seeing. The sound was the sound of the rodeo. It served her mainly as noise. She watched the motion on the screen because otherwise she would have to watch Lady and Juna making alternate trips downstairs carrying boxes and sewing machines and suitcases. She didn't let on she knew what was happening. She hadn't hit Charlene, there hadn't been a sign of blood, so why all the fuss? She hadn't known it was Charlene, had she? It was Charlene's fault, anyway, for not answering when she cried, "Who's there!" And what business had she on that fool ladder in the middle of the night? Anybody could make a mistake. She had a right to be jumpy, down here all alone. So why did Juna have to make a thing of it? Why couldn't she let well enough alone? She just liked attention. She didn't mean it. She wasn't going anywhere. All those boxes would just be to carry up again.

Juna came down the stairs and set a suitcase next to the growing pile in the hallway and went back up the stairs. Belle watched, then quickly looked back at the television. Let her go then. Serve her right. She wouldn't find another place like this one. She wouldn't find another cook like Lady or another friend like she herself had been. Where else would she get riding lessons? It was foolishness, just foolishness, as anybody could tell her if she would listen.

A clown was performing antics with an umbrella. Nothing but a chalk-white blob with a round red mouth at the center and an orange mop of wig, he ran before the bull, a large spotted bull, a mean, dangerous-looking thing. Behind him a cowboy picked himself up out of the arena and dusted himself off. You'd have to be crazy to get on a bull like that. Here came another one, the bull dumped forward and the rider's seat the lowest thing about him, the only part in contact with the animal, his knees crooked high and his skinny body slatted back against the crowd, bigger than the crowd, before he came off almost in a backward somersault, and here came the clown again with his umbrella.

"That's Carl Stevens, folks, from Wichita, riding last year in Cheyenne!" It was the Tula announcer's voice behind the picture but it wasn't even the Tula rodeo. Television could drive you batty, like a nest of boxes.

The camera switched to the catch pen. A loose bull, chased by a clown, trotted toward the opening in the fence, shied once, and feinted back toward the clown. The crowd laughed. Was that Tula? The bull trotted in a businesslike way into the mouth of the pen and the camera moved up in time to catch a hand snaking out to loose the rig and the bull's hind end crusted with manure and his little spilt-end tail awhip. Then he lunged, bucking, and crashed into the stockade. Belle found it boring. It was just like Kansas that worked with cows and bulls and steers every day of the week but Sunday to engage in the same old routine when it wanted to amuse itself. Why couldn't they put on a play? She'd been in *Arsenic and Old Lace* once. She could do it again if they asked her to. But it would be fun to do something different, something with a little heart in it. She longed for a little sweetness. Something modern but she couldn't think what and went immediately to the curtain calls. She had on a flowing, filmy thing, and she curtsied, low and graceful. There was a hush, and then a roar and somebody handed up roses and the write-up in the paper referred to her as Mrs. Burden, like Mrs. Siddon. It said Mrs. Burden's talents had matured, that she had reached the height of her powers as . . . She couldn't think of a heroine's name, and here came another idiot cowhand on a bull.

―――――

From high up amid stacked bales of hay, Charley listened to the MC calling the names of the calf ropers. The night before, she had dug out enough bales to make a hollow in the top of the stack about the size of a single bed. Now she lay with the walls of this bed rising around her and looked up at the sky. The sun was almost overhead but off a little to the south, already dropping toward cold weather. It left a shadow almost to her knees. If she wanted to shade her face, all she had to do was turn around. But she didn't want to turn around. She didn't want to move. She was sore and hung over and hungry. She hadn't found a broken bone or even an actual sprain. What hurt most was something inside, not in her body exactly, but in herself. Whatever it was felt bruised and battered and tried.

She had on a pair of shades she had found in the glove compartment of the Porsche. She didn't know how they got there. She never drove the car, just ran the motor now and then to keep up the battery. Last night she had driven a hundred miles up the Interstate without getting stopped, though she was going a hundred and twenty miles an hour. It was late. She mostly had the highway to herself. She discovered she liked the Porsche. She didn't know why she had denied herself all this time. It was suave and white and handsomely snouted, a ready henchman to her will. Her will was to go to Kansas City and find a way of having some shady fun, but she couldn't think what. She was surprised when she found herself doing a U-turn over the grassy median

224

and heading back toward Tula. She hadn't meant to go back. She hadn't meant to go to the rodeo, but just as she had found herself making the U-turn on the highway, she found herself turning off into the rodeo grounds at four a.m. A few people slept in their campers with the curtains pulled, and some were at a quiet all-night poker game in one of the concession stands. She found the haystack and parked behind it and stepped out through the sun-roof onto the top of the car and climbed up the bales and dug out a bed, stacking the bales she had removed higher all around it, and huddled under her jacket and tried to sleep but couldn't.

It was all over. Juna had seen her as she had never been but as now it seemed she had always known herself to be: vile, despicable, repulsive. Her own mother had been perfectly willing to put her out of her misery. It was a relief, wasn't it? No more striving and achieving. Nothing to run up like a flag each day and keep there, floating. Had it really been like that? She'd never thought so, but now it seemed as if it had always been like that. Now she could let go, lie down, she could rest in peace, she was free. But while she lay there shivering, a Janis Joplin line played over and over under her thoughts like its needle was stuck: "Freedom's just another name for nothing left to lose. . . ."

Huddled under her jacket, watching the stars go out, listening to the song, she thought she heard a soft step on the top of her car. She started and almost rose, but before she had time to look, a silhouette appeared over the bales of hay above her. The figure said, "Charley?"

"Crice, Warren, you scared the hell out of me."

He swung up and over the bales and into the nest beside her. She had to move over to make room. "You're shaking," he said. "I'm cold."

It was so narrow in the nest their shoulders touched. He didn't say anything or ask any questions and she was too tired to think. It was warmer with two of them. She dozed and woke to find that he had her hand, not tight, just letting her fingers lie on his while he looked at them in the moonlight and let them one by one fall down.

"Oh, Crice, Warren." She snatched her hand away. Then, she couldn't help it, she sobbed.

"Don't do that," he said.

"I will if I want to."

He sighed. "I reckon you will."

After a while, without meaning to, she dozed again, and when she woke, he had her head on his shoulder. She started up. "Warren! I mean it . . . you know I don't—"

"Yeah, I know you don't."

"What are you doing out here anyway?"

"Playing poker."

"You winning?"

He set his jaw and shook his head. "Naw. I'm losing. I'm not winning at anything." He looked at her. "I went out to take a leak and I saw your car."

"It's not my fault. I can't help it, you know."

"I know it," he said gruffly. "But what would you do if you were me?"

"I don't know. Look at somebody else."

"I am. I am looking at somebody else."

She didn't say anything. Then she said, "Who?"

"Reenie."

"Oh," she said. "That's good."

"Why? Why is that good?"

"Because I like her and because—"

"It's all in the family?"

"Yeah," she said, high on a falling scale, as if she were saying why the hell not.

He laughed, then sobered. "Too bad about us, though."

"No it's not!" She couldn't see his eyes, but she knew he was watching her face.

"Yes it is. I'm the one thing makes you feel the least bit female."

She thought about it. "No," she said. "that's not true."

"I don't know what else does," he scoffed.

"Juna."

It was quiet for a little lying there. He had his hat tipped forward. Finally he said, "You feel about her like I feel about you."

She nodded. It rubbed her head up and down against him. "What do you think about that?"

He sighed. "I think life's a bummer."

"It is not!"

He didn't say anything, so she didn't say anything. She dozed off again, and when she surfaced he was gone. At dawn she fell into a deep sleep, and when she woke up JoJo was hovering over the hay. "I seen the car," he said. "You gonter ride the broncs, Charley?" Only then did she begin to suspect what she was doing there.

She propped herself up against the bales and tipped her hat over her face to keep out a little sun and awaited JoJo's return. The sun was higher. She heard the sounds of the carnival that always set up on the grounds at rodeo time, motors being tinkered with and tried, and now and then snatches of tinny music. She peered out from between two bales to see the broncs in their corral, shaggy and rough-looking, and the scarred bulls in the bullpen—mostly Brahmas with an Angus and crossbreed or two. They looked so peaceful, fooling at the hay cakes scattered around, or standing backed in a corner, looking idly out at the world, their neck skin hanging. One of the Brahmas had a single horn curled down alongside his face. That one looked like it was figuring something out, standing in the middle of the pen eyeing the gate. She wouldn't ever want to ride a bull. Bulls are ugly and smart and full of surprises. And no sense in riding them. You

227

never ride bulls around a ranch. Just made-up meanness, all it was. Broncs were a different matter.

They were testing the microphones when JoJo climbed up over the top of the Porsche.

"Get your feet off my automobile," she said.

He whistled. "When you gone let me drive that baby?"

"I'm not."

"Aw, come on, Charley."

She took the corn dog and wolfed it down while he folded his arms on top of a bale and chucked at his chin with his thumb, a thickset boy with a blue powder burn on one cheek where once, cleaning a gun, he almost shot himself.

"Maybe I'll let you drive her," she said, and drank from the cardboard cup of coffee, "if you'll do me another little favor."

Juna looked around to see if she'd forgotten anything. She knew she hadn't but she looked anyway, the way in her travels she always came back one last time like her mother had taught her and looked around the room she'd slept in to see if she'd left anything behind. This time it was a mistake. She sank down on the bed and eyed desolation. The drawers hung open, and the closet door. All that was left was to run over the shelves with a dust cloth, close the drawers, bathe, and put on the clean clothes she had laid out. She remembered the first time she'd sat there, on the bed. She remembered lying back to try it out and looking up at the underjaw of Charley's elk. She couldn't laugh, but she smiled a little. She looked down at the sun on the old flowered rug and felt a wrench, as if she might burst into tears and weep at how much she was going to miss that rug. But time enough for all that once it was done.

She got up and dusted the shelves and closed the drawers and picked up a fallen hanger. Then she went barefoot down the hall and took the quickest bath she had ever taken in the crimson bathtub with the brass fixtures only now beginning to get a little green patina.

Usually she looked forward to the prospect of a change and turned her thoughts eagerly to what came next, but as she stepped out of the tub and stood naked on the furry carpet with the wet towel draping down her, she couldn't think what next. It was like the end of a book by Jane Austen, when you can't imagine a future because it was all wound up, finished, done. The feeling that came over her was so bleak that she began rubbing herself, vigorously, till she was red all over. She eyed the stud book face-down on the floor. She stooped and picked it up and turned to the fly leaf and looked a long time at Charley's name in the homely, barely legible scrawl.

She went back to what had been her room and put on clean clothes and avoided looking at the rug or at herself in the mirror, for the mirror mirrored the brass bed with its patchwork quilt and herself and Charley propped on the pillows against the head, eating popcorn and watching television, Mary Jane curled asleep at their feet.

She didn't look at the room again after she walked out. She went at a steady, purposeful clip downstairs, picking up the telephone as she swept through the dining room, and into the kitchen where Lady had set herself the job of cleaning the cupboards. It was a huge job, a once-a-year job, and she did it now to keep from feeling helpless. It was her least favorite feeling and it always set her to some Augean task, like cleaning the kitchen cupboards.

Juna ranged around the kitchen holding the telephone in her hand and dialing. Lady could hear the faint buzz of the busy signal against the noise of the calf roping coming from the television across the hall. "That's Pete Mackey, folks," the MC said.

Juna dialed again and listened. Lady heard the signal. It sounded like a calf tangled in barbed wire bawling in the distance. "It's either busy or nobody answers," Juna said. "But if it's busy, somebody's got to be there."

"Who you calling?" Lady asked. She was down on the floor, sitting on the blue-and-yellow linoleum with her feet out and pots and pans piled up around her.

"What are you doing?" Juna asked.

"Cleaning. Straightening. I got to do it when the mood hits me or it don't get done. Who you calling?"

"The taxi."

"You won't get a cab out here past the rodeo grounds today."

At the sound of their voices in the kitchen, Belle decided to act like nothing had happened. She laughed out loud. "Come see the clowns! You're missing all the fun!"

Juna walked over to the stove and poured herself a cup of tea and stood sipping, looking thoughtfully down at Lady. Then she picked up her purse and rummaged till she came up with her address book and stood thumbing through it, looking for a number. She found it and began to dial.

Charley was listening to the calf roping to take her mind off things. She didn't look over the edge of the haystack for she didn't want to lose her peculiar solitude, but she heard the clatter of hooves in the arena and imagined the calf rope snaking out, the loop finding the calf and the horse skidding down on its haunches. She saw the cowboy run down his rope and wrap and lift an arm to call time.

JoJo came back. "It might can be arranged," he said. "How much you got on you?"

Charley dug her hand into her pants pocket. She pulled the pocket out and it hung there sideways out of her jeans like KC's tongue, only paler.

"That ain't gonna do it," JoJo said.

She sat up and looked around. She spied Curtis May looking huge and awkward and out of place in a new, unfaded pair of jeans and a neckerchief, smiling at a couple of women in pink frontier pants passing arm in arm. "Wait here," she said.

JoJo took her place in the hollow among the bales and watched her climb down and go up to the bank president and start talking. A minute later she climbed back up and reached in her shirt and handed him a wad. He whistled. "How'd you do that?"

"I borried it."

"I wisht I had that kinda credit."

"Go on. Hurry up," she said. "I'll be right here."

She was still hungry. She climbed down again and bought herself a chiliburger and climbed back up and ate it. A line of cars crept into the parking lot off the highway. The high school band in its green-and-yellow corn huskers' uniforms played a rousing march, then took a break and scattered to the food concessions. The Ferris wheel creaked. Merry-go-round music came off and on on the wind.

JoJo came back. "Okey," he said. "It's all fixed."

She held up her wrist and looked at her watch, squinting in the sun. It might still be early enough. "Okey," she said, handing him the keys to the Porsche, "if you follow the tire tracks th'oo the field behind the pens, you'll come on a gate to the section road. Here's what I want you to do."

After she watched him climb down the pyramid of bales and let himself into the Porsche through the sunroof, she lapsed back into her nest and remembered her chaps. She cursed. She had worn them to the house the last time she used them. She spit out a hay stem she'd jabbed between her teeth and looked over the bales at the crowd. She eyed one of the stockmen over by the saddle bronc corral. He turned and walked toward her. She clambered down from her hiding place and caught up with him and walked in step. "What'll you take for them chaps you got on?"

Surprised, he paused and looked down at himself. The chaps were soft rough-outs, scuffed and worn, all different shades of tan from various scars and slicked-down smudges from horse lather.

They were scalloped and trimmed in buck-stitched suede and decorated with soft conches. He was short, maybe a couple of inches taller than she was, and he had a face that had been down the road. "What you want 'em fur?" he asked.

"I need 'em for a little while," Charley said.

He looked around, uncertain what to say to the little beev. "I reckon I might could let you use them, if it's just for a little." He reached down and unbuckled the chaps and took his riding glove off the strap where it always hung.

She took them. "Thanks."

He looked at her hand, then shook it. "I'm Clint Dent," he said.

"I'm Charley Burden." The chaps fit. They would do. They were beauts. She buckled them on, eyeing the glove in his hand. It looked like elkhide, the fingers curled over a palm stained and stiff and burnt dark with resin. But nobody would lend you his bucking glove. She would think about that later. The last she'd seen of her own resin-stiff glove, it lay on top of her bureau in what used to be her room, where she'd flung it after the last time she got down on Peanuts.

When she headed toward the chutes, Clint Dent followed. Since he'd quit bronc riding with a disk-shot back and prostatitis, he'd worked for the stock contractor. He wanted to see what she was up to in his chaps. He eyed the seat of her pants. She was all muscle. He weighed in at one forty-five and she looked like she'd be a good thirty pounds lighter. Light was good, but too much of a good thing was bad. If she had it in mind to ride a bronc, she was apt to get her killing.

10

Juna, at the window with a second cup of tea, saw the Ranchero turn off the highway and speed toward the house. The ground was dry after the recent rains but not dry enough this morning to send up dust. She missed the dust. Everything was different today.

The MC's voice in the background was listing the entries for the bucking events. She heard but she wasn't listening. She was watching with dread the approach of the Ranchero. Then the MC's voice rose up over a swell in the crowd noise. Belle shrieked. Juna turned, startled, toward the parlor bedroom.

"Did you hear that?" Belle cried, sitting straight up in bed.

Juna hadn't. Then the MC's voice said, "I repeat, in the saddle bronc riding Claude Holiday, Nate Mackey, Wilton Gibbs . . . and as I said, a hometown contestant, Charley Burden. . . ."

Belle swung her legs off the side of the bed and grabbed her cane. "Lady! I need help!"

Juna, beside her things, grasped the newel post, telling herself, "It's nothing to me," but her mind kept asking Charley *why*, and in spite of herself her heart knocked urgently with alarm.

The MC droned on. "Pete Dunovan, home from Texas to visit his granddad, Spike Mitchell, last year's winner and today's favorite . . ."

233

She watched, frozen, as Belle, all motion, tried to dress herself. Lady hurried past her in the hall. "What're you doing now?"

"Find me something to put on!"

"Where you think you're going?" But she went to the clothes press while Belle rolled up her rolled-down stockings. "You want the new pink suit?" Lady asked.

"Anything anything, quick!" Belle waved a hand. Lady handed her the suit and she put on the pants and jammed her feet into her shoes. Then she went with surprising agility past Juna into the dining room and grabbed up a wig and put it on, changed her mind, tore it off, and set it down askew on the head of the bust sitting there in its ladylike company and chose another, the black one she thought made her look Latin. She stopped and pointed. "What in the world is *that*?"

Lady in the door said, "That's the bust."

"The what?"

"The bust. The bust of Clay."

Belle looked from Lady to the foreign object there among her Styrofoam heads. "Nonsense," she said. "That doesn't look a thing like Clay."

Lady followed her past Juna till she dropped into her mechanical chair and headed for the porch.

Harvey paused at the head of the steps, his Ranchero parked behind him and his smile fixed. Belle purred out the door to the head of the ramp and said, "Catch hold of me, Harvey!" and he sprang to grab the back of the chair. They went recklessly down the ramp, Harvey on a startled slant and Lady behind them, calling, "Where you think you're going?" Juna had picked up one of her suitcases. "Harvey!" she shouted. "Wait!"

Harvey paused. "Come on!" Belle cried. "Hurry up!"

Harvey looked at Belle, then at Juna, and then, like a small boy commanded by his mother, he hurried the wheelchair down the walk. Belle stood up and he managed to get her into the Ranchero. She looked back at Juna on the porch. "Come on!

Hurry up! Didn't you hear? Charley's bronc riding again!" Her laugh set a flock of crows airborne out of the stubble.

The arena was empty. The calf roping was over. The MC was telling the history of rodeo. He had a bunch of dignitaries up in the box with him. He was going into introductions. Charley had heard it all before. She wasn't listening. She was standing outside the saddle-bronc corral, looking at the horses. One corral over, men were roping the bareback broncs, getting ready for the bucking events: the bareback broncs and the saddle broncs and finally the bulls. She didn't see the bronc that had bucked her off. Maybe it had killed somebody and they'd had to shoot him. Maybe he'd died of old age. Her hand, around a second cardboard cup of coffee, grasped so hard the cup collapsed. Coffee splashed out. It disgusted her and she threw the cup half-full into an oil drum trash barrel.

Behind the chutes the bareback riders lounged around or tended to their rig. One skinny youngster walked up and down, up and down, his lips moving, talking to himself, psyching himself up. In the background the MC's voice said, "Man and animal are paired purely by chance. The bareback bronc riders have drawn, folks. They know the name of their poison." The riders watched while the broncs went into the loading gates. Then they clambered onto the catwalk to eye them from the tops of the chutes and swap whatever last bits of knowledge they had about the broncs while they got their rigging in place. Up over her, at the back of a chute, hanging over the loading gate, the young cowboy she'd seen psyching himself up said softly, "Cheesus!" and laid his forehead a minute against the top of the chute where his bronc reared.

JoJo yelled. She turned in time to see the Porsche slide to a stop alongside the haystack. Juan sat stiffly upright beside him, looking as if he'd rather be somewhere else. She hurried over as

Juan lifted her bucking saddle out of the trunk. "No chaps," he said, then eyed the ones she had on. "No glove."

"I ran into him just as he was finished down't the old place," JoJo said breathlessly, kneeling to strap a pair of spurs on her heels. She looked down over her shoulder. He latched the strap across her instep and looped the narrow leather over the shank and under her heel to hold them in place. "Tighter," she said. "No, that's *too* tight." She bent and tested and redid a strap so they'd give, then hold, and when she straightened, Juan held onto her arm while he fumbled at his shirt pocket and brought something out and held it in front of her. Everything seemed a little weird, and she thought for a minute it was a mirror he wanted her to look into, but it was a picture postcard of a racetrack. The MC's voice sounded distant and disembodied, punctuated by static over the speaker system. The wind was coming up. All around behind the chutes the saddle bronc riders worked over their leather. You could hear the squeak of resin.

"I got you some resin," JoJo said.

She tried to look, but Juan had the postcard up in front of her face again, turned now to the writing side and a childish scrawl with a thick felt marker. "Marguerito," Juan said.

"For chrissake, Juan! Not now!" She pushed the card away.

Juan shrugged and picked up the Association saddle and carried it over behind the stands and dropped it on its skirts in the sparse, dry grass. Charley followed and knelt beside it and checked the rings and leather. She sat in it and stretched the stirrups out in front of her and reared back on the cantle and strafed a time or two.

Clint Dent lounged against an upright under the catwalk in the shade. She was doing it right. He turned and through slats of the chutes watched a bareback rider. The horse slid out of the chute in a spin. It sprang, leapt, and cut to the right. It sunfished and the rider flew off and hit the dust. Clint Dent spit out his wad. He'd been a saddle bronc rider himself.

He turned back and eyed the saddle she was working over with resin. It was a standard Association saddle, light, with a high, swelled pommel and free-swinging stirrup leathers.

"Whatchoo gone do for a glove?" he asked.

Charley could still see that seasoned glove hanging off his belt, but she didn't look at it.

She shrugged and went on rubbing.

The glove hit the dirt beside her. She eyed it lying there cupped like a hand. She looked up at him.

"See does it fit," he said.

She sat back on her haunches and drew it on. A feeling came over her of calm. The glove was a little big at the wrist but it fit over her knuckles. He had a small hand for a man.

"Better than nothing," he said.

He took a coil of whang from his shirt pocket and tossed it over. She picked it up and put it in her own shirt pocket, nodding, embarrassed. "Much obliged."

He took a can of Copenhagen out of his back pocket and fished in it with his fingers and came up with another little something to pack behind his lip.

The bareback event was drawing shouts from the crowd. It was time to get off by herself. She walked away from the loading gates and tried to get her head in place. She walked up and down along a corral fence, making various muscles let go and sag, but then she saw the man with his hat turned upside-down for the draw. Bronc riders converged on him behind the loading gates. Events were hurrying her along too fast. She needed a little time. She had to go back over.

When she walked away again, by herself, her hands were shaking. It was a chore to unfold the slip of paper. She held it open but couldn't for a minute take it in. Yellow Jack. Yellow Jack. She couldn't make sense of it, Yellow Jack. Behind her, the twisters began calling out the names of their broncs in hopes of getting information.

237

"Midnight Ace!"

"Cherry Coke!"

"Ride 'em short, Wilt!"

"Sky Diver!"

"Oh, man!"

"Anybody rode Buck Rogers?"

"He's a space case. He's a rank dude!"

Charley folded her bronc's name and put it in her shirt pocket.

"Aw, come on, Charley," JoJo said. "Wha'd you draw?"

She wasn't telling. Somebody pinned a number on her back and she shouldered her saddle and climbed the long ramp to the catwalk behind the chutes. She would draw a middling rein and take her chances. But JoJo ran along the ground below her. "Dammit, Charley! What's his name? Lemme see can I learn anything!"

But she walked on toward chute four. Clint Dent had stood outside the circle of bronc riders, watching as they drew. He shoved himself off the post holding him up and went up the catwalk behind her.

The other riders brushed past him. The MC was announcing. Charley leaned over the chute and looked down. As she looked, the horse inside butted his back end against the loading gate, reared a little, hopped, and went back down. She dropped behind the sidewall boards. Through them she saw buckskin, scruffy, a little long of coat. She got her hands out of the way just in time as he lunged again and fell against the side of the chute. "Ho there," she crooned. "We in this together, Jack. You'll do all right."

Juan came up behind her. He wasn't talking. She could see he wasn't going to give her anything. "Just this time," she said. "Just this once." But he kept his hands in his pockets and looked non-committally out into the arena. At chute one the gateman leapt back and something black lunged out. A second later pickup men closed in. The rider picked himself up, dusted himself off, looked at the horse and swore. The MC was announcing the second rider.

Charley watched as two slots over a cowboy straddled the chute and got down. She heard him say, "Okey!" She heard the gate latch fall. A raw-bone bay exploded into the arena, the cowboy raking the bronc's shoulders a moment too late. The cowboys on the chutes groaned and Clint Dent said, "He missed him out."

". . . looks like a goose egg," came over the mike.

Everything was moving too fast. Charley turned and watched while Clint Dent spat and rearranged his chew. Then he climbed over the side of the chute and looked at her through the wide-apart boards and said, "Let's get 'im saddled."

Charley lifted the saddle out over the buckskin bronc. She leaned out and let it down far forward on his shoulders. She expected an explosion. Instead his ears swiveled and a shiver hard enough to move the saddle ran down the length of his spine and waffled the skirts. She reached carefully and slid the saddle forward again.

"Gimme," Clint Dent said. He stuck his hand with a wire hook through the side boards, ready to grab, and she lowered herself down the side of the chute but saw Juan threading the cinch through, looking sideways up at her. She smiled. Clint Dent had caught the cinch and was putting it through the ring. Out in the arena, number three was riding to a roar of approval from the crowd.

"That's Claude Holiday on Cherry Coke!" the MC yelled.

The whistle blew and the pickup rider went in and Holiday tackled him around the waist and the big sorrel bucked out from under him.

The crowd went wild, hooting and clapping, and Holiday walked humbly back toward the chutes, grinning. But Clint Dent shook his head and said, "He made a show but it was easy. That horse won't win him no money."

"Ladies and gents, this puts Claude Holiday out front with

239

eighty-two points," the MC said. "The next rider is a hometown contestant, Charley Burden."

Charley felt her face warm up. She heard catcalls, laughter, some whistles, a scattering of applause. She reached down and patted the buckskin's neck, talking low. The bronc was very still. She went on talking while she put on the halter. His head shot up and caught her on the nose. A flash of light lit up the inside of her head but she held onto the halter and fumbled for the strap. The bronc settled a minute and she got it buckled up behind his ear. She snagged on her bucking rein.

———

The Ranchero sped toward the rodeo grounds, Belle up front with Harvey, her foot pressing the floor as if she had an accelerator under it. Juna and Lady in the truck bed, their backs against the cab, held onto each other. The wind blew Juna's hair around her face. It picked up Lady's skirt and wrapped it around her. The Ranchero headed for a line of traffic but without slowing swerved off the highway onto the shoulder and, to the tune of angrily honking pickup horns, raced along till it came to the gate.

An official, surprised, stepped out with a hand up to stop them but Belle's hand was already out the window to slap his. The official, surprised, found Ulysses S. Grant staring up at him from his palm. He looked back, amazed, while the Ranchero sped on by.

It pulled up beside a ramp into the stands and the doors opened. Harvey and Lady and Juna put down Belle's chair from the truck bed while she urged them to hurry, get her to the box, shouting also to Charley, who was at that moment straddling the chute, ready to get down.

The buckskin below was quiet. Then he reared suddenly and she swung up out of the way. He was over the gate with one hoof caught. One of the openers reached up with a cattle prod and knocked it off and he dropped back into the chute, thinking things over, twitching like flies were after him, but there weren't any flies.

Charley was shaking. She let Clint Dent climb up and edge the saddle forward again. The buckskin was ominously quiet. All around her, cowboys were calling to the riders who came after her.

"Ride 'em short, Joe!"

"Close up, Wilt! He eats sky."

Clint Dent was looking at her. She climbed back up and straddled the chute, ready to get down.

"He's a good bronc," Clint Dent said. "He ain't no easy ride. He can put you in the money. But he's mean. He spins to the left and he bucks with his nose in his frog, so ride 'em long."

She looked at him. She'd heard that before. The forked twig of a man with the lined face turned aside to spit. The juice strung out and landed, making a splatter welt in the dust. He wasn't from around Tula. She had never seen him before. He had loaned her his chaps and his glove.

"I work for the stock contractor," he said. "I know what I'm talking about."

The buckskin did a slow lunge. Her saddle rode forward, high on his shoulders, and back.

"Ride 'em short," he said, "or even middlin', he'll pull you over his head. Do like I say, you got a chance."

He talked to the buckskin and ruffled his mane to distract him while Charley, hanging onto the top of the chute with her free hand, let herself down. The saddle felt familiar, substantial, the resin helped her to seat herself, but it wasn't quite right, not yet. Clint Dent handed her the end of the cinch and she snagged it under her thigh. Juan's hand snaked out between the boards and held the thin-bowed stirrup. She put her toes in, keeping the spurs clear of the bronc. She felt him under her, alert and quivering, ready to come undone. She worked her hand into the glove and made a fist. It wasn't hers but it wasn't entirely wrong. She fished in her shirt pocket for the thong and wrapped it around the glove at her wrist and, holding the end between her teeth, pulled it tight and knotted it. She measured off some braided rein, stopped, then measured off some more, working it between her fingers. She tightened the cinch. She leaned back and pulled her feet up to his neck and lowered and reset them over the points of his shoulders, but she couldn't call in that feeling she had to have, the feeling of getting set like a screw. She waited. It wouldn't come. She turned her toes out and locked her ankles and put the spurs in the air where they'd drive down hard to mark the buckskin out. Still she waited, letting her shoulders fall. She settled herself once more, gave her hat a final yank, and threw her left hand up and back, and said, "Okey. Let me have him."

The gateman hit the latch and leapt aside. The gate fell open and the bronc slid out and spun to the left. She was raking her spurs up and back, watching his head, waiting for the rhythm, knowing there's no time to wait for the rhythm. She was snapped and jerked into the swells but she kept on stroking up and back till the stirrup leather snapped her foot behind the cantle. Clint Dent had told her true. He was a snuffer. There was a long line of rein from halter to fist, and his nose was on the ground. For a minute she was clear and lucid as the bronc turned in another spin, leapt, and cut to the right. Then he jackknifed and it was another story entirely. Her spurs arced, raking back and forth. She felt her seat go, but the buckskin rose under her and gave it back. He stood straight up but she dug in and stuck like a burr. She began to be able to read his mind.

The MC was hollering. "A beautiful kickoff! That's Charley Burden, folks, you all know Charley. She's got herself some bronc!"

Then everything gave at once. The bronc bucked forward and came up twisting in place and leaping. He bucked in a circle like a bull, then got his legs under him and reared again. This time he was going over. She didn't dare jump aside. That would end her ride. She felt herself coming off. She hung on. She waited. At the last minute, she flung herself aside and flew through the air. The hard dirt of the arena came up to meet her, and she felt the concussion when the bronc came down. Her shoulder doubled under her.

The MC was yelling, "No fault! No fault, folks. No fault to the rider if the horse goes down!" Oh Christ, let it be over. But it wasn't over. What the hell was she doing there?

Pickup men headed the bronc into the catch pen. She sat up and shook her head to clear it. She thought she had tried to get up but found she hadn't moved. She was sitting there with her legs crossed in the center of the arena, the crowd silent around her.

Juna had turned away in horror when the bronc reared and began to go over backward. She knew Charley was crushed. But nothing had happened. The crowd did not make that final kind of sound. Instead they hung there, suspended. She turned around and saw Charley flung aside in the dirt near the struggling bronc, not much different from the way she had lain the night before in the rectangle of light in the yard. When the MC said she had another chance, Juna's impulse was to run down the steep steps of the stadium and out to where Charley lay and grab her and yell in her face, "You don't have to kill yourself!" She had looked so small up there on the risen shoulders of the dun-colored horse, his black mane and tail lashing.

Then in the silence Belle started yelling like in her own dining room. She must hate Charley. What normal mother would yell as she was yelling, "Get up from there, Charley Burden! Get up from there this instant, do you hear me! You get back on that horse!"

Juna watched Charley rise and wobble in a circle and sit back down again. Was there time? Could she run down there and stop her? Did she want to stop her? Would she love her so much if she weren't wild and reckless and desperate? Oh God, she prayed,

243

surprising herself, let her do it and let her be all right and I'll unpack my things. But then she lost her nerve.

"Go stop her!" she cried to Harvey, bending there over Belle with his mustache drooping. Belle was talking to him, gesturing, taking his arm, and slowly, with her cane, moving toward where the MC stood like a crooner with his microphone. The MC was saying, "That's Charley Burden, folks, on a mean bronc. If the bronc goes down, the rider is not faulted. Charley Burden has a second chance. She can take it if she wants it at the end of the saddle bronc event."

Charley Burden wondered how many second chances she could survive.

"Charley Burden! This is your mother speaking to you!" Charley had the illusion the voice in her head was coming over the speaker system. "You get right up from there, do you hear me?"

She didn't believe her ears but obediently she stood up. Her knees, like jackknives with broken mechanisms, threatened not to lock. The arena spun around her. She swayed, steadied herself, and limped off toward the chutes. She couldn't hear the crowd. It was just a lot of pale, round blobs against the crazy quilt of denim and sheepskin and, finally, at top, the sky. She limped the long stretch back across the arena to the chute, not knowing if she would climb back up. She felt herself shaking all over. She put her hands on her hips to steady them. She wished the crowd would make a noise, yell at her, jeer, boo, do something. But the crowd was silent. Was she moving inside her own bubble like one of those children allergic to the world? But then she heard the hawkers yelling Popcorn! Peanuts! Corn dogs! Cokes!

At the gate she hesitated. A murmur ran over the crowd like a gust of wind. She looked at the chutes and saw Clint Dent up on top, looking down, watching her. She walked toward Clint Dent. Somebody was up there with him. Warren Hubble.

She climbed up the ramp and over the chute and looked down. It was déjà vu. The buckskin was there already. Clint Dent said,

244

"You got his number. That's howcome him to th'ow hisself down. He's plenty mad but you got 'im now if you'll just cahm down."

The bronc kicked out at the loading gate. His unshod hoofs struck with a sound like bullets. The whole chute shook under her. Warren handed her a cigarette. He held it in his hand while she took a drag and felt it sink to the bottom of her lungs. "Thanks, Hub." She was surprised at the sound of her voice. It was deadly calm.

Beyond her in chute five a cowboy said "okey" and the gates fell back. A rusty mare bucked out. Charley didn't watch. She was cutting out the crowd, the noise, the rodeo. Out past the wooden stockade fences, above the crowd, beyond the dust and the creak of the Ferris wheel when the music stopped, Kansas lay tawny in the golden autumn light with a line of trees scribbled between earth and sky, and she was riding. First she saw herself, then she felt herself out there, the bronc surging under her, her hand with the long, braided bronc rein up against her chest, her other hand way up behind her head, wafting like a leaf, her head bent and her hat sloped over her face. She was set like a screw. She could do no wrong. She had found the rhythm.

"Awright!" she said.

The gates swung back. The buckskin lunged to the center of the arena. She raked with her rowels. He sunfished in place. He bucked in a circle. He leapt, not high, but twisted in the middle. He lunged, reversing himself. She pitched up out of the saddle, and politely, like a gentleman, he came up under her, retrieving. The saddle felt slick now under her but she never lost it. She was seated like a screw. He could do as he liked. She watched his head. She had his beat. She was reading his mind.

She heard the buzzer. The crowd thundered. The MC shouted. The pickup men came alongside but she didn't want them yet. The bronc was demonstrating his higher education and it was easy. It was like sitting in a rocking chair at home. He

245

could go down again but it made no difference now. She was with him. The arena was the arena of her nightmare but she wasn't scared. The buckskin spun. The crowd spun around her. She heard the MC yelling, "It's a showboat!" And it was. The buckskin bucked straight out a couple of times. The pickup man was alongside. She fell sideways and tackled his waist and the bronc slid out from between her legs and her feet hit the ground running.

The crowd was hooting and hollering. The buckskin bucked off toward the catch pen. The crowd was catcalling. Then, over the mike, Belle's voice, wild with excitement, unintelligible. The MC said, "She did the whole ride and then some! Charley Burden comes in at eighty-nine! *Eighty-nine!*"

As she came out of the arena people converged on her, touching her, patting her back, trying to hug her.

"Our hometown girl can buck!" the MC said.

She found herself suddenly in the clear, alone, out in the arena in front of the MC's box. She looked up and saw Juna, but the crowd swelled back on her again. A solemn child handed her a pencil and a crumpled envelope. She wrote her name against her thigh.

She looked up for Juna again but saw Harvey Sears looking down on her, still smiling, though the slide in his eye was fixed. She heard Belle over the speaker. "Ladies and gentlemen . . . friends and neighbors . . . I'd like to take this opportunity . . ."

Reenie materialized with Creep behind her holding the baby. "Take a good look, Baba," she said. "That's your great Aunt Charley!"

Charley looked at the baby and Clay smiled up at her. A voice behind her yelled "Frederica!" She jumped, startled, and laughed.

The crowd in the stands was clapping. The corridor opened again and Juna was looking down the aisle of people at her and her heart faltered, hesitating. She was trying to be polite, to answer handshake with handshake, to respond to people she'd known all her life crowding up to her. But all of it—the crowd, the noise, the clapping—was once removed from where she stood. It was taking place on the surface while she was in the depths, barely able to hear or to see the light. She was embarrassed it was taking place before all these people. What she had set out to do was not what she had done. What she had set out to do was no longer clear, but everything else was clear in the crystal autumn light. It was like the time when as a child she had to do exercises the eye doctor prescribed. She had to look at these pictures, and she looked and looked and suddenly they fell into 3-D. It had been one of the most startling experiences of her life, and this was a lot like that: even though she was cool of face, not at all blushing, she was a little ashamed of the exhibition.

Clint Dent stepped up out of the crowd. She stopped and unbuckled the chaps and handed them over. She unwrapped the leather strap from her wrist and took off the glove and handed it back. "Thanks," she said.

"Wadn' nothing," he said, and she looked hard at him. Did Clint Dent know?

Warren Hubble, some way off, leaning on a fence and sucking a tooth, grinned a knowing grin at her and waved. Did that sucktooth, knowing grin mean Warren knew?

Juna walked up and they looked at each other. She couldn't read Juna's eyes. Then Juna reached tentatively out and hooked Charley's little finger with her own. "Idiot." she whispered.

Charley's breath caught in her throat. She threw back her head and laughed out loud with her eyes closed. Juna was inside her head where nobody had ever been before.

Belle, over the microphone, was warming up. ". . . pleased to be here today . . . at this event dear as you all know . . . to the heart of my late husband, Fletcher Burden. . . ."

There right in front of Charley blocking her way stood Will Askew looking like a Washington lawyer at a costume party, never quite comfortable in his sheepskin coat, and, hanging back a little, lighting his pipe, his daddy. Will reached out and gripped her arm. "Great going, Charley." And hiking his head toward Abner, "We've missed you. Haven't had a respectable game of checkers in lord knows when."

Abner puffed and threw away his match and looked up at her from under bushy brows that matched his brush mustache. "Lessen you've started playing checkers like you ride a bronc, come on over I'll beat the pants off you," he said.

The arena and the crowd receded. It felt like walking on something other than ground. They turned and walked the rest of the corridor, already closing behind them, to the MC stand, watching the MC trying to get his mike back, ready to go on to the finale, the bull riding, but Belle wasn't finished. "I'm here to tell you . . . I am proud . . . I am proud . . . of my daughter . . . Charlene Burden . . . I would like to take . . . this opportunity . . ."

People sidled up saying, "Great, Charley."

"Atagirl."

"Plain spectacular!"

Somebody reached out to touch her again while Juna held on to her arm and huddled close.

"I want you to know," came over the echoing speaker system so that, though Belle was right up there in front of them, they felt surrounded, "I'd like to take this opportunity to say . . ."

Nobody was listening, but their faces turned up to her, laughing, and she was on stage looking down at the world. Everybody was there. Curtis May and Mildred from the Plainsman's dining room, Ben Bunsen with his hands clasped at her like a prizefighter over his head, Raymond over by the ramp, and the Askews, father and son, all smiling up at her, and Darrel Thigpen . . . There was Thelma! She clutched the mike with her handkerchief and swayed, laughing, from side to side. "I'd like to take . . . this opportunity to recall . . . my arrival in Kansas . . ."

They roared up their approval.

". . . a bride from East Texas . . ."

They roared again.

". . . and take this opportunity to share with you . . ."

They clapped so hard she had to stop. She stood and waited, smiling down. They hooted and whistled, and there was her boarder, and Charley, looking up.

Charley watched the comedian's mouth stretch into a long thin smiling line, the mole snuggle up under the button nose. She squeezed Juna's arm to her side with her own as Belle shrieked and bowed, smiled and waved and bowed again. They were making too much noise to hear. They were laughing in appreciation of the wig, the hat, the long white gloves and the pink pantsuit.

". . . I'd like to take this opportunity to recognize . . ." Belle knew the part but she had to improvise the lines. They clapped so hard she had to stop. She waited, smiling down. And there, bless her heart, was Thelma. They hooted and whistled, they shouted up, and there beside Thelma stood Darrel Thigpen, reminding her she had to give Charley . . .

". . . this opportunity to say . . ."

She badly needed a curtain line and there beside Thelma stood her conscience looking up at her with that expectant smile.

". . . this opportunity to . . . to, uh, to present . . ." she began, but then caught herself and lifted her sights determinedly over Darrel Thigpen's head. He could wait a little longer. ". . . this opportunity to present . . . my lifelong friend . . ." She reached behind her for Lady, but Lady hung back laughing.

"I want all of you here today to know . . . how proud I am . . . to be part of this fair city . . . and our fair state. . . ."

They shouted her down but she went on talking, sliding an arm around Lady, trying to beckon Juna and Charley with her head—it would be so nice to have her family around her. The MC was trying to get his microphone back. The rodeo wasn't over. The bulls lay in wait in the chutes or lunged against the gates, but meanwhile the whole town of Tula, the whole wide country, was laughing, clapping, calling, faces turned up to her like sunflowers to the sun, giving her their complete and undivided attention. It was all applause. It was all grand. The only thing missing was the roses.